THE NEW MIGRATION IN EUROPE

Also by Helma Lutz

CROSSFIRES: Nationalism, Racism and Gender in Europe (*editor with Ann Phoenix and Nira Yuval-Davis*)

The New Migration in Europe

Social Constructions and Social Realities

Edited by

Khalid Koser
Research Fellow
School of African and Asian Studies
University of Sussex

and

Helma Lutz
Professor in General Education
Johann Wolfgang Goethe University
Frankfurt, Germany

First published in Great Britain 1998 by
MACMILLAN PRESS LTD
Houndmills, Basingstoke, Hampshire RG21 6XS and London
Companies and representatives throughout the world

A catalogue record for this book is available from the British Library.

ISBN 0–333–68311–0 hardcover
ISBN 0–333–72321–X paperback

First published in the United States of America 1998 by
ST. MARTIN'S PRESS, INC.,
Scholarly and Reference Division,
175 Fifth Avenue, New York, N.Y. 10010

ISBN 0–312–21005–1

Library of Congress Cataloging-in-Publication Data
The new migration in Europe : social constructions and social
realities / edited by Khalid Koser and Helma Lutz.
p.   cm.
Includes bibliographical references and index.
ISBN 0–312–21005–1 (cloth)
1. Emigration and immigration—Social aspects.   I. Koser, Khalid.
II. Lutz, Helma.
JV6225.N48   1997
304.8'094'09045—dc21   97–29473
                                                                CIP

This book is printed on paper suitable for recycling and made from fully managed and
sustained forest sources.

Transferred to digital printing 2001

Printed & bound by Antony Rowe Ltd, Eastbourne

Contents

List of Tables, Figures and Appendices

Acknowledgements

This book has evolved out of an international conference held at the University of Utrecht in April 1996. We would like to acknowledge the efforts of the Conference Committee, who made it such a successful conference. We would also like to extend special thanks to Angelique van den Braak, Eric Casteleijn and Marieke van Nimwegen for their invaluable support during the Conference and the preparation of this book. Kathy Davis and Dietrich Thränhardt commented constructively on the book and improved our Introduction greatly. We are grateful to Stephan Cremer and Rudolph Leiprecht for their encouragement and support. Finally we are indebted to Liz Gooster, who has worked tirelessly on sub-editing the book.

Khalid Koser, London
Helma Lutz, Amsterdam

Notes on Contributors

Jacqueline Andall is a Lecturer in Italian History and Society in the School of Modern Languages and International Studies at Bath University. She has researched and published in the field of gender and immigration in Italy.

Paolo Barbesino is a sociologist by training and is currently Research Fellow at the Graduate Research Centre in Culture and Communication, University of Sussex. He is the author of articles on both communicative approaches within the social sciences and the social construction of social knowledge. Since 1995 he has been leading an ethnographic research project on communication among migrants in urban settings co-funded by the Cariplo ISMU Foundation and the City Council of Milan.

Cristiano Codagnone was awarded a PhD in Sociology at New York University (1995). He is a lecturer in the Department of Sociology of Bocconi University in Milan. In 1996 he held an EC 'Human Capital and Mobility' Fellowship at the European Research Centre on Migration and Ethnic Relations (ERCOMER). His main topic of research recently has been the economic and democratic transitions of Russia and the other former Soviet republics, with a particular focus on the 'national question' and ethnic migrations.

Godfried Engbersen is Professor in Sociology at the Department of General Social Sciences at the University of Utrecht. He has published in the fields of the welfare state and social problems within urban areas; unemployment, poverty and undocumented immigration. He has published several books, which include *Publieke Bijstandsgeheimen* (Public Welfare Secrets) (1990) and together with K. Schuyt, J. Timmer and F. van Waarden, *Culture of Unemployment* (Westview Press, 1993). He is editor of the Annual Report on Poverty and Social Exclusion. During Spring 1996 he was visiting professor at the University of Berkeley, California.

Mirjam van Ewijk, a medical anthropologist, is a researcher and lecturer in the Department of General Social Sciences at the University of Utrecht. Her research interests are health and migration, focusing especially on mother and child care which she has conducted research in Turkey and the Caribbean, and also the illness careers of migrants. Her current research considers how asylum seekers cope with health problems, and institutional reactions towards TB in migrant populations in the Netherlands.

Paul Grifhorst, a social and medical anthropologist, is a researcher at the Department of General Social Sciences at the University of Utrecht. His previous research includes a study of informal labour organizations and health issues in Caribbean societies. His current research interests include health (care) issues in relation to social exclusion. He is currently working on a study of the illness careers of asylum seekers, and institutional reactions towards health needs in refugee populations in the Netherlands.

Felicitas Hillmann is a Research Fellow and project leader of the project 'International Mobility' at the Social Science Research Centre, Berlin.

Ronald Kaye is currently an Associate Senior Research Fellow at Leeds Metropolitan University. Previously he was Senior Lecturer in Politics at Glasgow Caledonian University until his retirement from full-time work in 1995. Since the mid-1980s he has carried out research in a number of areas within the field of refugee and asylum studies. The main published areas have been on exile politics, refugee non-governmental organizations, British refugee and asylum policy, and most recently media perception of refugees and asylum seekers.

Khalid Koser is Research Fellow in the School of African and Asian Studies, University of Sussex. Previously he was Research Fellow at the Migration Research Unit at University College London (1996), and Research Fellow at the European Research Centre on Migration and Ethnic Relations at the University of Utrecht (1994–6). The main focus of his research is forced migration, with a particular interest in refugee repatriation and social networks. He has conducted research on Afghan refugees in Pakistan, Mozambican refugees in Malawi, Iranian asylum seekers in the Netherlands, and is currently research-ing repatriation to Bosnia from the European Union. He has pub-lished a number of articles and book chapters on migration and refugee issues.

Helma Lutz is Professor in General Education at the Johann Wolfgang Goethe University in Frankfurt, Germany. She is also a Fellow of the Amsterdam School for Social Science Research (University of Amsterdam). Previous positions have included posts at the Universities of Utrecht and Amsterdam. She has published extensively on issues of gender, migration, ethnicity and identity in four European languages.

Joanne van der Leun is a researcher in the Department of General Social Sciences at the University of Utrecht. She has published on undocumented immigrants and criminality and, together with Robert Kloosterman and Jan Rath, on immigrants and their involvement within the informal economy. Her current research focus is on the question of whether or not the interface between public service bureaucrats and undocumented immigrants can be seen as 'bastard institutions'.

Annie Phizacklea is Professor of Sociology at Leicester University. Her research over the last 20 years has explored various dimensions of the relationship between migration, ethnicities and gender. Her last two books were (with Carol Wolkowitz) *Homeworking Woman: Gender, Racism and Class at Work* (Sage, 1995) and *Unpacking the Fashion Industry* (Routledge, 1990). Her latest book, *Gender, Migration and Globalisation will be published by Sage in 1998.*

Ann Phoenix is with the Department of Psychology, Birkbeck College, University of London. Her research interests include motherhood and the social identities of young people, particularly those associated with gender, 'race', social class and adoption. Her publications include *Young Mothers?* (Polity Press, 1991); *Black, White or Mixed Race? Race and Racism in the Lives of Young People of Mixed Parentage* (with B. Tizard) (Routledge, 1993); *Shifting Identities. Shifting Racisms* (edited with Kum-Kum Bhavnani) (Sage, 1994); *Crossfires: Nationalism, Racism and Gender in Europe* (edited with Helma Lutz and Nira Yuval-Davis) (Pluto, 1995) and *New Dimensions in Midwifery Care* (jointly published with several co-authors) (English National Board of Nursing and Midwifery).

Hilary Pilkington is Lecturer in Russian Politics and Society for Russian and East European Studies at the University of Birmingham. She is author of *Russia's Youth and its Culture: A Nation's*

Constructors and Constructed (Routledge, 1994) and editor of *Gender, Generation and Identity in Contemporary Russia* (Routledge, 1996). Her current research interests concern: forced migrations and their implications for ethnic and national identity in post-Soviet Russia; the relationship between Islam, ethnicity and nationalism in the Russian Federation; and the impact of globalization on Russian youth culture.

Hedwig Rudolph is Director of the Research Unit 'Organization and Employment' at the Social Science Research Centre, Berlin.

Richard Staring studied cultural anthropology at the University of Nijmegen and is currently completing his dissertation on Turkish undocumented immigrants in Rotterdam at the Faculty of Social Sciences (AWSB), University of Utrecht. He has published on the subject of commercial bank robbers in the Netherlands and is editor of *Focaal: Journal of Anthropology*.

1 The New Migration in Europe: Contexts, Constructions and Realities

Khalid Koser and Helma Lutz

THE NEW MIGRATION IN EUROPE

Over the past few years there has emerged an impressive array of academic literature on migration in the European context. A theme which unites much of this writing is that recent migration has a character which distinguishes it from earlier migration, and the generic term 'new migration' is now widely applied.

Shifts and Changes

This new migration has been identified in a number of ways. At its heart is the dynamic relationship between geopolitical and geoeconomic changes and evolving patterns and processes of migration (Castles and Miller, 1993; Gould and Findlay, 1994; Richmond, 1995). Nowhere have these changes had a greater impact than in Europe. The origins of the new migration in Europe are normally traced to 1989, since which date the conclusion of the Cold War and the collapse of communist regimes have resulted in the end of Europe's political division and the opening of borders between East and West. These changes are estimated to have triggered the migration of up to four million people in Europe between 1989 and 1994 (Fassman and Münz, 1994). At the same time, the outbreak of ethnically motivated wars and so-called 'ethnic cleansing' have precipitated the expulsion and flight of an estimated five million refugees from the territory of the former Yugoslavia alone (UNECE, 1995). There are also indications of large numbers of refugees and repatriates in the territory of the former Soviet Union (Salt and Clarke, 1996). While any estimations of migration are surrounded by the reservations of data deficiencies (Salt, 1995a), a number of commentators have suggested

1

that the extent of migration since 1989 in Europe allows for its qualification as 'new', as it outnumbers any other migration in Europe since the end of the Second World War (for example, Fassmann and Münz, 1994; IMR, 1993; King, 1993*a*; Münz 1996). There is at the same time a new geography of migration in Europe (King, 1993*b*). Recent migration has emerged from new countries of origin, the most significant numerically being the former Yugoslavia. While the dramatic geopolitical changes in the former Soviet Union and Eastern Europe have not resulted in the 'mass' migrations initially predicted, these are nevertheless also significant new countries of origin for migrants in Europe (Salt and Clarke, 1996; Rudolph, 1996; Thränhardt, 1996*a*). New countries of destination have also emerged within Europe (Thränhardt, 1996*b*). These include countries in Southern Europe (King and Rybaczuk, 1993) as well as in Central and Eastern Europe. The distinction between countries of origin and countries of destination within Europe has in this context become increasingly blurred, as traditional countries of emigration have become countries of immigration at the same time.

This new geography of European migration has often been associated with new types of migration. Intensified short-term movements (Salt and Clarke, 1996) and transit migration (Wallace *et al.*, 1996), for example, have been substantial in Central and Eastern Europe. At the same time, progress made towards the elimination of barriers to the movement of goods, employees, capital and services has increased the salience of regional migration within an integrated Europe (Rees *et al.*, 1996). The new migration has also been associated with changing migrant profiles more generally. Most commentators speak of an increasingly wide range of migrant 'types' (see, for example, Collinson, 1993; Salt 1995*b*). Among the most significant are highly skilled workers, clandestine migrants and asylum seekers (White, 1993). A substantial literature deals with each of these three types, but an important overall comment is that together they embody an increasing polarity in migration flows. In particular, this is manifested by a bipolar distribution according to skills, occupation and income (Champion, 1994).

Family fragmentation has been another result of modern migration, bringing about the growing participation of women in mass migration. There is a general view that the tendency towards a feminization of migration flows is another of the main features of the new migration (Castles and Miller, 1993), although empirical evidence for this trend is still not conclusive (Zlotnik, 1995). In her contribution to this volume, Annie Phizacklea (Chapter 2) suggests that migration statistics, through their exclusive focus on 'legal' migrants, are in effect gender-biased. The data include only those female migrants who use legal channels to enter Europe, normally as the spouse of a legal migrant under the system of family reunification, and furthermore they say nothing about the motivations of these 'legal' female migrants. On a global scale, women are increasingly pioneering migration flows by seizing their chances to work outside their home countries, either legally or illegally (Hondagneu-Sotelo, 1994; Mitter, 1989; Morokvasic, 1993). In Europe, this development is characterized by a growing number of female migrants in sectors of the economy which exhibit employment growth, and especially in the service sector (Rudolph, 1996). A growing number of female migrants are also reported as being exploited in the prostitution and entertainment industries, although reliable data are generally unavailable (Hummel, 1993; Miera, 1996; Morokvasic, 1994; Schenk, 1993).

Responses

It is becoming clear that the new migration in Europe bears a significance which outweighs these changing patterns and processes alone. Migration has assumed a growing importance on political agendas. Dramatic changes in policy responses have taken place, often with negative consequences for its targets (Cornelius *et al.*, 1994). New migrants, and particularly undocumented migrants and asylum seekers, have become the focus for a brand of moral panic in many European societies, in which they represent a broader social symbol of immigrants who abuse the welfare state, commit crimes and threaten the employment of established citizens.

In this context, the new migration has been associated with the current resurgence of racist and extreme nationalist movements in a number of European societies (Billig, 1995; Miles, 1993; Solomos and Wrench, 1993). The construction of 'frontiers of identity' against 'the other' has intensified (Cohen, 1994) and diversified along gender lines (Lutz, Phoenix and Yuval-Davis, 1995). The geography of the new migration has added further complexities, incorporating as it does new countries of origin within Europe. In the territories of the former Soviet Union the new migration has intersected not only with questions of identity, ethnicity and citizenship, but also with definitions of territory and nation (Chinn and Kaiser, 1996), a process reflected as a consequence of war in the territories of the former Yugoslavia (Zarkov, 1995).

Political responses have in turn been associated with the increasing vulnerability of many migrants, from asylum seekers deprived of welfare, through undocumented migrants indebted to smugglers, to women exploited in entertainment industries and in prostitution. At the same time, however, a new brand of transformative politics has emerged out of the new migration. Migrants have adopted new migration strategies which have often undermined the efforts of restrictive immigration policies. As many authors in this volume demonstrate, new restrictions can trigger new forms of resistance. Although power and knowledge are unequally distributed between policy makers and their targets, migrants are not simply victims and passive recipients of these policies; they also have the capacity to mobilize resources and create or broaden their own spaces of control.

Responses 'from below' do not embody only migrants' strategies. There has also emerged an 'industry' based on the activities of smugglers and traffickers which has flourished in the context of tightening political restrictions. In this way migrants are mobilizing social networks which stretch beyond the domain of family or kin. Furthermore, these strategies of resistance increasingly have found support in immigrant communities, sometimes transcending the divisions of 'race', and often of class, culture and religion too (Cohen, 1994). The new migration has in this way become the locus for the redefinition of rights-based liberalism in many industrialized democracies (Cornelius *et al.*, 1994).

New Migration?

The characterization of recent migration in Europe as 'new' seems plausible at an empirical level, in the context of increasing numbers, shifting geographies, changing migrant profiles, feminization, new policy responses and changing migration strategies. At a more conceptual level, however, historical analysis shows us that the application of the term 'new' to a social phenomenon is arbitrary and therefore debatable – transitions are permeable and boundaries can be blurred.

Describing a phenomenon as 'new' corresponds with the modern desire to order and arrange societies according to certain characteristics, of which the expression of time in sequential structure is a major principle. It is, however, an example of an a posteriori description, and these have in other contexts been challenged at a later date on the basis of different ordering principles. In the US context, for example, the in-migration of predominantly Southern and Eastern Europeans around the turn of the century (1873–1910) was called the 'New Migration', while the next major migration (1916–21), formed mainly by the internal migration of Afro-Americans from the agricultural South to the industrialized North, became known as the 'Great migration'. It is significant, however, that the latter was much smaller in size (some 500,000) than the former (around 9.3 million). These movements were perceived and labelled in terms of the migrants' collective ethnic and national characteristics, rather than in terms of numbers.

Another example, this time from the European context, is the widespread notion that migration is historically a 'new' phenomenon, often associated with the expansion of capitalism and the Industrial Revolution and defined as emerging in the late eighteenth and the nineteenth centuries. This view has recently been challenged by historians, who argue that Europeans have moved within and to and from Europe in relatively large numbers for at least the last 500 years (Lucassen and Lucassen, 1996). In this way, new insights from migration historians have not only demonstrated earlier explanations to be seriously flawed, they also question the characterizations and definitions of migration movements through labels such as 'old' and 'new'. It follows that the description of recent migration in Europe as 'new' is still preliminary, and the validity of the notion of 'new' migration stands to be tested and proved in the long term.

This Book

At an empirical level, this book provides a window on contemporary migration in Europe. The contributions cover a range of migrant 'types', including highly skilled migrants, undocumented migrants, asylum seekers and refugees. Their geographical coverage includes Eastern Europe and the former Soviet Union, and migrants from a wide variety of origins. They combine studies of host country populations as well as newly arrived migrants, and cover a wide range of important contemporary issues including identity, criminality, disease and the measurement of migration.

Our aim, however, has been to elevate this book above the status simply of an up-to-date overview of the new migration in Europe by developing a conceptual approach. This book proceeds from the assumption that the new migration in Europe is more than just a label, and might better be conceived of as a social concept, or a social institution. It is, however, a concept which is poorly understood, and the contributions in this volume attempt to capture its meaning. The volume emerges out of an international conference which focused on a series of critical questions, including the extent to which the description 'new' is conceptually valid, how the new migration is defined socially and by whom, and how the new migration is experienced by migrants themselves.

The diverse chapters in this volume demonstrate that the new migration is a broad and complex concept, covering a bewildering array of patterns, processes, diversifications and interactions. They reveal that the concept has multiple and dynamic definitions, and different meanings for different interest groups. They show in addition how the meaning of the new migration has become the focus of competition and sometimes conflict between policy makers, new migrants and resident populations – indigenous and immigrant – in Europe. In this way, the book as a whole can be read as a demonstration of the value of a conceptual approach to a subject which all too often has been subject to analysis no deeper than empirical description, and the study of which has tended to follow a limited political agenda.

In an effort to move the research agenda beyond these restrictions, this book identifies three new research strategies. The first is to place the new migration into comparative and historical context. The second is to investigate how the concept of the new migration has become socially constructed. The third is to focus on the social realities of the new migration. The remainder of this Introduction identifies how the discrete chapters contribute towards an understanding of the new migration through these research strategies.

THE NEW MIGRATION IN CONTEXT

As demonstrated in the previous section, a theme which unites much of the existing literature is that the new migration is conceived of as a discrete phenomenon, with defining characteristics which distinguish it from previous migration in Europe. In contrast, if there is a theme that pervades this book as a whole, it is that the new migration should be placed in context.

One way of assessing the significance of changing migration in Europe is to place it in an historical setting (Cohen, 1991). In their review of old paradigms and new perspectives on historical perspectives on migration studies, Lucassen and Lucassen (1996) argue that historians have successfully challenged existing migration typologies, dichotomies and classifications. Hilary Pilkington (Chapter 5) provides illustration of this process through a study of forced migration in post-Soviet Russia. The people who fall into this category belong predominantly to Russian-speaking communities which were located in the former Soviet republics. Their return can therefore be considered the final stage in an historical migration cycle. At the same time, Pilkington demonstrates how rival conceptions of the collective identity of 'Russianness' have arisen between returning and resident Russians. In this way she reveals a dichotomy in Russia which is far more complex than simply a distinction between recent and previous migration.

Implicit in historical approaches to the new migration is another method of contextualizing the new migration, namely looking outside mainstream migration theory with its roots in sociology and geography, and attempting to integrate other disciplinary approaches. Annie Phizacklea (Chapter 2) places a premium on such an interdisciplinary approach, by arguing that recent empirical changes in migration have generally not been echoed in theoretical developments. In her theoretical analysis of the feminization of the new migration, Phizacklea therefore incorporates insights from feminist theory. This approach enables her to demonstrate how women's experience of migration is mediated by immigration policies and rules which often in very subtle ways continue to treat women as confined to a male-regulated private sphere.

The different experiences of the new migration by men and women highlights the point that migration is not an undifferentiated process. Another way of achieving a contextualized understanding of the new migration is through a comparison of its different elements. Cristiano Codagnone (Chapter 3) disaggregates the multiple migration flows which constitute the new migration in Russia. He demonstrates how much of the migration in and from the Russian arena is not in fact new. The emigration of Jews and ethnic Germans, and the return of ethnic Russians from the Transcaucasian and Central Asian Republics, are all movements which have been occurring since the 1970s. Codagnone concludes instead that in the context of social, economic and political changes in both Russia and Europe, these movements might more accurately be considered not new, but newly relevant.

Highly skilled migrants are another example of a migration type which has until recently been 'invisible' (Salt, 1995*b*). In part this relates again to disciplinary boundaries, as many migration researchers have often been reluctant to consider as migration the relatively short-term movement of people with no intention to settle in the destination country. Another reason is that highly skilled migrants rarely give rise to political debate as they tend to be well-paid and middle-class and are not perceived as constituting a problem. Hedwig Rudolph and Felicitas Hillmann (Chapter 4) demonstrate how a large component of highly skilled migration is shaped by the strategies of large companies which are internationalizing their activities in the context of globalization.

The four chapters in the first part of this volume adopt a variety of methods for contextualizing the new migration to serve different purposes. None of them denies that the new migration embodies new characteristics, although they do imply that these new characteristics are neither uniform nor consistent in their impact upon migration in Europe. They do, however, suggest that there is a very real sense in which an emphasis on the new character of migration has been at the expense of properly analysing underlying processes, many of which can by no means be described as new.

SOCIAL CONSTRUCTIONS OF THE NEW MIGRATION

Simultaneously with the new migration, a 'new Europe' has emerged. Political transformations, and most significantly the collapse of the Soviet bloc, have brought into sharper focus questions surrounding the definition of Europe and its boundaries (Balibar, 1990). Before 1989, Europe was often conceived of as the then European Economic Community (EEC) and the other parliamentary democracies of Western Europe. The nature of organizing principles which can unify the new Europe, however, has become subject to competition and conflict, at the centre of which are located new migrants.

In the quest for the intrinsic character of Europe, discourses of culture, politics and space have become closely entwined with discourses of nationalism, racism and 'home' versus 'otherness' (Räthzel, 1994, 1995). The new racist nationalism (Lutz, Phoenix and Yuval-Davis, 1995), which is gathering force in contemporary Europe, is centrally concerned with notions of defending home, space and territory against 'the other', a category which has come to include immigrants, asylum seekers and ethnic minorities. Essed (1995) has coined the term 'Europism' to describe the defensive discourse involved in the construction of a 'pure Europe' as a symbolic continent which is cleansed of foreign and 'uncivilized elements' in its territory. Elements of 'Europism' can be found in what Habermas (1992) has called the 'chauvinism of prosperity', focusing on the current process of European self-definition through defending its prosperity and the institutions of the welfare state against greedy, indigent 'outsiders'.

The new migration as a social concept cannot be understood in isolation from the uncertainty and confusion over the economic, political and social orientation of the new Europe. In this context, Ann Phoenix (Chapter 6) argues that attempts to understand racism require a focus on the white majority as well as on black or other minority experiences. In the context of new migration, originating as it has predominantly within Europe, the ways in which whiteness is differentiated have become more evident than previously. Phoenix identifies the evolution of new 'hierarchies of whiteness', and in this way she demonstrates how the processes of racialization and ethnicization are essentially socially constructed.

Clearly this study of the construction of differences has important implications for understanding contemporary conceptions of and attitudes towards migrants. One implication is that the social construction of migrants is a differentiated process. Along with 'race' and ethnicity, another important variable can be gender. Focusing on an historical case study, Jacqueline Andall (Chapter 7) examines Catholic and State constructions of female migrants in the domestic sector in Italy. As a result of such constructions, these women were subject to a double invisibility as women and workers. National discourses of gender did not address women's specific situation as *female* migrants, categorizing them instead only as migrants. This positioning in turn contributed to their invisibility as workers since most were located within a marginalized and feminized sphere of the economy. Andall's contribution not only elucidates the gendered notions of visibility and invisibility of migrants, but also emphasizes the role of the Church as a major agent of the construction of society in two different spheres, the public and the private. Migrants are differentiated and localized within and by these spheres.

That the social construction of migrants can differentiate them is clear. This theme of differentiation, however, also applies to the *process* of social construction. Different people or actors can construct the same concept in different ways. Paolo Barbesino (Chapter 8) provides a concrete example of this differentiation. He focuses on the social construction of data on recent migration in Italy. At an empirical level, he demonstrates a lack of integration between the agencies responsible for collecting and analysing data. At a more conceptual level, he argues, the outcome is a whole range of national conceptions of the significance of the new migration.

In contrast to Barbesino, Ron Kaye (Chapter 9) focuses on the social construction of a specific type of new migrant, namely asylum seekers, and more specifically, on the media as an agent of social construction. Employing the technique of media analysis, Kaye demonstrates the systematic use of pejorative language in certain UK newspapers about asylum seekers, labelling them as 'bogus' or 'phoney' refugees. Kaye concludes that in this case the media do not set the agenda, but rather appear to be intermediary agents following the political agenda. In any case, the outcome is the socialization of readers into thinking of asylum seekers as undeserving 'cheats'.

The new migration, like any social concept, is subject to social constructions. The four chapters in the second part of this volume try to understand this process of social construction. It is generally clear that the new migration has been constructed as a 'problem', and that the roots of this construction lie at least in part elsewhere in the new Europe. The process, nevertheless, is differentiated, and the new migration is defined differently by, and has different meanings for, different people and groups. A central challenge in properly understanding the concept the 'new migration' is to try to distinguish these social constructions from social realities.

THE NEW MIGRATION AS A SOCIAL REALITY

It is impossible to understand the social realities of the new migration in isolation from changing immigration policies. The new migration has risen to the top of the political agenda in most European countries, as well as in most other industrialized democracies. The extent to which subsequent changes in policy-making have been a response to changes in migration is, however, very hard to discern. In some cases it is possible to demonstrate a correlation between the timing of new regulations and national peaks in numbers (Salt, 1995*a*). In other cases policies have been directed quite specifically towards certain types of migrants, especially asylum seekers and undocumented migrants (Loescher, 1989; Widgren, 1990). On the other hand, it is clear that the 'ceiling argument' as a policy instrument is arbitrarily employable. In the case of the *Aussiedler* (ethnic Germans migrating from the former Soviet Union and Eastern Europe), an immigration movement which outnumbers any other in contemporary Germany, it has until only very recently been consciously avoided (Münz, 1996; Rudolph, 1996). Immigration control has often emerged out of political, social and economic imperatives which have little direct relationship with migrants and migration (Cornelius *et al.*, 1994). The four chapters in the last part of this book tend, however, not to dwell upon the philosophy and practice of policy-making. Instead they focus on the impacts of these changing policies. They look at how changing rules and regulations have become pervasive influences in the lives of migrants; and they demonstrate how complying with or contesting immigration policies have become the central dynamic in how migrants experience the new migration. These contributions focus on four different sites in which the social realities of the new migration are experienced: illegalization, criminalization, risk strategies and medicalization.

The impacts of immigration policies are far from straightforward, and are surrounded by contradictions. An almost inevitable outcome of restrictive policies, as Khalid Koser (Chapter 10) shows, has been the creation of unauthorized migration, often referred to as undocumented or 'illegal' migration. Paradoxically it is this brand of migration probably more than any other that has provoked public hostility towards immigrants generally, which has in turn placed pressure on governments to adopt more restrictive policies (Cornelius *et al.*, 1994). In this context, an increasing proportion of the new migration is becoming 'illegal'. Koser shows, for example, how Europe's new 'illegal' migrants are also asylum seekers and refugees. He also suggests that 'illegal' migration has assumed a dynamic of its own, as it now supports an important 'business' revolving around smugglers, traffickers and other intermediaries. Most significantly, Koser demonstrates that by being forced to adopt illegal strategies in their quest for asylum, asylum seekers are being exposed to sources of political, economic and social vulnerability.

The relationship between 'illegal' migrants and criminal activities is explored in another context by Godfried Engbersen and Joanne van der Leun (Chapter 11). They present a detailed analysis of the involvement of undocumented migrants in the Netherlands in recorded criminal activity. Their analysis focuses on the creation of opportunity structures for crime, and shows how these arise when migrants are denied access to the wage labour market or to supportive social networks. They conclude that new and planned regulations, such as the Compulsory Identification Act in the Netherlands, will increasingly coerce undocumented migrants into criminality.

A theme which arises from the contributions of Koser and Engbersen and van der Leun is the coercion of migrants into strategies which are associated with risks for them. Richard Staring (Chapter 12) finds a similar pattern in the context of another strategy. He looks at the attempts by undocumented migrants in the Netherlands to legalize their situations, and focuses specifically upon the strategy of marrying a Dutch national. This is another strategy around which a 'business' has grown, and which is associated with threats for the migrants involved. Staring shows how pursuing the marriage strategy can exacerbate the dependent and subordinate positions of undocumented migrants in their own communities.

Employing illegal migration strategies with its associated threats is a reflection not only of the absolute premium which people like asylum seekers place upon migrating, but also more generally of a determination on the part of migrants to overcome new regulations. Non-compliance is the theme of the contribution by Mirjam van Ewijk and Paul Grifhorst (Chapter 13). They explore attempts to control and discipline asylum seekers through the process of 'medicalization'. They demonstrate how asylum seekers articulate protest and resistance to this process of attempted control, and thereby show how 'medicalization' has become a contested concept.

NEW RESEARCH AGENDAS

This book cannot pretend to provide a comprehensive overview of recent migration in Europe. It does not systematically categorize or cover all the distinct migrant types which are relevant in contemporary European migration. Similarly, there exist gaps in its geographical coverage. We would have liked, for example, to pay more attention to Southern Europe as an emerging arena for new migration. There are also issues specific to particular migrant groups or European countries which are missing. A case in point is Germany, where a new '*Gastarbeiter*' system has recruited labourers from Eastern European countries, where between 1988 and 1992 some 1.4 million ethnic Germans (*Aussiedler*) arrived, and where at the same time the German constitution nevertheless has been changed in order to prevent (non-European) asylum seekers from entering the country.

Germany alone could serve as a case study for changing migration patterns, for the diversification of migrant groups (including Jewish immigrants from the former Soviet Union), and for new immigration policies. The case of Germany also illustrates how these developments can be contradictory and confusing, and contribute towards an increasing complexity of the European population. The changing social and demographic landscapes of Europe are characterized by two distinct and contradictory processes. On the one hand, Europe has adopted a 'fortress mentality'; on the other hand, it has developed into a 'new immigration continent' (Thränhardt, 1996*b*). Underlying these changes are new political and economic forces: the breakdown of borders and the transnational mobilization of capital in a global economy respectively. Saskia Sassen has observed that:

> There are strategic sites, for example the formation of the European Union and the internationalization of advanced urban economies, where it becomes clear that the existence of two different regimes for the circulation of capital and the circulation of immigrants poses problems that cannot be solved through the old rules of the game.
>
> (Sasssen, 1996: 25)

Charting 'new rules' is an urgent area for further research. Any effort to provide an overall view of the new migration must also take into account the numerous strategies adopted by people to overcome regulations, limitations and borders, and must fully appreciate the risks that are being taken to this end. In this context, we are aware that the contributions in this book cover only those migrants who in one sense at least have 'succeeded'. This book provides no insight into people who have been unable to migrate in the context of restrictions upon entry; neither does it consider 'unsuccessful' migrants who have become 'trapped' *en route* to their destination or even died in transit, nor those migrants who have been returned to their countries of origin or elsewhere. All of these are important research gaps, the existence of which may reflect the political nature of European research agendas and their tendency to focus on 'visible' phenomena.

The new migration is a concept that we have only begun to explore in this volume. It is a concept, nevertheless, which we believe worthy of further investigation. The contributions point to the potential of a conceptual perspective. They uncover some of the processes that underlie changing migration patterns; they illuminate interactions between phenomena hitherto often considered discrete and independent; and they have practical applications. They demonstrate, for example, how a conceptually informed approach to contemporary migration in Europe can provide a platform for rational debate and informed decision-making. Contextual analysis reveals that the distinction between the new migration and previous migration in the European context is in fact far more blurred than is often proposed.

In this context, it is shown that there is a degree to which the new migration is therefore a social construction, employed by governments at least in part with the aim of legitimizing political responses, the roots of which lie elsewhere. New immigration policies nevertheless are pervasive in the lives of new migrants, and it is suggested that there is a very real sense in which new migrants in Europe today are more vulnerable than ever before.

Vulnerability, however, is experienced differently by migrants, and is differentiated along the lines of gender, class, age and ethnicity. We need more and better studies to analyse how people cope with increasing vulnerability. Further investigations also need to take into account the development of new hierarchies outside and within settled immigrant communities. In this context, the issue of cross-national and inter-ethnic coalition building should be investigated as a proof for changing and shifting solidarities.

In every European society discourses of domination can be distinguished from discourses of social inclusion and resistance to exclusionary forces. All over Europe, people have engaged in developing anti-racist and anti-nationalistic strategies and providing (material and emotional) supply and shelter. One example is the sanctuary movement for asylum seekers, a phenomenon which could be interpreted as an indication of the transnationalization of identities and loyalties. Without denying the sometimes devastating consequences of immigration constraints on the individual, emphasis therefore needs to be placed on the opportunities resulting from migration movements. That migration can be enabling and not just constraining has emerged from migrants' literature (King *et al.*, 1995). As well as embodying cultural cross-fertilization, migrant writers are increasingly successful in challenging national discourses by inscribing the 'other' into the existing selective and exclusive European cultural discourse.

Historians have taught us that migration has always been part of European history, and that European history is in this way a history of migrations (Moch, 1992). Political forces ultimately need to acknowledge that migration was and is a dynamic element of contemporary societal changes. New migrants will keep on coming, and many of them will stay.

REFERENCES

Balibar, E., 'The Nation. Form, History and Ideology', *Review*, 13 (3) (1990), 329–61.

Billig, M., *Banal Nationalism* (London: Sage, 1995).

Castles, S. and M.J. Miller, *The Age of Migration* (London: Macmillan, 1993).

Champion, A. G., 'International Migration and Demographic Change in the Developed World', *Urban Studies*, 31 (4–5) (1994) 653–77.

Chinn, J. and R. Kaiser (eds), *Russians as the New Minority* (Oxford: Westview Press, 1996).

Cohen, R., 'East–West and European Migration in a Global Context', *New Community*, 18(1) (1991) 9–26.

Cohen, R., *Frontiers of Identity: The British and the Others* (London: Longman, 1994).

Collinson, S., *Europe and International Migration* (London: Pinter, 1993).

Cornelius, W.A., P.L. Martin and J.F. Hollifield (eds), *Controlling Immigration: A Global Perspective* (Stanford: Stanford University Press, 1994).

Essed, P.H., 'Gender, Migration and Cross-ethnic Coalition Building', in H. Lutz, A. Phoenix and N. Yuval-Davis (eds), *Crossfires. Nationalism, Racism and Gender in Europe* (London: Pluto, 1995) 48–64.

Fassman, H. and R. Münz, *European Migration in the late Twentieth Century* (Aldershot: Edward Elgar, 1994).

Gould, W.T.S. and A.M. Findlay (eds), *Population Migration and the Changing World Order*, (London: Belhaven, 1994).

Habermas, J., 'Citizenship and National Identity: Some Reflections on the Future of Europe', *Praxis International*, 12 (1) (1992), 1–19.

Hondagneu-Sotelo, P., *Gendered Transitions* (California: California University Press, 1994).

Hummel, D., 'Lohnende Geschäfte: Frauenhandel mit Osteuropäerinnen und der EG-Binnenmarkt', *Beiträge zur Feministischen Theorie und Praxis*, 34 (1993), 59–69.

International Migration Review (IMR), Special Issue: The New Europe and International Migration, 26 (98) (1992).

King, R. (ed.), *Mass Migration in Europe: The Legacy and the Future* (London: Belhaven, 1993a).

King, R. (ed.), *The New Geography of European Migrations* (London: Belhaven, 1993b).

King, R. and K. Rybaczuk, 1993, 'Southern Europe and the International Division of Labour: From Emigration to Immigration', in R. King (ed.), *The New Geography of European Migrations* (London: Belhaven, 1993) 175–206.

King, R., J. Connell and P. White (eds), *Writing across Worlds: Literature and Migration* (London: Routledge, 1995).

Loescher, G., 'The European Community and Refugees', *International Affairs* 65 (4) (1989) 617–36.

Lucassen, J. and L. Lucassen, 'Migrations, Migration History, History: Old Paradigms and New Perspectives', in J. Lucassen and L. Lucassen (eds), *Migrations, Migration History, History: Old Paradigms and New Perspectives* (Bern: Lang, 1996) 1–29.

Lutz, H., A. Phoenix and N. Yuval-Davis (eds), *Crossfires: Nationalism, Racism and Gender in Europe* (London: Pluto, 1995).

Miera, F. (1996) 'Zuwanderer und Zuwanderinnen aus Polen in Berlin in den 90ger Jahren. Thesen über die Auswirkungen der Migrationspolitiken im Spektrum von Niederlassung, neuer Gastarbeit und Prekarisierung', Discussion Paper, Wissenschaftzentrums Berlin für Sozialforschung (1996).

Miles, R., *Racism after Race Relations* (London: Routledge, 1993).

Mitter, S. (ed.) *Information Technology and Women's Employment. The Case of the European Clothing Industry* (Berlin and New York: Springer Verlag, 1989).

Moch, L. P., *Moving Europeans* (Bloomington & Indianapolis: Indiana University Press, 1992).

Morokvasic, M. (1993), ' "In and out" of the Labour Market: Immigrant Women in Europe', *New Community*, 19 (3) (1993), 459–84.

Morokvasic, M., 'Pendeln statt Auswandern. Das Beispiel der Polen', in M. Morokvasic and H. Rudolph (eds), *Wanderungsraum Europa. Menschen und Grenzen in Bewegung* (Berlin: Edition Sigma, 1994) 166–87.

Munz, R., 'A Continent of Migration: European Mass Migration in the Twentieth Century', *New Community*, 22 (2) (1996), 287–300.

Rathzel, N., 'Harmonious Heimat and disturbing Auslander', *Feminist Psychology*, 1(4) (1994) 81–98.

Räthzel, N., 'Nationalism and Gender in Western Europe: The German Case', in H. Lutz, A. Phoenix and N. Yuval-Davis (eds), *Crossfires. Nationalism, Racism and Gender in Europe* (London: Pluto, 1995) 161–89.

Rees, P., J. Stillwell, A. Convey and M. Kupiszewski, *Population Migration in the European Union* (London: John Wiley, 1996).

Richmond, A. H., *Global Apartheid* (Toronto: Oxford University Press, 1995).

Rudolph, H., 'The New Gastarbeiter System in Germany', *New Community*, 22(2) (1996), 287–300.

Salt, J., 'International Migration Report', *New Community* 21(3) (1995a) 443–64.

Salt, J., 'International Migration and Migration Control in Europe: Perspectives for the 1990s', paper presented to the Institute of British Geographers Annual Conference, University of Northumbria at Newcastle (1995b).

Salt, J. and J. Clarke, 'International Migration in Central and Eastern Europe', *New Community*, 22(3) (1996), 513–29.

Sassen, S., Transnational Economies and National Migration Policies', Annual Lecture, IMES, Amsterdam (1996).

Schenk, W., 'GrenzgängerInnen', *Beiträge zur feministischen Theorie und Praxis*, 34 (1993), 69–74

Solomos, J. and J. Wrench (eds), *Racism and Migration in Western Europe* (Oxford: Berg, 1993).

Thränhardt, D., 'European Migration from East to West: Present Patterns and Future Directions', *New Community*, 22 (2) (1996a), 227–42.

Thränhardt, D., 'Europe: A New Immigration Continent. Policies and Politics since 1945 in Comparative Perspective', in D. Thränhardt (ed.), *Europe: A New Immigration Continent* (Münster: Lit Verlag & Transaction, 1996b), 13–74.

UNECE, *Population Trends and Population Related Issues in Countries in Transition: The Need for International Assistance* (Geneva: UN Population Activities Unit, 1995).

Wallace, C., O. Chmouliar and E. Sidorenko, 'The Eastern Frontier of Western Europe: Mobility in the Buffer Zone', *New Community* 22(2) (1996), 259–86.

White, P., 'The Social Geography of Immigrants in European Cities: The Geography of Arrival', in R. King (ed.), *The New Geography of European Migrations* (London: Belhaven, 1993), 47–66.

Widgren, J., 'Asylum Seekers in Europe in the Context of South–North Movements', *International Migration Review* 23(3) (1990), 599–605.

Zarkov, D., 'Gender, Orientalism and the History of Ethnic Hatred', in H. Lutz, A. Phoenix and N. Yuval-Davis (eds), *Crossfires: Nationalism, Racism and Gender in Europe* (London: Pluto, 1995) 105–120.

Zlotnik, H., 'The South-to-North Migration of Women', *International Migration Review*, 29 (1) (1995), 229–54.

Part I
The New Migration in Context

2 Migration and Globalization: A Feminist Perspective
Annie Phizacklea

INTRODUCTION

The theoretical aim of this chapter is to work towards an account of global labour migration which includes an examination of transformative politics. To this end, the chapter explores several cases of global labour migration, some of them involving global networking, in which a change in the balance of power and a measure of justice in favour of the supposedly 'powerless' have been sought, and to some extent, achieved. The argument put forward here is that these 'success stories' are a result of collective agency operating across ethnic and national boundaries, and in some instances across class and gender boundaries as well.

The chapter is divided into four sections. The first is a summary and critique of what are generally agreed to be the main theoretical approaches to the study of global labour migration. The second section endeavours both to borrow from and to build on these theories as a means of better understanding processes of global migration from a feminist perspective. The third section attempts to analyse a number of globalized industries that are built upon the labour and services provided by migrant women. The final section looks at the role of alliance-building and campaigning in these industries.

A NOTE ON THE USE OF THE TERM 'GLOBAL'

The use of the word 'global' rather than 'international' here begs the question of whether or not there has been a fundamental transformation of international, social, economic and political relations which now makes them truly global. I maintain that the processes of globalization were initiated in the fifteenth century, when European powers set out on their 'great voyages of discovery' and began to carve up and

21

colonize large tracts of the world. Globalization therefore always has been about linkages and inequalities between regions on a global basis.

There are nevertheless a number of factors present in the late twentieth century which have acted to accelerate the level of cultural and economic interdependence on a global scale, making such processes more nearly global than simply international. These include: the growing importance of the multinational company; the elimination of national barriers to trade and investment; rapid developments in transportation systems and in information and communication technologies which have transformed the ordering of time and space in our lives, such as the Internet, satellite television, and so on. Set against the massive internationalization of capital flows and subsequent economic interdependence, however, the international flow of labour remains under the jurisdiction of individual nation-states which jealously protect their right to decide who is allowed entry and on what terms.

THEORIZING GLOBAL MIGRATION

Statistics on migration flows are notoriously unreliable but there are at least 100 million people in the world today who have left their home country in order to seek a livelihood or safety elsewhere.[1] Over half of all these migrants are women, and 20 million of this 100 million are officially classified as refugees or asylum seekers, 80 per cent of whom are women accompanied by dependent children. The literature on migration increasingly acknowledges what is referred to as the 'feminization' of migration (see, for instance, Castles and Miller, 1993), but this phenomenon has had little impact on theorization or on the development of social policy. Some would challenge what they refer to as 'the conventional wisdom' that female migration has outnumbered male migration since 1974 (for example, Zlotnik, 1995: 229). The argument is that 'the majority of women who migrate internationally do not do so for work purposes. That is especially the case of women migrating legally from developing to developed countries' (Zlotnik, 1995: 230).

This statement however reflects the single largest problem in analyses based on official figures: that they take account only of documented migration in a period (since 1974) when stringent immigration controls have operated to stop both men and women from the 'developing' world legally entering the 'developed' world for the purposes of work. Family reunion is one of the few mechanisms available to women through which to enter legally a 'developed' nation, but this says nothing about their subsequent employment status. In addition, it is only when we look at the outcome of amnesty/regularization programmes that the scale of undocumented migration becomes apparent. For instance, in 1986 the US Immigration Reform and Control Act (IRCA) included provisions for the legalization of undocumented migrants who could satisfy a series of criteria. Some 1.2 million Mexicans submitted applications for legalization, about half of these being women (Hondagneu-Sotelo, 1994). As will be seen later in the case of migrant domestic workers, the overwhelming majority of whom are women, undocumented workers constitute a significant proportion of the labour force.

In this chapter I am not concerned with the migration of well-qualified, usually professional migrant women workers moving from one affluent country to another and whose relatively 'scarce' skills can be sold for generous rewards on the world labour market.[2] While it is claimed that 'globalization requires and fosters their [the highly qualified] mobility across borders' (Böhning and Oishi, 1995: 796), my concern is with those migrants (including refugees) who through poverty, unemployment, persecution or war, or rapid social and economic change (such as the transformation in the employment structure of the former Soviet Union and Eastern Europe), are forced to seek a livelihood outside their country of origin, regardless of their qualifications.

Such a group includes women living permanently or for long periods of time outside their country of origin, as well as those migrating for relatively short periods of time on fixed-term work contracts. Others may have migrated in order to join husbands or relatives already working abroad and others are forced to leave their home countries due to unrest, persecution and violence. For none of these women is the migration decision a simple one, nor is it one which can be compared automatically with male migration decision-making patterns.

Over the last 20 years accounts of international migration basically have fallen within one of two schools of thought, the first of which I term here the 'orthodox model', the second the 'structural model'. In an otherwise excellent literature review, Goss and Lindquist (1995) refer to these models as 'functional' and 'structural' respectively. The problem with referring to any model so closely guided by rational choice theory as 'functional' is that rational choice theorists have been at pains to avoid the teleological explanations of Marxists and non-Marxists alike and to put the 'rational' actor back, as they see it, in her or his rightful place. I argue that structural analyses have also erred in the direction of functionalism, in this case, 'capital-logic'. I would endorse nevertheless Goss and Lindquist's view that the assumptions underlying the orthodox model have been adopted by many 'developing' country governments with the expectation that the encouragement of migration will have both socially and economically equilibrating consequences

Goss and Lindquist go on to adopt Giddens' structuration thesis as a way out of what they see as the sterile agency/structure dichotomy. I thus evaluate here the potential of structuration in helping to develop an adequate and transformatory model of migration. Most importantly, while poststructural models have had little impact on migration theory, they have had a considerable impact on feminist theory and therefore on feminism's attempts to overcome the criticisms of the last decade. These criticisms have focused on the accusation that feminism's totalizing view of 'women' has in fact been based on a 'subject' who is white, middle-class and located in the affluent world.

The Orthodox Model

The theorization of international migration sometimes takes a neo-classical economic form rooted in development economics. From this perspective, migration is seen as a combination of 'push' and 'pull' factors, individuals being propelled to leave their home country because of underdevelopment, economic hardship or political persecution and drawn towards certain migrant destinations which offer employment and higher wages (Todaro, 1969). The model thus presupposes that individuals make rational choices on the basis of the evidence available to them.

Even though rational choice theorists have never been very good at indicating precisely how the actions of individuals translate into macroeconomic processes, many 'developing' country governments have adopted the orthodox model on the assumption that it will produce equilibrating social and economic outcomes. Many governments have encouraged their surplus labour to work abroad because they view migration as a solution to a number of domestic problems such as unemployment and poverty, and the potential for political unrest that these may unleash. During the period of the Marcos rule, for instance, the Philippine government advertised its ability to package and deliver ready-made workers to labour-importing countries. Migrants also send home remittances which can further alleviate poverty and help service foreign debts. It is also assumed that migrants will acquire useful skills while abroad.

A range of problems is associated with this orthodox model. It lacks an historical and political economic context and what are presented as individual, rational 'choices' are usually circumscribed by at least some factors which are outside of the control of individuals. We know, for example, that the preferred migration destination for Jamaicans until the early 1950s was the 'land of opportunity', the US. This is not surprising. The introduction of restrictive immigration legislation, however, cut off the US as a Jamaican migrant destination. Jamaicans then turned to the UK because they had freedom of access to the labour market and right of residence as Commonwealth citizens and also because some British employers had started recruitment schemes in the Caribbean. The UK was not necessarily Jamaicans' favoured 'choice' and throughout the 1950s their migration responded reasonably accurately to the level of job vacancies (Peach, 1968). But then in 1962 Britain also restricted labour migration from the 'black' Commonwealth and from this date onwards Jamaicans again had to look elsewhere, initially turning to Canada and then, as immigration quotas changed once more, back to the US.

The point to be emphasized here is that migratory 'choices' are circumscribed by factors not subject to manipulation by individuals such as immigration policy and the administration of immigration rules. These factors to a large degree determine the migratory decision. It is, for instance, such laws and rules which determine the 'legal' or 'illegal' status of the migrant, not the activities of the individual migrant. It is moreover these laws and rules which operate in such a way as to reproduce a very traditional notion of a migrant woman's place within a male-regulated private sphere, not only defining her status on entry but defining her subsequent right of residence and employment.

In addition, those countries which encouraged migration as a 'rational' solution to their domestic problems soon discovered that few benefits flow from the migration strategy. Usually it is the most skilled and resourceful people who migrate, even though their skills often go unrecognized in the migration setting. And because they are underemployed they rarely acquire new skills. Remittances may ease economic hardship for individual families, but many migrants are saddled with their own debts both at home and abroad.

Thus while orthodox theories are successful in stressing the role of human agency, the complexity of hierarchically structured social relations and institutionalized constraints on the exercise of individual choice are not considered.

Structural Accounts: The Political Economy of Migration

By the early 1970s a very different account of migration, rooted in Marxist political economy, began to play an increasingly important role in migration theory. Drawing in particular upon the theories of dependency and world systems, the pioneering research of scholars such as Stephen Castles and Godula Kosack, Manuel Castells and Marios Nikolinakos stressed not only the political economy of migratory processes but the common class position shared by migrant workers in the migratory setting. With hindsight we now identify these accounts as overly economically determined analyses which are driven by capital logic, leaving little space for the role of human agency unless it is to act in the interests of the 'historic' collective agency – the global working class.

At the end of the 1970s I began to explore the possibilities of developing a gendered analysis of migration within this political economy-based model. But my early attempts were still caught within a structural straitjacket, which cast migrant women as a racialized and gendered class fraction, whose migration was largely determined by the uneven economic development of capitalism on a global level. The social and economic relations of class remained primary in the analysis with gendered and racialized relations providing additional texture.

Thus if the orthodox accounts are guilty of voluntarism, structural accounts can be criticized for their mechanistic, capital-logic approach to global migratory processes. I argue that a more flexible and less economistic conceptualization of structure is needed if we are to understand contemporary migratory processes in a gendered way. Giddens' structuration thesis marked an attempt to move away from a rigid agency and structure division by viewing structure as a set of rules and resources which are integral to the conduct of individual and collective actors. In this he challenges the view of structure as necessarily external and constraining to individual and collective agency. Instead he views structures as both constraining *and* enabling because they are both medium and outcome of 'the practices they recursively organise' (Giddens, 1984: 25). Structures therefore produced, reproduced and transformed through actors drawing on rules and resources. According to this model our knowledge of the social world will reflect both the constraints and opportunities presented by structures and, while both knowledge and power are unequally distributed, Giddens maintains that even the powerless have the capacity to mobilize resources and secure 'spaces' of control. In the final section of this chapter I describe several instances in which this process has occurred. These cases represent a form of transformatory politics which fly in the face of what many now regard as the bland political pluralism arising from the emphasis on 'difference' in much current feminist theorizing (see for instance Mary Maynard's critique, 1996). First, however, I consider briefly the problems that arise from these poststructural accounts.

DIFFERENCE AND DIVERSITY

Poststructural accounts have had little impact on the theorization of global migration though they have had a significant impact on the way in which feminist theory has attempted to come to grips with charges of universalism. Given Western feminism's tendency to universalize the experience of Western, affluent women, a recognition of difference and diversity is welcome. It is clear that migratory flows incorporate not only different nationalities, but also people of different ethnic, linguistic and religious affiliations. Some migrants have documents, others do not, some have left to join families, or simply to seek work, while others have been persecuted. The bases of difference and diversity are endless. Nevertheless it needs to be emphasized that there are also real dangers in an emphasis on difference and diversity if it obscures the very real material inequalities between women which that diversity represents.

Mary Maynard has argued that the notion of 'difference' as used in the literature of Women's Studies treats differences 'as existing all on one plane, in the same way and on the same level. So many forms of difference are created that it becomes impossible to analyse them in terms of relations of inequality and power' (Maynard, 1996:15). Maynard adds that this preoccupation with difference emphasizes what divides women rather than what they might share. The attempt to build alliances across boundaries of class, ethnicity and nationality can then seem futile. But as we shall see, such alliances *are* built and in the process the seemingly 'powerless' mobilize resources and secure 'spaces' of control, however limited these spaces may sometimes seem.

At this point it is worth summarizing what is being retained and rejected from each of the models discussed. The orthodox model of migration may be guilty of voluntarism but at the same time it recognizes the possibility of strategic action on the part of the individual and collective actor. Structural models have played down the role of human agency but their emphasis on political economy is in my view vital for any analysis of migration. Structuration theory provides a 'middle road' by collapsing the distinction between agency and structure and Giddens' notion of the 'dialectic of control', in other words how the less powerful carve out spaces of control for themselves, is an important analytical tool in the building of a transformatory model. Poststructural conceptions of difference and diversity are welcome, but on the other hand they are unhelpful if they abandon the notion of social relations as hierarchies of power and privilege.

MIGRANT WOMEN: THE CONSTRUCTION OF DEPENDENCY AND ITS TRANSFORMATION

In this section I look at the factors which need to be considered in a gendered account of migration, showing that the factors which stimulate migration may be different for women as compared with men. Structuralist accounts as described above would consider the ways in which colonialism and the trade and investment practices of postcolonialism have produced vast regional inequalities on a global scale. In the short to medium term economic development does not reduce the pressure on individuals to migrate in search of a livelihood; on the contrary, it actually increases that pressure because of the economic and social dislocation that accompanies the development process. But the penetration of the cash economy, the mechanization of agriculture and the industrialization process itself are not gender-neutral in their impact. For instance, deprived of traditional subsistence activities on and around the land, it is often women who become a relative surplus population in the poorer 'developing' countries of the world. Even though these same countries have been the favoured sites for low-wage manufacturing production by multinationals from the late 1960s onwards, the supply of women workers continues to outstrip available employment. But it is also important to understand migration as an escape route for women who find themselves locked into what they consider to be oppressive patriarchal social structures with rigid notions of what constitutes 'proper' behaviour for women.

Breda Gray's exploration of twentieth-century Irish women's migration is useful here. The proportion of women migrating from Ireland in this century has always been equal to or has surpassed that of men (Gray, 1996: 166). Official explanations for the high rate of female migration in the 1920s and 1930s nevertheless pointed to the impact of Hollywood which 'further unbalanced already flighty female minds' (Lee, 1990, cited in Gray, 1996: 166). A search for economic independence and an escape from a society which had institutionalized patriarchy in a range of ways were not considered as motivations for female migration. Gray also considers O'Carroll's research on Irish women's migration to the US in the 1980s, which suggests that women 'seem to be seeking to escape from repressive legislation and economic hardship' (O'Carroll, 1995, cited in Gray, 1996: 168). When asked if they wanted to return to Ireland, many of O'Carroll's respondents replied that they would only return if attitudes to women there changed. Mirjana Morokvasic's analysis of women migrating from former Yugoslavia in the 1960s points to the operation of similar factors (Morokvasic, 1983). Seen within this context migratory flows do not represent simply an enforced response to economic hardship, but also a recognition on the part of gendered individual actors that migration may provide an opportunity to escape a repressive environment.

While migration may hold out the prospect of earnings and a 'better life' for some women, increasingly restrictive immigration controls and entrenched notions regarding migrant women's place in industrial and post-industrial labour markets constantly work against the fulfilment of those aspirations. For women who enter under family reunion regulations, immigration laws act to reproduce a very traditional notion of woman's dependency within a male-regulated private sphere. Women who have no means of legal entry are confined largely to privatized spheres of work (for instance, domestic service and the sex industry, which are often not regarded as 'work' at all), which are bounded by a highly racialized sexual division of labour.

The vast majority of individuals who enter countries under regulations allowing for family reunion are female. In cases where a woman has entered as the spouse of an employed male she may be bound to an unhappy, even violent marriage by immigration laws which render her right of residence dependent on that of her husband (Potts, 1990). If a woman in this situation divorces she becomes liable to deportation. The legal entry of spouses and dependants is allowed only if a sponsor can provide evidence that he or she can support and accommodate them without recourse to 'public funds'. Not only is the family then forced to settle without state support, in many cases there is a waiting period before legal access to the labour market is granted. Many migrant women, lacking work permits and thus denied access to the formal labour market, are forced into undeclared work.

Even those migrant women who have a legal right to work may experience racial discrimination and disadvantage which confines them to low-paid jobs because racialized segregation is as deeply etched as gender segregation in most affluent society labour markets. In the UK, for instance, despite formal sex equality in immigration law, the application of immigration rules is both sexist and racist. If a British Asian woman asks for permission for her non-British Asian husband to join her she is likely to be refused because it is very often claimed that the primary purpose for their marriage was to get him into Britain. If British Asian men or white British women seek permission to bring in their spouses their motives are far less likely to be questioned (Bhabha and Shutter, 1994). It would appear that Asian women are only allowed to follow and be dependent upon men.

The distinction between what goes on in the public sphere and is defined as a public as opposed to a private act has serious implications for women refugees. The term refugee refers to people who have fled their country to avoid persecution, but the definition of persecution in the Geneva Convention relates very much to the public, particularly the political, sphere (Bhabha and Shutter, 1994). The problem is that much persecution that women face occurs in the private sphere. A woman's refusal to abide by customary rules of marriage may threaten her safety, for example, but this would not constitute sufficient grounds for granting her refugee status. An Iranian woman who sought asylum in Canada after being beaten and sacked from her job because she had not worn her veil in her own home was sent back to Iran because it was argued that she risked prosecution not persecution, that her injuries were not permanent and that she had not been deprived of her livelihood.

The fact that women's experience of migration is mediated by immigration policies and rules which often in very subtle ways continue to treat women as confined to a male-regulated private sphere (the implication being that what goes on in that sphere should be treated as private) has meant that many of the fastest growing industries involving migrant women are built around those understandings.

THE SEX AND MARRIAGE INDUSTRIES

Over the last 20 years we have witnessed the rapid growth of the sex-related entertainment industry in affluent and newly industrializing countries. Prostitution and other forms of sex-related 'entertainment' have become very big business for many countries where this industry has become an integral part of tourism. While women from many parts of South East Asia and Africa have been deceived and 'trafficked' by the sex industry for a relatively long time, women from Eastern Europe and the former Soviet Union are now also part of this lucrative trade. The traffic in women is largely illegal and undocumented. Many women are recruited as entertainers, but when they arrive at their destination they realize that the only entertainment they are expected to provide is sex. Others, indebted in their home country, may be trafficked as bonded labour, but because they are very often illegal migrants any attempt to break free of the trafficker or pimp will result in deportation (Truong, 1990; Truong and del Rosario, 1994).

A related growth industry is that of 'mail-order' brides; whereas in the past women from South East Asia were 'favoured' for their 'submissiveness', now Eastern European women are being promoted on cost grounds, as the following extract from *Bild*, a German newspaper, indicates:

> Whereas a Thai is unprepared for cold German winters – one has to buy her clothes – a Pole brings her own boots and fur coat. And she is as good in bed and as industrious in the kitchen.
>
> (*Bild*, 9 January 1991, cited in Morokvasic, 1991)

To reiterate, trafficked women are often deceived or coerced into an illegal migration and at the migrant destination remain under the physical control of their procurers, who hold their passports and return tickets. If they come to the notice of the state, deportation is likely to be the result for the worker as an illegal alien while the employer is likely to go free. The burden of proof is shifted to the woman, who in the eyes of the state is an undesirable alien. In the same way, if a mail-order bride wishes to leave the relationship which secured her entry into the migration setting, she too will be liable to deportation. Once women are shifted out of the private sphere it is immigration law rather than family law or laws against trafficking which determines their status (Truong and del Rosario, 1994).

Even those women working legally in the sex industry may have no protection under labour laws because the work that they do is not regarded as work. For instance the 40,000 women working legally within the Japanese 'entertainment' industry, mainly Filipinas, are classified as 'guests' and non-workers (Anderson, 1997). But guest visas last only for three months which is not enough time for the women to have earned enough to repay the 'debt' incurred through their migration and 'deployment' in Japan (which according to the *Far Eastern Economic Review*, October 1993, can be somewhere between $15,000 and $20,000).

THE MAIDS INDUSTRY

By the early 1980s it was estimated that less than 15 per cent of families in the US conformed to the idealized notion of a bread-winning husband, a housewife and 2.4 children. The vast majority of households contained either dual-earner couples or were single-headed (Anderson, 1988). Other affluent societies have followed suit and the reality of the working mother and a diminishing role of the state in the care of the very young and the elderly has resulted in a massively increased demand for domestic workers in affluent societies. Research in the US indicates very clearly that more affluent women can buy their way out of performing many tasks traditionally associated with women's 'role' in the private sphere by employing poorer (often undocumented) migrant women to perform them instead. A case that has become known as the 'Zoe Baird incident' is a classic illustration of this process. In 1993 Zoe Baird, President Clinton's first nominee for Attorney-General in the US, admitted that she and her husband had employed an undocumented alien as a live-in domestic servant and her husband, also undocumented, as a chauffeur. Not only is the employment of undocumented workers outlawed in the US, but the Bairds also admitted to non-payment of social security and other taxes in respect of the couple (Macklin, 1994: 14).

It has been suggested that while in theory it is illegal for employers to hire undocumented workers, in reality the Immigration and Naturalization Service in the US refrains from investigating such employers. While on the one hand this situation makes it more attractive for undocumented migrants to seek work in private households as they are less likely to be detected, on the other hand it greatly increases their potential exploitation by employers who can implicitly or explicitly use the threat of deportation to intimidate them (Macklin, 1994: 30). Macklin goes on to argue that: 'the grim truth is that some women's access to the high-paying, high-status professions is being facilitated through the revival of semi-indentured servitude. Put another way, one woman is exercising class and citizenship privilege to buy her way out of sex oppression' (Macklin, 1994: 34). The demand for migrant domestic workers cannot be seen however simply as a function of the desire of indigenous women to pursue full-time careers. In many countries, for example Taiwan, live-in servants are a mark of social status. Bridget Anderson's work shows how in the Gulf States and in Britain migrant domestic workers are treated by the state as members of households, and consequently have no immigration status in their own right. This non-recognition as an employee leaves such workers, virtually all of whom are women, vulnerable to physical, mental and material abuse. As in the case study discussed above, they are trapped by an immigration law which ties them into what can be a wholly unsatisfactory, even physically dangerous relationship with their employer. If they leave their employment, they will be liable to deportation (Anderson, 1993).

Anderson's current work in Europe indicates the widespread demand for migrant domestic workers, a large proportion of whom are undocumented. Even in countries such as France, where nearly one million families are registered as employers of domestic workers (payment of domestic workers is tax deductible in France), there is also evidence of large numbers of undocumented migrant domestics, for instance an estimated 17,000 live-in Filipinas (Anderson, 1996). Other countries in Europe have introduced measures to regularize domestic work and domestic workers. In Spain, for example, there is an annual quota of migrant domestic workers of around 9000. This quota has been used largely to regularize the position of migrant women already resident but in an undocumented position, but it ties the recipient to a particular employer (Anderson, 1996). Anderson's work also points to the crude racist stereotypes that are often applied to different nationalities in the migrant domestic workforce. Not only do employers express clear preferences, making it clear that certain groups need not apply for job vacancies, but they pay different wages according to nationality. Preferences are also made clear to recruitment agencies even though such practices are outlawed by anti-discrimination laws in many European countries.

Thus women from poor countries such as Mexico, Sri Lanka and the Philippines allow women in more affluent countries to escape the drudgery of housework in conditions which sometimes approximate to a contemporary form of state-facilitated slavery. The increasing incidence of paid domestic work highlights the hollowness of the supposedly new 'spousal egalitarianism'. The hiring of a full-time domestic worker means that patriarchal household and work structures can go unquestioned, women pursuing a career *and* a family need not 'rock the boat' and any guilt over exploitation is assuaged by the knowledge that a less fortunate woman is being provided with work. Thus racialized and class privileges are preserved as well as patriarchal structures and privileges.

TRANSFORMATIVE POLITICS

While these case studies illustrate the diversity of the experience of migration and the persistence of inequalities between women on a global scale, they also paint a picture of migrant women imprisoned in institutionalized forms of dependency. One of the most pressing questions remaining is that of the possibilities for transformatory politics, for organization and coalition-building across different classes, ethnic groups and nationalities when these categories represent hierarchies of power and privilege. The means by which the seemingly powerless carve out spaces of control need to be explored.

Self-organization and activity have often been forced upon migrant workers in the face of racism. In many cases organizations representing particular nationality groupings initially have been set up with a social function. Yet it is these very organizations which have shown themselves capable of transforming their role through networking to take on a political campaigning function, as illustrated by Filipino women's organizations in Europe, for example. In 1979 the Commission for Filipino Migrant Workers was set up to support Filipino migrants in Britain, many of whom are maids and are totally isolated (Anderson, 1993: 59). Women of all nationalities who had escaped from abusive employers have been helped by the Commission, but it became increasingly clear that a campaign to change the immigration law relating to the position of domestics was essential. An organization called Kalayaan was formed, representing a coalition of migrant and immigrant groups, trade unions and concerned individuals who have campaigned to change the law as well as providing practical help for migrant domestic workers in Britain (Anderson, 1993).

Macklin reports a similar process of coalition-building among black, immigrant and women's organizations around the issue of domestic work in Canada in the 1970s. From the 1950s onwards the

Caribbean Domestic Scheme operated to recruit young Caribbean women without dependants as live-in domestics. As the scheme developed it became increasingly restrictive, denying these women any possibility of converting their status from that of tied migrant worker to immigrant. While Caribbean women were deemed to be excellent domestics, it transpired that employers were paying them up to $150 a month less than their white counterparts. Macklin observes 'that the notion of women of colour as at once uniquely well suited to domestic service yet (or perhaps therefore) worth less money than white women is a recurring paradox' (Macklin, 1994: 17). There was in addition increasing evidence of abuse at the hands of employers and immigration officials. In 1977, seven Jamaican women were threatened with deportation because they had not originally declared dependants in Jamaica when they obtained their visas. The case provided the springboard for a broader-based campaign to gain for domestic workers the same immigration rights as other groups of workers whose labour was deemed socially necessary. In 1981 the coalition-based campaign succeeded in changing federal immigration law so that foreign domestic workers could apply for landed immigrant status from within Canada (Macklin, 1994: 18).

In the Netherlands local women's groups have taken up the cause of undocumented migrant sex workers who would face deportation if they were personally to publicize and campaign against the bonded conditions under which they work (Truong and del Rosario, 1994). There are many other instances of coalition-building amongst diverse groups which only underline the point that a recognition of diversity and difference does not preclude a role for collective agency across hierarchies of class, ethnicity, nationality and gender.

In this chapter I have attempted to look at contemporary migration flows in a gendered way and also to put the role of collective agency back into the frame. I have emphasized the problem that we have in considering the scale and nature of women's migration at a global level because official statistics are based on documented migration. This creates problems for any analysis of migration irrespective of gender, but it creates particular problems for analysing women's migratory patterns in the post-1974 years because they have occurred in the context of stringent immigration controls in the 'developed' countries aimed at halting all but a trickle of labour migration from the 'developing' world. Yet analysis of these 'trickles' and where they are permitted could form the foundations of the larger picture. The sex and domestic worker industry case studies have been presented here in the hope of illustrating how we can piece together that larger picture and the role that the state (which continues to guard jealously its jurisdiction over immigration) plays in producing and reproducing patriarchal structures. In this final section I have attempted to show that the seemingly least powerful actors on the global stage have none the less carved out spaces of control, often managing to secure a measure of justice through legislative change.

NOTES

1. As far as global labour migration is concerned the ILO estimated that in 1994 there were 30–5 million economically active persons plus 40–50 million dependants (ILO, IOM, UNHCR, 1994: 2).
2. I am not suggesting that this is unimportant, in fact it is an area which requires further research. For instance, a few years ago there was some media attention given in the UK to the number of well-qualified women who were taking up opportunities provided by the freedom of movement provision of the Single European Market to secure jobs in other parts of Europe which they believed the 'glass ceiling' prevented them from obtaining in the UK. There was no reference as to whether black or minority ethnic women were among those 'benefiting'.

REFERENCES

Andersen, M., *Thinking about Women: Sociological Perspectives on Sex and Gender* (New York: Macmillan, 1988).

Anderson, B., *Britain's Secret Slaves* (London: Anti-Slavery International, 1993).

Anderson, B., 'Overseas Domestic Workers in the European Union', Report for Stichting Tegen Vrouwenhandel (Utrecht, 1996).

Anderson, B., *Labour Exchange: Patterns of Migration in South-East Asia* (London: CIR, 1997).

Bhabha, J., and S. Shutter, *Women's Movement: Women under Immigration, Nationality and Refugee Law* (London: Trentham Books, 1994).

Böhning, W. and N. Oishi, 'Is International Economic Migration Spreading?', *International Migration Review*, 29 (3) (1995) 794–9.

Brown, W., 'Finding the Man in the State', *Feminist Studies*, 18 (1) (1992) 7–34.

Bryan, B., S. Dadzie and S. Scafe, *The Heart of the Race* (London: Virago, 1986).

Castles, S., and M. Miller, *The Age of Migration* (New York: Macmillan, 1993).

Far Eastern Economic Review, October 1993.

Forbes-Martin, S., *Refugee Women* (London: Zed, 1991).

Frobel, F., J. Heinrichs and O. Kreye, *The New International Division of Labour* (Cambridge: Cambridge University Press, 1981).

Giddens, A., *The Constitution of Society* (Cambridge: Polity Press, 1984).

Goss, J. and B. Lindquist (1995) 'Conceptualising International Labor Migration: A Structuration Perspective', *International Migration Review*, 29 (2) (1995) 317–51.

Gray, B., 'The Home of our Mothers and our Birthright for Ages? Nation, Diaspora and Irish Women', in M. Maynard and J. Purvis (eds), *New Frontiers in Women's Studies* (London: Taylor and Francis, 1996) 164–87.

Hertz, R., *More Equal than Others* (Berkeley: University of California Press, 1986).

Hochschild A. and A. Machung, *The Second Shift* (New York: Viking, 1989).

Hondagneu-Sotelo, P., *Gendered Transitions* (Berkeley: University of California Press, 1994).

Kofman, E. and R. Sales, 'Towards Fortress Europe', *Women's Studies International Forum*, 15 (5/6) (1992) 29–40.

Macklin, A., 'On the Outside Looking in: Foreign Domestic Workers in Canada', in W. Giles and S. Arat-Koc (eds), *Maid in the Market* (Halifax, Canada: Fernwood Publishing, 1994) 13–40.

Maynard, M., 'Challenging the Boundaries: Towards an Anti-racist Women's Studies', in M. Maynard and J. Purvis (eds), *New Frontiers in Women's Studies* (London: Taylor and Francis, 1996) 11–30.

Mitter, S., *Common Fate, Common Bond* (London: Pluto, 1986).

Morokvasic, M., 'Women and Migration: Beyond the Reductionist Outlook', in A. Phizacklea (ed.), *One-way Ticket: Migration and Female Labour* (London: Routledge, 1983) 13–31.

Morokvasic, M., 'Fortress Europe and Migrant Women', *Feminist Review* 39 (Winter) (1991) 69–84.

Mouzelis, N., *Sociological Theory: What Went Wrong?* (London: Routledge, 1995).

Peach, C., *West Indian Migration to Britain* (Oxford: Oxford University Press, 1968).

Phizacklea, A., *Unpacking the Fashion Industry: Gender, Racism and Class in Production* (London: Routledge, 1990).

Phizacklea, A. and C. Wolkowitz, *Homeworking Women: Gender, Racism and Class at Work* (London: Sage, 1994).

Potts, L., *The World Labour Market* (London: Zed Press, 1990).

Rowbotham, S. and S. Mitter (eds), *Dignity and Daily Bread* (London: Routledge, 1994).

Sen, G. and C. Grown, *Development Crises and Alternative Visions: Third World Women's Perspectives* (London: Earthscan, 1988).

Shah, N., A.-Q. Sulayman and M. Shah, 'Asian Women Workers in Kuwait', *International Migration Review*, 25 (3) (1991) 464–86.

Todaro, M., 'A Model of Labour Migration and Urban Unemployment in Less Developed Countries', *American Economic Review* 59 (1969) 138–48.

Truong, T.-D. *Sex, Money and Morality: Prostitution and Tourism in South-east Asia* (London: Zed, 1990).

Truong, T.-D. and V. del Rosario, 'Captive Outsiders: Trafficked Sex Workers and Mail-order Brides in the European Union', in J. Wiersma (ed.), *Insiders and Outsiders: On the Making of Europe II* (Kampen: Pharos, 1994) 39–61.

Tyree, A. and K. Donato, 'A Demographic Overview of the International Migration of Women', in R. J. Simon and C. B. Bretell (eds), *International Migration: The Female Experience* (New Jersey: Rowman and Allanheld, 1986) 21–41.

Zlotnik, H., 'The South-to-North Migration of Women', *International Migration Review* 29 (1) (1995) 229–54.

3 The New Migration in Russia in the 1990s
Cristiano Codagnone

INTRODUCTION

This chapter presents a general and largely empirical overview of recent migration flows in Russia and, to a lesser extent, other post-Soviet states. As in other chapters in this book, the concept of 'new' migration is discussed critically here. One of the central themes of the chapter is that some of the migration flows characterizing Russia in the 1990s are better considered newly relevant rather than genuinely new.

Post-Soviet emigration has risen towards the top of the political agenda in Europe, and the former Soviet Union has been conceived as a potential source of massive 'new' immigration into 'Fortress Europe' (see Brym, 1991, 1992; Heitman, 1991). In Russia, meanwhile, the return of ethnic Russians from what is termed here the 'new abroad', referring to the former Soviet Republics, has similarly become the topic of heated public debate. Relying on official statistics and on reasonable estimates presented during the author's interviews with Russian scholars and officials of the Federal Migration Service (FMS), it is suggested in this chapter that the political and symbolic importance assumed by post-Soviet migration both in the West and in Russia tends to outweigh its numerical significance. More specifically, it is demonstrated that emigration to the West, while having increased in recent years, has done so in only a limited fashion, and has been less relevant than immigration into Russia.

An overview of this balance between emigration and immigration is provided by considering the component changes of the Russian population (see Table 3.1). Between 1990 and 1994 a total positive migration balance of 1.63 million has more than offset the 1.36 million by which deaths have exceeded births. Further indirect proof comes from a 1996 FMS proposal that the draft legislation 'On Emigration and Immigration' be re-oriented to focus 'On Immigration in the Russian Federation', because 'emigration flows are not so significant' and can therefore be regulated within the existing legal framework (FMS, 1996: 5).

Table 3.1   Components of population change in Russia, 1986–94

Year	Population at beginning of year (000s)	Annual population change (000s)			Population at end of year (000s)
		Total increase	Natural increase	Net migration	
1986	143 835.2	1 279.7	983.7	296.0	145 114.9
1987	145 114.9	1 228.4	964.4	264.0	146 343.3
1988	146 343.3	1 034.5	783.0	251.5	147 400.5
1989	147 400.5	662.9	580.0	82.9	148 040.7
1990	148 040.7	502.0	338.0	164.0	148 542.7
1991	148 542.7	161.6	110.0	51.6	148 704.3
1992	148 704.3	−30.9	−207.0	176.1	148 673.4
1993	148 673.4	−307.6	−737.7	430.1	148 365.8
1994	148 365.8	−59.7	−869.7	810.0	148 306.1

Source: Goskomstat (1995: 7).

DATA PROBLEMS AND ANALYTICAL DISTINCTIONS

The usual warning about the limits of official migration statistics applies to the data presented in this chapter. The statistics on emigration outside the border of the former Soviet Union come from the Ministry of the Interior records of individuals who received exit visas for permanent residence abroad and actually left the country. They do not include those who exited with tourist visas and personal invitations and eventually settled abroad. The statistics on the migrations between Russia and all former Soviet republics were obtained by the combined elaboration of first, the arrivals and departure records compiled by local militia bodies at the border, and second, data on the registration (*propiska*) and out-registration (*vypiska*) of permanent residence. At the regional level the system of internal passport system is still in use, and life without a *propiska* can be quite difficult; as a result the data on migrations internal to the former Soviet Union can be considered relatively reliable, especially for ethnic Russians. On the other hand, regional authorities often refuse to register the residence of immigrants of other former Soviet nationalities (especially Transcaucasians) after they have been admitted to Russia, thus their number is underestimated by official statistics.

A difficulty of a more conceptual nature arises in the analysis of migration generally and concerns the analytical distinction between different migration 'types'. This problem is exacerbated in the post-Soviet context because of the coincidence of widespread socioeconomic crisis, the outbreak of ethnic and civil wars, and the simultaneous processes of empire break-up and the birth of new 'nationalizing' states[1] in which national minorities find themselves disadvantaged. The distinction in this context between economic migrants, ethnic repatriates and refugees thus becomes blurred. For the purposes of lending coherence to the structure of this chapter, a broadly geographical typology of migration is adopted here, as follows:

1. Migration between Russia and the 'old abroad' (all countries previously external to Soviet borders).
2. Migration between Russia and the 'new abroad' (all countries previously internal to Soviet borders). This category is synonymous with what many researchers term the 'near abroad'. The term 'new abroad' is used here to emphasize the contrast with the previous category, the 'old abroad'.
3. Migration within Russia.

At the same time, this geographical typology broadly corresponds to different migration profiles. Migration in relation to the 'new abroad' tends to be characterized by forced migration and post-colonial repatriation, whereas socioeconomic factors appear to be more salient in explaining migration to and from the 'old abroad'. Internal migration is similarly of a broadly socioeconomic nature, although it can be distinguished from economic migration to the 'old abroad' in that the latter stems from the specific history of population redistribution during the Soviet era. A final qualification is that for the purposes of this chapter, refugees from areas of open conflict or widespread tensions in the ethnic autonomous North Caucasian republics (for example North Ossetia and Chechnya) into other areas of Russia, although formally inside Russian borders, are grouped together with refugees from the 'new abroad'.

MIGRATION TO AND FROM THE 'OLD ABROAD'

The flows between Russia and the 'old abroad' can be divided into emigration to Western countries (including Israel) and immigration from Asian and African countries.

Emigration

The term 'ethnic migration' is commonly used to refer to the outmigration from the Soviet Union of Jews, ethnic Germans, ethnic Greeks and other groups to their respective 'historic homelands' (see, for example, Brubaker, 1992; Fassmann and Münz, 1994; Vichnevsky and Zayontchkovskaya, 1991). While in practice these ethnic migrations have been of a largely economic nature, they may be distinguished from simple economic migration because of the advantages which derive from entitlement to citizenship in the destination countries.

As summarized by Vichnevsky and Zayontchkovskaya (1991), specialists divide emigration from the USSR in the twentieth century into three distinct waves, the first two forced, the third more spontaneous. The first wave followed World War I and the Russian Revolution, the second occurred during and in the aftermath of World War II, while the third began in the 1950s and consisted mainly of ethnic migration. This third wave was limited numerically because emigration was not completely liberalized until 1988 (Voynova and Ushkalov, 1994).

Western diplomatic pressure on the Soviet Union in the 1970s none the less led the regime to allow the emigration of some 340,000 people between 1973 and 1980 (Fassmann and Münz, 1994: 531). It has been noted by both Russian and Western researchers that ethnic migration continued to predominate after emigration was liberalized in 1988 (Brubaker, 1992; Fassmann and Münz, 1994; Manfrass, 1992; Pushkareva, 1992; Shevtsova, 1992; Vichnevsky and Zayontchkovskaya, 1991; Voynova and Ushkalov, 1994). Around 790,000 Soviet citizens emigrated between 1988 and 1990, representing a considerable but not enormous increase (Vichnevsky and Zayontchkovskaya, 1991: 9). Considering Russia alone, some 582,000 people emigrated to the 'old abroad', between 1988 and 1994 (see Table 3.2), with the annual average between 1990 and 1994 standing at just over 100,000 departures. Most emigrants (86.3 per cent) went to Israel, Germany and Greece, again underlining the prevalence of ethnic migration.

Although the official statistics presented thus far tend to underestimate the actual numbers of emigrants, it is unlikely that unreported emigration is of a level sufficient to warrant the gloomy predictions mentioned earlier.[2] Such predictions were based on the assumption that worsening economic conditions and rising unemployment would be followed by waves of economic migrants. The most recent Russian statistical yearbook (Goskomstat, 1996) confirms the general impression of a socioeconomic crisis in Russia in the 1990s, yet mass outmigration has not occurred. This presents a challenge to the standard assumptions of migration theory and suggests that economic deprivation alone does not determine mobility decisions. Overpopulation and poor economic conditions also characterized rural areas of Soviet Central Asia before the 1990s, yet indigenous nationalities showed a low propensity to migrate, not only to more developed Soviet republics but even to the cities of their own homeland (Patnaik, 1995).

Table 3.2 Emigration from Russia to the 'old abroad' by main destinations, 1988–94 (000s)

Destinations	1988	1989	1990	1991	1992	1993	1994
Israel	8.0	21.9	61.0	38.7	21.9	20.4	16.9
Germany	9.9	21.1	33.7	33.7	62.6	72.9	69.5
USA	0.6	0.6	2.3	11.0	13.2	14.8	13.7
Greece	0.1	1.8	4.1	2.0	1.8	1.7	1.0
Others	1.5	2.0	2.4	2.7	3.3	3.8	4.1
Total	20.8	47.6	103.6	88.3	103.1	113.9	105.2

Source: Goskomstat (1995: 402).

Immigration

A new phenomenon of the 1990s is the growing influx of undocumented immigrants and asylum seekers from Asian and African countries. Although there are no precise statistics available, these migration flows have become a priority problem for the FMS and for other governmental structures responsible for regulating migration. While at the end of 1993 the total number of undocumented immigrants in Russia was estimated at 100,000 (Slater, 1994: 40), the FMS figure for the end of 1995 was 500,000, a total expected to rise by 100,000 annually (Regent, 1995: 70).

Reasons for such flows include the permeability of borders at the periphery of the former Soviet Union (especially in the Transcaucasus and Central Asia) and the weak control of the new borders between Russia and the former republics. A further indirect cause, according to the FMS, is the premature ratification of the 1951 Geneva Convention and the related 1967 protocol on refugees by the Russian Parliament at the end of 1992 (FMS, 1995: 9). This made Russia a 'country of first resort' at a time when its borders were effectively open and no relevant legislation existed to deal with asylum seekers. This situation attracted asylum seekers who, whether 'bogus' or 'bona fide', easily crossed the porous Russian borders in the hope of proceeding to Western countries (Regent, 1995: 70). Many who were refused access to the West found themselves in an indeterminate legal status in Russia because of the lack of legislation.

Immigration to Russia from the 'old abroad' can be divided into two categories:

1. transit migration consisting of both asylum seekers and undocumented migrants (mainly from Ethiopia, Somalia, Sri Lanka, Iraq) trying to enter Western countries;
2. permanent and temporary economic migration comprising mostly Chinese but also Vietnamese citizens.

Transit migration, which lately has attracted the attention of international organizations, is not unique to Russia but also concerns Belarus and Ukraine (Markus, 1994*a*, 1994*b*) and also the Baltic republics.[3] These countries often represent the final destinations within the former Soviet borders for such migrants. Given the post-Soviet states' lack of experience and financial resources to deal with this situation, these migrants, once they have bounced off the closed walls of 'Fortress Europe', find themselves in shaky temporary camps in very poor living conditions.[4]

The new immigration of petty traders and temporary labourers from China is raising some serious concerns in Russia. Although this flow is also directed towards Moscow, where their number is estimated at about 50,000 (Komarova and Tishkov, 1996: 42), the majority enter and operate in the border areas of the sparsely populated Russian Far East. Since this region, as will be shown later, is characterized by a large outmigration of Russians, the influx from China is perceived as a possible geopolitical threat. According to Russian demographer Leonid Rybakovskiy, who took part in a round-table discussion on migration:

> We, strictly speaking, do not know if in our country Chinese immigrants number 500,000 or one million. But it is very clear that the problem is of a geopolitical nature as it concerns territories that we could sooner or later lose.[5]

Apart from such long-term geopolitical concerns, the immigration of Chinese labourers into the Far East of Russia has already caused some tensions: the employment of 15 Chinese in the maritime *kray* factories has sparked protests from Russians losing job opportunities but also from Chinese authorities, who claim that the labourers are kept in a sort of slave colony (*Segodnya*, 8 July 1995). Despite some local resentment and the declared intentions of Moscow to curb such migration flows, attractions for migrants are substantial. First, the weakness of border controls allows many Chinese living in the border areas to cross them repeatedly. Secondly, there is a real demand in the cities and towns of the Russian Far East for the cheap goods brought on to the market by Chinese traders, since they are supplied only poorly by Moscow and other commercial centres. Finally, the out-migration of Russians is forcing many factories to draw in cheap labour from China. These factors seem to suggest that immigration from China, and possibly from other nearby Asian countries, into the Russian Far East is a phenomenon that Moscow authorities will have to address for the foreseeable future.

MIGRATION TO AND FROM THE 'NEW ABROAD'

In theory, at least three different migration flows between Russia and the 'new abroad' can be distinguished. These are:

1. forced migration from areas of ethnic and civil wars;
2. repatriation of ethnic Russians to Russia as well as of other nationalities from Russia to their homeland;
3. economic migrations.

Yet in practice it is often difficult to determine boundaries between these categories, especially for ethnic Russians. The 1993 law on 'forced migrants' and the way in which the FMS has granted this status show that the return of ethnic Russians from any post-Soviet state is equated with forced migration regardless of whether the migrants come from peaceful Turkmenistan or from war-ridden Taji-kistan.[6] The rationale behind this interpretation is that these people are not repatriating voluntarily to their homeland but are forced to do so by nationalizing state policies reflected in language and citizenship laws which discriminate against them. Interviews with Russian experts in Moscow revealed that even where migrants came from areas of severe economic crisis, they were seen not as economic migrants but as forced migrants because of the perceived differential effect of nation-alizing policies on ethnic Russians and titular nationalities. The super-ficial nature of the divisions between these three categories should thus be recognized in relation to the discussion below.

Forced Migration

The first inflows of individuals escaping from ethnic conflict, mainly
into the Southern provinces of Krasnodar and Stavropol, date back to
the late 1980s after the outbreak of the Nagorno-Karabakh conflicts
and of the Ferghana valley pogroms against Meshketian Turks (Ter-
Sarkisyants, 1994; Yamskov, 1995). Since that time several other
ethnic conflicts and civil wars in Georgia, Moldova, Tajikistan and
in the Russian Caucasus have forced large numbers of individuals
to migrate. The number of people granted the official status of
'forced migrant' or 'refugee' in Russia has been recorded by the
newly created FMS only since July 1992. The total at the end of
1995 amounted to a little over one million (see Table 3.3). This
figure is not, however, an accurate indicator of the number of 'forced
migrants', strictly defined, who have arrived in Russia. First, it

Table 3.3 Annual and total number of forced migrants and refugees
registered by the Russian Federal Migration Service

Region of departure	1992	1993	1994	1995	1992–95
Tajikistan	65 448	68 598	24 320	26 974	185 340
Russia:	21 826	91 125	23 040	34 868	17 059
Chechnya	21 588	39 823	22 008	33 769	117 188
Ingushetia	0	834	161	254	1 249
N. Ossetia	180	48 700	534	376	49 790
Kazakhstan	283	7 665	63 533	88 681	160 162
Uzbekistan	3 247	18 366	59 574	59 209	140 396
Georgia:	24 817	66 063	17 451	10 774	119 105
Abkhazia	2 106	9 092	3 397	2 076	16 671
Azerbaijan	32 860	44 479	13 751	12 963	104 053
Kyrgyzstan	897	20 074	32 588	17 767	71 326
Moldova	10 341	4 323	2 682	2 688	20 034
Latvia	92	4 156	5 929	5 426	15 603
Estonia	56	1 992	2 784	3 171	8 003
Turkmenistan	54	450	2 208	4 574	728
Armenia	126	1 864	3 382	1 653	7 025
Ukraine	19	262	1 904	2 263	4 448
Lithuania	41	468	1 190	720	2 419
Belarus	0	17	108	188	313
Not shown	234	690	74	31	1 029
Total	160 341	330 592	254 518	271 950	1 017 401

Source: FMS, Moscow.

does not include those who arrived before 1992. Secondly, according to the FMS in Moscow, only between 20 and 30 per cent of those potentially entitled to such a status actually apply for it. Finally, many of those registered could better be described as repatriates: Table 3.3, for instance, shows a marked increase after 1993 of those arriving from Kazakhstan and Uzbekistan where no open conflict was registered.

Table 3.4 Russians in the other Soviet republics: census data, 1959–89

Republic	1959	Total (000s) 1979	1989	% of republic's total population 1959	1979	1989
Ukraine	7 091	10 472	11 365	16.9	21.1	22.1
Kazakhstan	3 974	5 991	6 228	42.7	40.8	37.8
Uzbekistan	1 090	1 666	1 654	13.5	10.8	8.4
Belarus	659	1 134	1 342	8.2	11.9	13.2
Kyrgyzstan	624	912	917	30.2	25.9	21.5
Latvia	556	833	906	26.6	32.8	34.0
Moldova	293	506	562	10.2	12.8	13.0
Estonia	240	409	475	20.1	27.9	30.3
Tajikistan	263	395	395	13.3	10.4	7.6
Azerbaijan	501	475	392	13.6	7.9	5.6
Lithuania	231	303	344	8.5	8.9	9.4
Georgia	408	372	341	10.1	7.4	6.3
Turkmenistan	263	349	334	17.3	12.6	9.5
Armenia	56	70	52	3.2	2.3	1.6

Source: Soviet Census 1959, 1979, 1989.

There are numerous estimates of the actual number of strictly defined forced migrants in Russia. According to the UNHCR, by 1993 there were 2 million from the Transcaucasian republics of Georgia, Armenia and Azerbaijan alone (Slater, 1994: 41). On the other hand, Goskomstat estimates that just 20 per cent of all immigrants arriving from the 'new abroad' are forced migrants (Komarova and Tishkov, 1996: 36), a ratio which, applied to the period 1989–94, would put their total number at only about one million.

In the context of such inaccuracies in the quantitative assessment of this phenomenon, Table 3.3 gives a qualitative indication of the flow. It shows how in the early years the most numerous arrivals were those from Georgia, Azerbaijan and Tajikistan, whereas since the beginning of the war in Chechnya internal refugees from the Russian Caucasus have almost reached the level of those from

Tajikistan. The FMS estimate that some 480,000 people fled the Chechnyan Republic in 1995 and that a further 117,000 had already left between 1992 and the start of the war (*Nezavisimaya gazeta*, 2 April 1996). The prospects for the new inflow of refugees from the 'new abroad' and from the unstable autonomous republics of North Caucasus in the near future are difficult to predict, and depend on the evolution of unresolved open ethnic conflicts but also on thus far latent tensions.

Post-Soviet Repatriation

The return of ethnic Russians (henceforth simply Russians) from some of the former Soviet republics began before the 1990s. As shown in Table 3.4, the total number of Russians in Georgia and Azerbaijan had already begun to decrease in the period between 1959 and 1979, while in the Central Asian republics their number either decreased or remained stable between 1979 and 1989.

Although during the 1960s Russia registered a net outmigration of about 1.1 million, by the 1970s this had shifted to a net immigration of considerable proportions (see Table 3.5). At the same time, all the other republics, with the exception of the Baltic and the other two Slavic republics, experienced net outmigration during the 1980s.

Table 3.5   Soviet inter-republican net migration, 1961–89

Republic	Net migration (000s)		
	1961–70	*1971–80*	*1981–89*
Russia	−1 114	673	1 605
Belarus	−160	−84	12
Moldova	68	−58	−47
Ukraine	530	199	177
Estonia	93	60	47
Latvia	144	104	81
Lithuania	49	68	100
Armenia	144	85	−333
Azerbaijan	−69	−96	−256
Georgia	−94	−162	−62
Kyrgyzstan	130	−99	−140
Tajikistan	120	3	−118
Turkmenistan	10	−9	−55
Uzbekistan	414	150	−591
Kazakhstan	414	−562	−779

Source: Subbotina (1992: 84).

This net outmigration from the Transcaucasus and Central Asia and net immigration into Russia were both, to a considerable extent, the result of the movement of Russians (Kaiser, 1994; Komarova and Tishkov, 1996; Perevedentsev, 1993; Subbotina, 1992; Topilin, 1992). Russians had also begun to depart from the ethnic autonomous republics of North Caucasus as early as the 1970s and 1980s (Yamskov, 1992: 39–40). Large-scale Russian emigration to other Soviet republics occurred after World War II and was stimulated by the campaign for the socioeconomic equalization of all territories of the Union. Consequently skilled workers, technicians and other qualified personnel moved from the centre towards the less developed periphery.

This reverse flow from the Southern republics can be explained by a complex of socioeconomic and ethnic factors. The demographic explosion of titular nationalities in the Southern republics and their increasing urbanization, at a time when the first signs of economic stagnation became evident, increased the level of ethnic competition. This led to worsening ethnic relations between the titular nationalities and Russians, and the latter began to emigrate. With the collapse of the Soviet Union the combination of socioeconomic and ethnic factors encouraging Russians to repatriate have become more pressing and have accelerated a process which was already unfolding.

The picture is quite different in the Baltic republics (especially Estonia and Latvia), where the immigration of Russians continued until the late 1980s. Russian emigration from Estonia and Latvia in the 1990s is thus a new phenomenon and can be considered a 'forced' repatriation. It can be seen from Table 3.6 that between 1989 and 1994 more than three million Russians returned, while 1.4 million emigrated, resulting in a net balance of almost 1.6 million. It should be noted here that Russians were only part of the total net immigration into Russia (2.3 million) from the 'new abroad' between 1989 and 1994. About 600,000 were immigrants of other titular nationalities. Table 3.7 shows that since 1993 Russia registered net inflows of Russians from all former Soviet republics. These inflows have been consistent throughout the period considered for Transcaucasian and Central Asian republics and have increased for Kazakhstan after 1992. It is worth noting that the increase of inflows from Latvia and Estonia occurred only after 1991, confirming the novelty of the phenomenon. These data however must also be read in the context of the initial number of Russians in each republic in 1989. If we divide the total net migration of Russians (1990–4) by their number in 1989 in each republic, the rates presented in Table 3.8 are obtained. Hence, even though the total net outmigration of Russians is highest for Kazakhstan, at almost 500,000 (see Table 3.7), the fact that there were more than six million Russians in Kazakhstan in 1989 casts a new light on this figure. From this perspective, Russians in fact emigrate most intensively from the Transcaucasian and Central Asian republics, continuing a trend which had started much earlier than 1989. The new Russian outmigration from the Baltic republics is significant but still limited.

Table 3.6 Migration between Russia and the 'new abroad'

| | Arrivals (000s) | | Departures (000s) | | Net migration (000s) | |
	Total	Russian	Total	Russian	Total	Russian
1989	854.3	396.0	691.6	334.5	162.7	61.5
1990	913.0	491.7	625.7	291.8	287.3	199.9
1991	692.0	394.1	587.1	276.4	104.9	117.7
1992	925.7	612.0	570.0	251.8	355.7	360.2
1993	922.8	594.8	369.1	175.4	553.7	419.4
1994	1 146.3	726.9	231.7	114.5	914.6	612.4
Total	5 454.1	3 215.5	3 075.2	1 444.4	2 378.9	1 771.1

Source: Goskomstat (1995: 422–3).

Table 3.7 Net migration of Russians to and from the 'new abroad' by republic, 1990–94 (000s)

Republic	1990	1991	1992	1993	1994
Ukraine	−4.9	−24.7	−12.3	38.5	101.0
Belarus	5.6	−2.0	−4.6	1.2	13.3
Moldova	3.1	4.1	11.1	4.0	7.6
Lithuania	5.1	4.5	10.2	13.4	5.4
Latvia	3.5	5.2	19.7	19.4	19.3
Estonia	2.8	3.6	18.7	10.6	8.2
Georgia	9.5	18.0	29.6	33.8	24.2
Azerbaijan	42.9	17.6	35.1	22.9	19.0
Armenia	3.6	3.3	5.6	6.4	4.6
Uzbekistan	40.2	27.9	65.2	50.7	93.5
Kyrgyzstan	16.1	15.5	41.4	66.4	42.9
Tajikistan	31.7	14.4	47.1	40.9	25.8
Turkmenistan	4.4	4.7	10.9	6.7	13.0
Kazakhstan	36.3	25.6	82.4	104.4	234.3

Source: Komarova and Tishkov (1996: 29).

Table 3.8 Ratio of Russian net outmigration from the former Soviet Republics, 1990–94

Republics	Ratio of Russian net outmigration (%)
Armenia	45.1
Tajikistan	40.4
Azerbaijan	35.0
Georgia	33.7
Kyrgyzstan	19.8
Uzbekistan	16.7
Turkmenistan	11.8
Lithuania	11.2
Estonia	9.2
Lativa	7.7
Kazakhstan	7.7
Moldova	5.3
Belarus	1.0
Ukraine	0.8

Source: Elaboration of census data (1989) and migration data in Table 3.7.

Table 3.9 shows the movements of non-Russian titular nationalities between Russia and the 'new abroad'. Most nationalities, with the exception of Armenians, registered net outflows between 1990 and 1992, but net inflows in 1993 and 1994. The data on total immigration into Russia for 1993–4 show that most arrived from their own republics, where no ethnic 'push' factors are at work (Goskomstat, 1994: 402–3 and 1995: 422–3). It can thus be argued that such immigration of non-Russians into Russia from former Soviet republics is of a socioeconomic nature. The same line of reasoning can also be applied to the outmigration of Russians from Ukraine and Belarus which began in 1993, because it is unlikely that strong ethnic 'push' factors are at work in these two Slavic republics. These preliminary conclusions seem to suggest that to some extent migrations from the 'new abroad' into Russia are purely socioeconomic. This means that both Russians and non-Russians, when looking for better economic opportunities, do not necessarily undertake migrations to the West but also move to Russia.

In terms of the short-term prospects, there are again conflicting estimates. The official FMS forecast predicts a minimum of 2–3 million arrivals and a maximum of 4–6 million (Regent, 1995: 66).

Yet figures presented by Russian scholars are more conservative. Demographers such as Rybakovskiy limit the pool of potential Russians repatriates to those still living in the Transcaucasian and Central Asian republics (with the exclusion of Kazakhstan).[7] At the time of writing, the minimum scenario presented by the FMS seems more realistic, unless there is an outbreak of new ethnic and civil wars and a dramatic deepening of the economic crisis in the 'new abroad'.

Table 3.9 Net migration of other nationalities in and out of Russia

Nationality	1990	1991	1992	1993	1994
Ukrainians	22.0	−25.9	−64.3	11.0	79.2
Belarus	19.4	−0.9	−10.6	−5.9	10.1
Moldovans	−2.1	−2.0	−3.0	0	3.2
Lithuanians	−0.7	−0.8	−0.1	0.2	0.4
Latvians	−0.4	−0.3	0	0.3	0.5
Estonians	0	−0.1	0.2	0.3	0.3
Georgians	−2.7	−3.1	0.4	6.1	12.5
Azer	−3.9	−3.8	−2.9	4.7	13.1
Armenians	16.1	10.5	23.6	42.7	60.7
Uzbeks	−3.2	−4.5	−2.9	0.3	3.7
Kyrgyz	−1.5	−2.1	−2.1	−1.0	0.1
Tajiks	−0.4	−0.6	0.5	2.9	3.9
Turkmenians	−0.5	−1.6	−2.1	−1.2	0
Kazakhs	−2.9	−6.6	−10.8	−6.8	1.1
Others	49.3	29.0	69.7	80.8	113.4

Source: Goskomstat (1995: 422–3).

Internal Migrations

Although they have attracted little attention in the West, internal movements have been numerically the most significant migration flows affecting Russia in the 1990s thus far:

> According to Goskomstat's data, between 1990 and 1992 alone the total volume of internal migration amounted to 11 million individuals. It consisted mainly of interregional and rural–urban migration. (*Federal'naya Migratsionnaya programma*, 116–31)

In 1993 and 1994 internal migration, although declining relative to previous years, was still of considerable importance, at 2.9 and 3 million respectively (Komarova and Tishkov, 1996: 18). In terms of migration to and from the 11 so-called 'economic districts', the most

evident trend is the net outmigration from the North, eastern Siberia
and the Far East (see Tables 3.10 and 3.11).

Table 3.10   Russian internal migration in 1993 and 1994

Economic district	Net migration to/from other districts (000s)	
	1993	1994
North	−30.8	−39.1
North West	−5.9	17.7
Central	10.4	53.0
Volgo-Vjatskii	6.2	13.7
Central Black-Earth	23.2	24.7
Povol'zhe	30.7	31.3
Northern Caucasus	35.3	73.8
Urals	1.3	15.0
West Siberia	−4.2	−7.6
East Siberia	−23.6	−20.0
Far East	−78.0	−120.0

Source: Goskomstat (1994: 384-99; 1995: 404-9).

Table 3.11   Net migration rates by economic district, 1979–88 and 1989–94
(average annual net migration per 10,000 population)

Economic district	1979–88			1989–94		
	Total	Urban	Rural	Total	Urban	Rural
Russian Federation	13	57	−98	19	18	23
North	7	40	−93	−51	−43	−75
North West	56	67	−5	15	9	58
Central	34	61	−78	31	28	44
Volga-Vjatki	−27	47	−168	18	35	−21
Central Black-Earth	−18	71	−132	72	77	64
Povol'zhe	−1	58	−142	50	53	41
North Caucasus	4	51	−56	64	42	93
Urals	−28	21	−161	11	16	−2
West Siberia	58	108	−60	11	6	24
East Siberia	5	47	−95	−26	−15	−54
Far East	45	61	−2	−100	−86	−145

Source: Goskomstat (1995: 428-30).

These sparsely populated areas, characterized by harsh living conditions (extreme climate, poor infrastructure, lack of consumer goods)
but endowed with precious natural resources (oil, gas, diamonds,
gold) have always represented a problem for Soviet planners, who

have struggled to attract and retain the necessary labour force there
(Rybakovskiy and Tarasova, 1989). None the less, through economic
incentives such as wage differentials and the so-called 'northern coef-
ficients',[8] migrants, mostly from central and southern rural regions of
European Russia, were attracted to these areas between the mid-1970s
and the mid-1980s. The net migration rates for the periods 1979–88
and 1989–94 demonstrated in Table 3.11 show that after 1989 positive
rates became negative in the three areas concerned, whereas the
opposite occurred in central rural areas such as Volgo-Vyatsky, Central Black-Earth and Povol'zhe.[9] These outmigrations from the
North, Siberia and the Far East have a clear socioeconomic character.
The turning point was 1989 when the deterioration of the economy
began to be felt. With the deepening of the economic crisis in
the 1990s, the Moscow authorities have been unable to maintain the
economic incentives to remain: wage differentials were eroded by
the inflationary process following market reforms and the rising
costs of transport made consumer goods scarcer and on average
more expensive than in other parts of the country.

The other component of internal migration is the movement of
people between cities and rural villages, a flow traditionally intense
in Soviet times.[10] This type of migration continued in the 1990s but
paradoxically market reforms have caused a sort of de-urbanization
process (Rybakovskiy and Tarasova, 1994). In 1992, for instance, the
movement from cities to the countryside exceeded the reverse flow by
113,000 (*Federal'naya migratsionnaya programma*, 1994: 124).
Although this figure decreased in subsequent years, Table 3.11
shows that in certain areas immigration in relative terms is higher in
the countryside. It is worth mentioning that the highest rural net
migration rate has been registered in the densely populated North
Caucasus, a phenomenon with clear implications for the already tense
ethnic relations in the region. The increase of settlement in rural areas
through the arrival of both Russian and non-Russian refugees and
migrants raises the potential for inter-ethnic conflict by intensifying
the already critical scarcity of land and housing.

DISCUSSION AND CONCLUSION

The empirical overview presented in the previous sections has confirmed the three main hypotheses put forward at the beginning of this
chapter. First, former Soviet citizens have emigrated to Western Eur-

ope and North America in relatively limited numbers. Secondly, the repatriation of ethnic Russians has been significant but not massive. Thirdly, in both cases these migrations are not completely 'new' but instead represent an acceleration of processes already at work, as in the case of the emigration of Jews and ethnic Germans to Israel and Germany or of ethnic Russians returning from Transcaucasian and Central Asian republics.

At the same time there are two other flows which have attracted less attention, but which in fact may be more deserving of the term 'new'. Numerically the most significant phenomenon is represented by inter-regional and rural–urban migration within Russia, including the striking new trend of outmigration from areas of the North, Siberia and the Far East. A completely new migration flow is the arrival in Russia of asylum seekers and undocumented migrants from Asian and African countries, most of whom aspire to move to Western countries, although Chinese migrants tend either to settle in Russia or to commute back and forth across the Russian–Chinese border.

The repatriation of ethnic Russians from the 'new abroad' is of great political and symbolic meaning for Russian politics today, where it represents one of the most important issues at stake in the ongoing debate on Russia's geopolitical interests in, and policies towards, other post-Soviet states. For this reason it has attracted considerable attention from the mass media and from politicians, whose apocalyptic forecasts are highly responsive to political agendas. Similar predictions of waves of immigration from the post-Soviet area into the European Union are also widely subscribed to and diffused by the media and politicians in Europe. It can be argued that such scenarios have been at least partially instrumental in legitimating and reinforcing the concept of 'Fortress Europe' and the restrictive immigration policies derived from this construction.

Relations between Western democracies and the former Soviet Union are paradoxical with regard to migration. First, after pressuring the Soviet regime to liberalize emigration in the 1970s and early 1980s, Western leaders in the 1990s have begun to depict such emigration as a possible new invasion of the West in order to legitimate preventive policies. Secondly, Russia and other post-Soviet states have rushed to adopt the 1951 Geneva Convention on refugees, as one of the measures necessary to pass the 'exams of democracy', thus stimulating transit migration towards Europe which their 'democratic examiners' do not want to receive.

Russian migration in the 1990s has theoretical as well as political implications. The lack of large-scale emigration from the post-Soviet space represents one of those cases in which, as Zolberg (1989) suggests, scholars of migration must engage in new thinking to explain why massive migration does not occur despite the existence of strong socioeconomic incentives to do so. In other words, we need to theorize not just why people move but also why they stay. Russians who migrated from the Far East for socioeconomic reasons did not go to Europe but to the central and southern region of European Russia from which they originally emigrated and where they could rely on friends and relatives. The same reasoning applies to Ukrainians who began to emigrate to Russia after 1993. Jews and ethnic Germans have emigrated much more than other nationalities, mainly because they have had most to gain from migration to specific destinations.[11] Current restrictive migration policies in Europe are probably more effective than is generally believed, and may have partially neutralized the socioeconomic factors that otherwise may have attracted more immigrants from Russia and other former Soviet republics.

Yet the excessive emphasis often placed on socioeconomic factors paradoxically shares the flaws of both structuralism and individualism. The differential economic conditions in the world economy are viewed as directly imposing themselves on individuals, who at the same time appear as atomized entities making rational choices between the costs and benefits of migration. To avoid such problems, migration theory must draw from and contribute to the current debate on agency and structure more than it has to date. Heisler (1992) proposes an examination of how migrants are influenced by institutions and norms at both the national and the international level as a starting point for the development of migration theory.

The dominant nationalities of Eastern Europe, with the very specific exception of East Germans, historically have never migrated West in great numbers (Fassmann and Münz, 1994: 534). This important empirical observation demands an explanation which takes into account socioeconomic as well as cultural, and perhaps most pertinently, institutional factors. Detailed analysis of such influences, for instance the traditional lack of internal and external freedom of movement typical of both Tsarist and Soviet Russia (Dowty, 1987: 63–7) would shed more light on post-Soviet migration and, further, contribute to our understanding of international migration in general.

NOTES

1. For a discussion of the significance of the 'nationalizing state' applied to the post-Soviet context, see Brubaker (1992).
2. Some statistics on immigration from Russia and other former Soviet republics have been compiled from the data registered in European countries and reported by Thränhardt (1996: 228–9). These data confirm that immigration into Western Europe from the former Soviet Union has been fairly limited.
3. The (perceived) significance of this phenomenon led the prime ministers of the three Baltic states to sign a treaty in June 1995 on the readmission of illegal immigrants and to discuss co-operative measures to halt transit migration (*Omri Daily Digest*, 128, 3 July 1995).
4. According to the Moscow newspaper *Moskovskiy komosomolets* (22 July 1995), the Russian government intended to concentrate most 'illegal' immigrants in a huge camp in a very unhealthy area of the capital. In late 1995 news emerged of refugees staging a hunger strike against the poor living conditions in the Latvian camp of Olaine (*Omri Daily Digest*, 172, 5 September 1995).
5. This quotation is from page 11 of the proceedings of the round-table discussion of 3 April 1996, *Migratsiya: bedstvie ili blago*, published by the Institute of Ethnology and Anthropology of the Russian Academy of Sciences.
6. The Law on 'Forced Migrants' (*vynuzhdennye pereselentsy*) and the Law on 'Refugees' (*bezhentsy*) were both adopted in 1993 and distinguish between ethnic Russians and members of other national groups entitled to Russian citizenship, who can apply upon arrival for the official status of 'forced migrant', and members of all other nationalities, who can only be granted the status of 'refugee', which excludes them from certain privileges attached to 'forced migrant' status.
7. See *Migratsiya: bedtvie ili blag*, op. cit.: 13.
8. Those who worked in such areas were allowed to retire earlier.
9. It should be noted that the rates in Table 3.11 also include immigration and emigration to and from other Soviet republics and that the net loss of population, for instance from the Far East, is also due to the outmigration of Ukrainians to Ukraine and so on (Perevedentsev, 1993: 69).
10. This component of internal migration overlaps only partially with the previous one because it often occurs within the same region.
11. Anti-Semitism in the Soviet Union has been shown to be only one reason behind Jewish emigration (Benifand, 1991). Ethnic Germans were one of the most integrated of the non-Russian nationalities; hence it is difficult to see 'anti-German' discrimination as a primary determinant of migration.

58   *Cristiano Codagnone*

REFERENCES

Benifand, A., 'Jewish Emigration from the USSR in the 1990s', *Innovation*, 3–4 (1991) 35–50.

Brubaker, W., 'Citizenship Struggles in the Soviet Successor States', *International Migration Review*, 2 (1992) 269–91.

Brym, R., 'The Emigration Potential of Russia and Lithuania: Recent Survey Results', *Innovation*, 3–4 (1991) 29–32.

Brym, R., 'The Emigration Potential of Czechoslovakia, Hungary, Lithuania, Poland and Russia: Recent Survey Results', *International Sociology*, 4 (1992) 387–95.

Dowty, A., *Closed Borders: The Contemporary Assault on Freedom of Movement* (New Haven: Yale University Press, 1987).

Fassmann, H. and R. Münz, 'European East–West migration, 1945–1992', *International Migration Review*, 3 (1994) 520–38.

Federal Migration Service (FMS), *Problemy i perspektivyi deyatel'nosti FMS Rossii*, (Moscow: FMS, 1995).

Federal Migration Service (FMS), *Tezisy doklada na zasedanie Kollegii FMS Rossii 1–3–96*, (Moscow: FMS, 1996).

Federal'naya Migratsionnaya programma, *Etnopolis*, 1 (1994) 116–31.

Goskomstat, *Demograficheskiy ezhgodnik Rossiyskoy Federatsii, 1993* (Moscow: Goskomstat, 1994).

Goskomstat, *Rossiyskiy statisticheskiy ezhegodnik Rossii, 1995* (Moscow: Goskomstat, 1995).

Heisler, M.O., 'Migration, International Relations and the New Europe: Theoretical Perspectives from Institutional Political Sociology', *International Migration Review*, 2 (1992) 596–622.

Heitman, S., 'Soviet Emigration in 1990: A New "Fourth Wave"?', *Innovation*, 3–4 (1991) 1–15.

Kaiser, R., *The Geography of Nationalism in Russia and the USSR* (Princeton: Princeton University Press, 1994).

Komarova, O. and V. Tishkov, 'Rossiyskaya Federatsiya. Migratsii i Migratsionnaya politika', in V. Tishkov (ed.), *Migratsii i novye diaspory v postsovetskikh gosudarstvakh*, (Moscow: Institute of Ethnology and Anthropology of the Russian Academy of Sciences, 1996) 11–54.

Manfrass, K., 'Europe: South–North or East–West Migration', *International Migration Review*, 2 (1992), 388–412.

Markus, U., 'Migration to and from Belarus', *RFE/RL Research Report*, 26 (1994*a*) 45–7.

Markus, U., 'Immigrants in Ukraine', *RFE/RL Research Report*, 26 (1994*b*) 48–53.

Patnaik, A., 'Agriculture and Rural Out-migration in Central Asia, 1960–91', *Europe-Asia-Studies*, 1 (1995) 147–69.

Perevedentsev, V., 'Migratsiya naseleniya v SNG: opyt prognoza', *Polis*, 2 (1993) 69–79.

Pushkareva, N., 'Puti formirovaniya russkoy diaspory posle 1945 g.', *Etnicheskoe Obozrenie*, 6 (1992) 18–30.

Regent, T., 'Migrant-Ne perekati-pole', *Mezhdunarodnaya Zhizn'*, 4–5 (1995) 65–73.

Rybakovskiy L. and V. Tarasova, 'Sovremmennye problemy migratsii naseleniya SSSR', *Istoriya SSSR*, 2 (1989) 68–81.

Rybakovskiy L. and V. Tarasova, 'Vnutrirossiyskaya migratsiya naseleniya: nyneshnyaya situatsiya i prognoz', *Sotsiologicheskie Issledovaniya*, 1 (1994) 31–8.

Shevtsova, L., 'Post-Soviet Emigration Today and Tomorrow', *International Migration Review*, 2 (1992) 241–57.

Slater, W., 'The Problem of Immigration into Russia', RFE/RL Research Report, 26 (1994) 39–44.

Subbotina, I., 'Migratsii russkikh v inoetnicheskikh sredakh', *Racy i Narody*, 7 (1992) 76–98.

Ter-Sarkisyants, A., *Mezhnatsional'nye otnosheniya v Krasnodarskom krae (1993 g.): osnovnye tendentsii razvitiya* (Moscow: Institute of Ethnology and Anthropology of the Russian Academy of Sciences, 1994).

Thränhardt, D., 'European Migration from East to West: Present Patterns and Future Directions', *New Community*, 22(2) (1996) 227–42.

Topilin, A., 'Vliyanie migratsii na etnonatsional'nuyu Strukturu', *Sotsiologicheskie Issledovaniya*, 7 (1992) 31–43.

Vichnevsky A. and J. Zayontchkovskaia, 'L'émigration de l'ex-Union Soviétique: premices et inconnues', *Revue Européenne des Migrations Internationales*, 3 (1991) 5–29.

Voynova V. and I. Ushkalov, 'Sovremennye emigratsionnye protsessy v Rossii, *Sotsiologicheskie Issledovaniya*, 1 (1994) 39–49.

Yamskov, A., *Sovremmenye problemy i veroyatnye napravleniya razvitiya natsional'no-gosudarstvennogo ustroystva Rossiyskoy Federatsii*, (Moscow: Institute of Ethnology and Anthropology of the Russian Academy of Sciences, 1992).

Yamskov, A., 'Involuntary Ethnic Migrations and Resulting Social Problems in the Stavropol Province', paper presented at the international conference 'Development-induced displacement and impoverishment', Oxford, 2–5 January 1995.

Zolberg, A.R., 'The Next Waves: Migration Theory for a Changing World', *International Migration Review*, 3 (1989) 403–30.

4 The Invisible Hand Needs Visible Heads: Managers, Experts and Professionals from Western Countries in Poland
Hedwig Rudolph and Felicitas Hillmann

INTRODUCTION

The focus of this chapter is the mobility of highly skilled people in the context of processes of transformation in Eastern Europe. We use the migratory space between Poland and Western Europe as an example of the structure and dynamics of such flows. Our underlying assumptions are that flows of skilled migrants are highly institutionalized and that they reflect recent changes in the global division of labour. Since statistical data on the phenomenon of highly skilled migration flows to Poland are incomplete, our aim in this chapter is to use our own empirical data to focus on specific aspects of these flows and to explore the potential of a migrant institution perspective as a theoretical framework for further research. We attempt to combine in our conceptual framework an institutional approach with that of the individual actor, differentiating between several 'layers' of migration.

We begin in the first section with a short history of migratory movements to and from Poland, with special reference to skilled labour migration. In the second section we discuss briefly the contributions of network concepts in the context of migration studies, and recent critiques of the network approach, leading to Goss and Lindquist's concept of the migrant institution, which we adopt in our empirical study. In the third section, we present the (preliminary) results of our fieldwork, which was an empirical investigation into the mobility of managers, experts and professionals from Western countries to Poland, using the institutional framework mentioned above. We discuss three types of international migrant institution in this context, although the main focus of our analysis is the dynamics of the internal labour markets of large companies/multinationals. We concentrate particularly on two sectors which are of major strategic importance in the transformation from a managed to a market economy which Poland (in common with other East European countries) is undergoing: food and telecommunications. Our initial results suggest that multinational companies are of particular significance in shaping the flow of highly skilled migration to Poland and hence this chapter is based on the outcomes of semi-structured interviews with high-level managers in some 50 multinational companies/ joint ventures, as well as on interviews with experts, managers and professionals. The main findings of our study as well as the advantages and limitations of our approach are discussed in the concluding section.

MIGRATION FLOWS BETWEEN POLAND AND WESTERN COUNTRIES – THE RECENT PAST AND THE PRESENT

It is no surprise that there is more data and debate on the migration from Poland to Western countries than vice versa. During the years immediately succeeding World War II, mass migrations from Poland formed part of the huge refugee flows from Eastern Europe, which amounted to approximately 15.4 million people. The expulsion of seven million ethnic Germans from Poland also contributed to these migrations (Fassmann and Münz, 1994: 521). The outflow from Poland was directed mainly towards East and West Germany.

Migration flows declined between 1950 and 1992: approximately 1.43 million emigrants from Poland to Western Germany are registered for this period, again mainly ethnic Germans. Three waves of emigration nevertheless can be distinguished within this period: 1956–7 (approximately 216,000 migrants); 1976–82 (approximately 242,000 migrants); and 1987–90 (approximately 753,000 migrants).[1] These movements were supported and, to some extent, incited by the German government, but there were also internal push factors for emigration, such as the anti-Semitic campaign led by the Polish state and the imposition of martial law in 1980–1, when many highly skilled Poles left the country. In 1986, measures which made legal emigration possible were introduced in Poland. While Okólski (1994: 137) assumes that the role of networks in Polish emigration in the 1980s was relatively insignificant, Morokvasic (1994: 181) emphasizes the role of the *Polonia* and of networks in the migration of Poles to Western countries during this decade. The year 1989 is considered to be the turning point for migration trends in Poland. While the rate of emigration among Poles has decreased in the 1990s, diverse and complex migration patterns of 'transit' migration to Poland have emerged. Poland has become one of the main transit routes for migrants from Eastern Europe (especially from Russia, Ukraine, Bulgaria and Romania) to West European countries (IOM, 1994). So-called 'pendulum migration' emerged as an important phenomenon and obtaining legal access to the German labour market as a *Saisonarbeiter* or as a *Werkvertragsarbeitnehmer* became possible (Rudolph and Hillmann, 1995).

Labour migration to Poland is a recent occurrence which gathered momentum only in the 1990s. While in 1991 nearly 12,000 work permits were issued to foreigners by the Polish authorities (IOM, 1994: 28), the number has fluctuated since the end of 1992. Official statistical data indicate that access to economic sectors in Poland for foreigners is segmented according to ethnicity. Europeans and Americans are employed more frequently as specialists and consultants, while nationals of Asian countries hold executive positions in sectors in which they invest, for example restaurants, trading companies, and so on (IOM, 1994: 29). Asian nationals are most often employed however in the food industry (60 per cent of all Vietnamese, for example, work in this sector) and by trade companies. Conversely, 61 per cent of all work permits issued to Germans are for executive positions, while East Europeans work disproportionately as artists and teachers/trainers. These ethnic divisions in the labour market for foreigners were clearly discernible in 1995 (see Table 4.1). The table also shows that in the first half of 1995, a total of 4813 work permits were issued. In addition, 560 permits were granted to foreigners employed by foreign-based companies operating in Poland.

Empirical evidence indicates that Polish science and research institutions lost about a quarter of their human capital between 1981 and 1991. Around two-thirds of these former scientists moved to other types of employment, while roughly one in three emigrated to Western countries (Hryniewicz *et al.*, 1992). Since 1994, an 'inverse brain drain' can be identified, that is, the inflow of human capital to Poland exceeds the outflow. One reason for this phenomenon is that the percentage of emigrants having a very low standard of education has markedly increased (amounting to nearly 70 per cent of all emigrants). Another indicator of this feature is the fact that more immi-

Table 4.1 Work permits for foreigners according to type of work and region of origin (1994 and first half of 1995)

Region	Year	All management functions	Owners	Experts, specialists and consultants	Administrative personnel	Medical professions	Teacher trainers	Artists	Skilled manual work	Unskilled manual work	Other
East European Countries	1994	419	213	400	116	61	230	654	549	1814	146
	1995 Jan.–June	195	117	141	14	28	161	268	22	15	74
West European Countries	1994	1232	420	392	108	7	302	12	24	2	31
	1995 Jan.–June	858	203	210	17	38	124	4	8	9	10
Germany	1994	247	127	103	28	0	12	3	5	0	18
	1995 Jan.–June	175	75	45	4	2	4	1	2	1	1
Total	1994	1651	633	792	224	68	532	666	573	1816	177
	1995 Jan.–June	1053	320	351	31	66	285	272	30	24	84

Source: Sprawozdanie z badania sondazowego zezwolenia na prace udzielane cudzozziemcom przez wojewodzkie urzedy pracy w okresie 1994; 1 January 1994–30 June 1995.

grants than emigrants occupy managerial or professional posts at the time of registration (Okólski, 1995: 13).

Although the data on the direction, volume and dynamics of flows of highly qualified persons are fragmentary, we suggest that the migration processes they portray are indicative of fundamental social and economic changes. We argue that the migration patterns observable in Poland are an outcome and an instrument of the transformative process which the country is undergoing. Specifically, the restructuring of the economy to a market-based one is assisted to a great extent by the transfer of knowledge and skills. The functioning of markets is not guaranteed merely by the abolition of price fixing, the convertibility of the zloty and the introduction of Western administration systems. The transfer of so-called 'soft skills' and organizational learning, we suggest, is also required. In this context Western professionals have critical functions.

We have analysed the interrelation between processes of transformation and processes of migration, focusing on the highly visible segment of skilled labour migration. We argue that Western managers, experts and professionals in Warsaw represent the 'visible heads' who are creating the 'invisible hand of the market' with the aim of transforming Poland. Estimates of the number of foreign experts working and living in Warsaw oscillate around 3000, excluding the considerable number of experts who circulate between Poland and their home countries. Since data on the flow of Western experts to Eastern European countries are few and fragmentary, our fieldwork[2] was conducted by interviewing different types of professionals, concentrating on two sectors which are of particular importance in the transformation process: food and telecommunications.[3] We adopted an approach which is relatively new in the study of migration, that of the dynamic institutional approach developed by Goss and Lindquist (1995). This seemed to us to represent the most comprehensive theoretical framework for our empirical results. In the following section we summarize the institutional approach and discuss how we adapted the concept to our own empirical research.

NETWORKS AND INSTITUTIONS IN THE ANALYSIS OF MIGRATION

At the most general level, a network is defined 'as a specific type of relation linking a defined set of persons, objects and events' (Knoke and Kuklinski, 1991: 175). People, objects and events are conceptualized as nodes or actors in the network which are related through 'ties' or 'links'. The most simple version of a network is the dyadic one (two partners), but there are also very complex versions in which many different partners interact. Fundamental to the concept of networks is the assumption that personal relationships are central features in the lives of individuals, both enabling and constraining their behaviour. This perspective is broadened by the recognition that economic activities, too, are embedded in a social context (Portes, 1995: 8).

When the concept of networks was first adopted in the study of migration in the 1960s (for example, MacDonald and MacDonald, 1964; Tilly and Brown, 1967), the focus was on the adaptation of migrants to the receiving country using personal networks. This reflected the nature of migration research in general in the 1960s and 1970s, which was characterized by the concept of assimilation and the idea of the 'melting pot'. This perspective also represents, however, the current state of social network research, in that nearly all recent structural analyses are 'concerned with issues of social integration and the normative rights and duties that prescribe the activities of bounded groups' (Milardo, 1988: 15).

Some time after the first research on networks in migration, Lomnitz (1977) attempted to establish a conceptual link between migrants' individual actions or household strategies and macrostructural constraints of migration. This approach was later adopted more widely (see Dumon, 1989; Massey, 1990; Pessar, 1982; Schminck, 1984). A recent approach to networks in the migration process is pitched purely at the macro-level: national migration systems are interpreted as migration networks (Salt, 1989). Again, these macro-level networks are said to be characterized by the nature and strength of links between the participants (countries).[4]

In short, migrant networks reflect the features of social networks. They are defined as webs of interpersonal interactions of kin and non-kin migrants and migrant associations. According to Gurak and Caces (1992: 153), the important functions of such networks include buffering migrants from the costs and disruptions of migration. At the destination, networks represent social capital for immigrants, facilitating job search, hiring, recruitment and training (Waldinger, 1994). It has been argued, however, that other important issues are not adequately covered by this framework, for example, the conditions under which networks operate in the host society, the level of exclusion of newcomers through networks, the varying importance of networks for different labour market sectors, and the links between the shape of networks and the type of migration (Gurak and Caces, 1992). Other critiques of the network approach go further. 'It is still not clear how these networks operate as social entities beyond the sum of the individual relationships of which they are constituted' (Goss and Lindquist, 1995: 351). Networks are 'treated as a causal category by virtue merely of their empirical existence without an adequate theorization' (*ibid.*). Goss and Lindquist maintain that an institutional approach to international migration is better suited to elucidating the relative role of structure and agency in the migration process.

In the context of his research on immigrant niches, Waldinger (1994) also suggests using an institutional approach to explain the integration of migrants into labour markets. He – among others, such as Lim (1987) and Salt (1989) – stresses the role of internal labour markets. Groups of 'seedbed' immigrants implanted in these labour markets 'quickly directed new immigrants into the appropriate places in the bureaucracy' (Waldinger, 1994: 12). Portes (1981) emphasizes the determinant role of internal labour markets in oligopolistic institutions; conversely, in the secondary labour market segment, immigrants mostly are hired according not to their skills, but to their ethnicity.

Goss and Lindquist (1995) argue that the concept of migrant networks should be broadened in order to serve as an integrative approach to the study of international labour migration. They suggest that the theory of structuration developed by Giddens may be more capable of 'transcending the macro–micro dichotomy' than contemporary migration theory. Social structures exist objectively as rules and resources. Rules 'include the dimensions of semantic rules (interpretative filters of the individual to decode the reality) and moral rules (norms of social behaviour based on modes of legitimation)' (Goss and Lindquist, 1995: 331). Resources are defined as 'the means which facilitate and constrain the actions of individuals' (*ibid.*). The predominant resource types are authoritative and allocative resources. Migrants' actions are interpreted as:

> a complex articulation of rules and resources which presents constraints and opportunities to individual action. Individuals act strategically within institutions, but the capacity for such action is differentially distributed according to knowledge of rules and access to resources which, in turn may be partially determined by their position within other institutions. (Goss and Lindquist, 1995: 345)

Networks which represent sedimented structures in time and space are defined as institutions. Institutions are expected to coordinate and reproduce the social system. The establishment of international migrant institutions, that is, the conditioning of access to overseas employment by the operation of specific rules and the mobilization of resources, is defined by Goss and Lindquist as the 'institutionalization of migration'. Taking into account the interrelations between structure and agency in the migration process, this approach could be a means of attaining a more holistic picture of the dynamics of international migration. In the following section we adopt such a framework in an attempt to identify rules and resources for different 'layers' of migration networks/institutions for highly skilled labour between Western countries and Poland. The term 'layers' is used here to refer to segments of the labour market, which are distinct but which have a (limited) degree of permeability between them.

HIGHLY SKILLED LABOUR MIGRATION WEST–EAST

In this section, we focus on the inflow of West Europeans to the Polish labour market and present findings from our recent empirical research. We identify two different types[5] of international migrant institution in the primary labour market: political organizations and multinational companies; and the network of freelance professionals. In our exploration of their role in facilitating highly skilled migration, we operationalize the concept of institutions as developed by Goss and Lindquist (1995) by identifying specific 'rules' and 'resources'. Finally in this section, we examine the linkages which exist between these migrant institutions or 'layers'.

Political Organizations

A substantial number of the foreign experts working in Poland (and in other countries in Central Eastern Europe) are sponsored by international and national organizations which participate in EU programmes such as the Poland and Hungary Action for Reconstructing the Economy (PHARE) and Technical Assistance to the Commonwealth of Independent States (TACIS) or are involved in the transformation process in other ways.

The history of the PHARE programme can be divided roughly into three phases: in the first period of about two years, food, humanitarian and medical aid were quite important. The focus soon shifted however to the transfer of 'know-how' about restructuring the state and about management, education and technical assistance for the privatization process. In recent years the third phase of the programme has been oriented towards the provision of financial support for large infrastructure programmes and towards adaptive measures in view of integration into the European Union. Between 1993 and 1995 the PHARE programme promoted activities in the fields of economic and regional restructuring; development of human resources; reform and consolidation of the public sector; and infrastructural development. During the years 1990–4, Poland received a quarter of the total investment made under the PHARE programme (OECD, 1996: 71).

Published studies and the statements of experts indicate that EU policy is incoherent and confused: projects are numerous, but are often not interconnected. Specific data on the implementation of the programmes are not easy to obtain; the situation is described by the experts involved as 'chaotic'. It is clear that as a result of the EU programmes, a substantial but unknown number of experts has been transferred, with the movement overwhelmingly occurring from West to East (Salt, 1989). As a concrete example, data from the *Centrum für Internationale Migration und Entwicklung* (CIM), the German public recruitment agency for highly skilled manpower, reflect this trend. The so-called integrated experts recruited and transferred by this organization are given local work contracts in the target countries, but the German government provides the funds for topping up their salaries. The demand for these highly skilled and experienced experts is increasing and easily surpasses the financial resources available for the programme.

Poland is the major recipient of this inexpensive support in Central Eastern Europe: in 1994, 25 of the 70 integrated experts on CIM's staff in this region were employed in Poland. These experts are earmarked for specific organizations with crucial functions for the promotion of the privatization process, such as the Polish bank for development, the bank for export promotion and the agency for regional development (which supports in particular small and medium sized enterprises) (CIM, 1994: 30f). The countries of Central Eastern Europe are particularly eager to take advantage of the problem-solving capacity generated by the German unification process. Consequently, experts from the new *Bundesländer* are increasingly welcome (contrasting with initial negative prejudice). Their 'assets' include knowledge of the country and of the language, constituting cultural capital that enhances the efficiency of co-operation (CIM, 1994: 42). This cultural capital is also increasingly appreciated by private consultancies.

The rules of access to this migrant institution are similar to those of international diplomacy: a high professional standard combined with 'political sensitivity'. The criteria for the selection of candidates also take into account specific idiosyncrasies of the target country's political élites (such as the aversion to experts from the former GDR during the first phase of transformation mentioned above). Generally, official German representatives in the target country participate in the definition and assessment of the project to be staffed. This multi-stage process is supposed to minimize risks and to allow an optimal matching of requirements with personnel. In the Polish case described, the balance of interests is even more delicate since the experts, although they receive financial subsidies from German authorities, hold contracts with the Polish government. Professional expertise is their most important asset. The 'state of the art' in their field of specialization may however produce a variety of solutions to the problems at hand. Conflicting loyalties may thus arise if some solutions seem more attractive to Polish colleagues, others to the German ones. Hence the complexity of rules in this segment of the labour market clearly reflects the composite structure of resources and the fact that international aid can rarely be understood as a purely charitable act.

Multinationals and Joint Ventures

The second 'layer' within the labour market for the highly skilled is that of managers and professionals working for multinational companies.[6] Here, the relevant migrant institutions are the internationally operating internal labour markets of these large companies. In Poland, the spatial concentration of foreign companies is very marked in some cases, for instance the telecommunications sector, in which most firms have their offices in Warsaw and are clustered in the newly constructed, modern trade centres in just four or five areas of the city. In contrast, the food industry is regionally dispersed and is particularly well represented in less developed regions such as central and eastern Poland. These patterns of location clearly reflect different strategic options for future expansion. As important political decisions concerning the opening of the Polish telecommunications market were still pending at the time of our interviews, representatives of foreign telecommunication companies attempted to stay within arm's length of the 'political headquarters' in Warsaw.

The dominant motives for foreign company investment in Poland are the large Polish market and the proximity of the huge market of Russia. Representatives of some of the Western telecommunications companies state that their Polish outlet is, at the moment, rather marginal with respect to the global development of their enterprise. Their presence in Poland is mainly of a strategic nature: they intend to be prepared to expand instantly and rapidly when the situation permits, to serve the 'hungry' market. Other companies feel put on the spot:

All our competitors have subsidiaries in Poland, so we cannot afford to wait. Now is the time to establish a presence in Poland.
(Polish manager of a South Asian electronics company)

Foreign managers are central agents in creating a first footing in the country and their experience may in some senses be likened to that of a 'pioneer', clearing the ground before recruiting local staff and creating a team:

You must understand that it is very hard to find the adjustment to East European conditions for multinational companies, they really feel sometimes lost with the Polish legal system and how you register a company and so on. Us, also, it took almost one year to register our company. I was working here for one year almost illegally. I had to open the office here, from the scratch, and we were in bad shape on the Polish market.... For almost eight months I was alone, without anything.
(Manager of one of the world's largest computer companies)

In the food sector, the strategies of foreign companies/joint ventures are different. Firms in the food sector are also much larger in general than in the telecommunications branch, employing an average of 360 people. In the first phase of the transformation process, foreign investment was low and took place through the establishment of joint ventures with relatively small foreign engagements. Since 1993, foreign investment in this sector in Poland has generally taken one of three forms: first, the construction of brand new processing plants; secondly, the acquisition of shares in privatized enterprises or the investment of capital in these enterprises; and thirdly, the establishment of joint ventures, in which the state contributes the assets of the enterprise and the foreign company provides cash for investments or increases of working capital. By the mid-1990s, there were approximately 60 major foreign investments in this sector, representing

Germany (196), the US (14), the Netherlands (five), France (four), the UK (three) and Austria (also three) (Urban, 1995).

'Very few of the multinational companies act without expats and sometimes even the trend to substitute them is only declared,' one respondent stated. Indeed, the majority of the multinational firms/ joint ventures in our sample had non-Polish managers at the top level of the organization in Poland. Around 72 per cent of foreign managers and experts in the food sector occupy positions at the upper level; in the telecommunications sector, the figure is around 80 per cent. Their dominant function is central management, where the recruitment of foreign experts is considered to be 'indispensable'. In the food sector, finance and marketing (functions that did not exist in the socialist economy) divisions are staffed mostly by expatriates.

Foreign managers/experts are characterized by a high level of 'cultural homogeneity' in terms of their countries of origin, age range, sex-ratio and educational background. Around a third of foreign managers and experts come from the UK, a sixth from the US (these two countries together comprise 50 per cent of all foreign experts); other significant countries of origin are France, the Netherlands and Germany. This pattern is difficult to interpret because the figures above do not match the corresponding national division of foreign company headquarters in Poland.

These managers and experts are relatively young, most often between 30 and 39 years of age. Some, mainly consultants, are even younger (around 24 years old). There is a correlation between age and the position held in the company hierarchy: in upper-level management, expatriates are mostly around 40 years old. Secondments abroad are more likely to be offered and accepted during the earlier phases of a career (often indicating access to the 'fast track').

Very few female foreign experts are employed, and when they are, they are often in personnel management. This is unsurprising since women are under-represented in managerial positions in general. That the gender ratio is even less balanced among expatriates reflects obstacles to international mobility which often arise from women's personal circumstances. The harsh working conditions in Poland during the transformation period may also have made a transfer of female managers less likely. On the other hand, Poland, like all former socialist countries, has a long tradition of affirmative action policies which made women holding positions of power more 'normal'.

Solid professional experience is said to be more important than the level of formal education. Yet nearly all the foreign managers and experts interviewed had a university degree, with a predominance of technical and economic backgrounds. A high standard of formal education thus seems to be a necessary, though not sufficient, condition for access to managerial positions. The focus on professional experience makes sense given that successful management of the processes of transformation occurring in Poland cannot be achieved using only academic knowledge of business techniques.

The policies of recruitment of highly skilled foreign personnel differ between the sectors. In the food sector, the internal pool (that is, internal labour markets) is most important except for the highest positions, to which staff are recruited externally via head-hunters. The American dream of rising 'from dishwasher to millionaire' is part of the career concept. One company expects to double its volume of sales every five years, thus frequently creating new positions. The slogan is: 'move up or move out'. In the telecommunications sector, the pool for managerial recruitment is more often external. This is related to the fact that 'hopping' from one company to another is more widespread in this sector and that the significance of individual networks outside the company is much more important for the managers. Career prospects are relatively short-term and less stable than in the food sector. The interest in state-of-the-art technology and the 'young' image of this branch encourage 'flexible thinking' among managers; the desire to adapt quickly to new conditions and to develop new technologies are the main incentives for changing companies.

No non-Polish managers (irrespective of their company and their former employment) had to accept a lower-level position when transferred to Poland. In fact, a great majority of the managers and experts retained the same level, especially in the telecommunications sector. The wider scope of responsibilities and discretionary power is most often cited as the attraction of a position in Poland. Thus higher income is not the only, and sometimes not even the most relevant, incentive for non-Polish managers and experts to move to Poland. Despite this, they do, on average, earn about 20 per cent more in Poland than in their former positions.

Not all non-Polish managers and experts are 'real' expatriates in the sense that they receive an 'expat-package' (including higher salary, insurance payments, a free car and other fringe benefits such as flights home, subsidies for apartment rent, and so on). Another category of foreigners, who have the same kinds of positions as the expatriates but do not benefit from these extras, are the so-called 'hybrids'. A 'hybrid' status can be taken as an *ex-post* indicator of weaker bargaining power at the time of recruitment (for instance, because these people were already in the country). Once a person is hired as a 'hybrid' s/he has very little chance of being promoted to an expatriate position.

Another type of skilled employee is of special importance in the Polish case. A number of managers and experts (in our sample about one third) are Polish return migrants. Often they are the children of Polish emigrants who left the country in the early 1980s:[7]

> A large number of them are coming back here. From the group of people I knew in Canada (there were, with me, four people from the class of my high school), around 25 people, already half is back here. Most of them were in professional positions down there. Not the highest. And all of them, except one who opened his own business, are working with multinationals.
>
> (General manager of one of the largest multinational software companies)

These people have a Polish cultural background, but received their education in the West, often in Anglo-Saxon countries, thus becoming part of the '*Polonia*'. Several Polish return migrant clubs in Warsaw, for example the Pink Club and the Eagle Club, provide a social space in the 'home-country' for them:

> There was just a small group of us who felt that people returning from abroad had certain things in common in terms of their outlook, but also in terms of having to adjust to Poland having returned – despite the fact that most people travelled to Poland quite often and obviously had friends and relatives here. Nevertheless, when you actually return to stay here permanently, you then do at first feel a little bit alienated in that you've got used to something else abroad than what you actually find here in Poland. Communist propaganda for so many years was that anyone who leaves Poland was a bit of a traitor. It has taken its toll. That image is still there. ... Most of the people who joined the club simply wanted to have the opportunity to meet people who are in rather similar situations.
>
> (Manager of a club)

The people in the club come from different backgrounds, but all are engaged in white-collar professions. Virtually all the Western countries are represented at the monthly meetings, though the UK, the US, Germany and France predominate. One female expatriate from Perth, home to one of the largest Polish communities in Australia, who works as a consultant, names as one of her motives for coming to Poland (beside the recessionary economy in Australia), that she 'wanted to catch up with my roots'.

We can thus observe a threefold division of this segment or 'layer' of the labour market: first, non-Polish people with expatriate status; second, non-Polish people without complete expatriate status; and third, Polish people. The presence of foreign managers and experts is directly related to the transformation process[8] and the ability to create functioning socio-economic relationships.

Over time, as each company established its presence, the US-based staff have a tendency to return because their position then becomes marginal, as the local people have received training, understand the mindset and the corporate culture of the company that they represent. Then they are able and – surprise, surprise – are more competent and able to develop these markets on behalf of the parent company themselves.

(A Polish expert in the telecommunications sector, who has a Western educational background)

In general, the substitution of foreign managers and experts by locally recruited people proceeds quickly. Expatriates are very expensive, whereas a Polish senior manager earns about half or even a quarter of an expatriate's salary. In the companies in our sample, foreign managers and experts were, as a rule, substituted after about five years. In our group of interviewees, the average stay of foreign managers and experts was about two or three years. In the telecommunications sector, professional contacts established with dealers and distributors sometimes serve to recruit the necessary local personnel:

Mostly we work on internal resources, people from the field. We do our own head-hunting. You can use some other companies, it is not as if you lack the money for it; it costs around $8000 in Poland to get somebody, in management position. For the workers and so on we would be paying $3000 and $4000. But it is not an issue of the money. We don't have much time to get people we must train from the start. That is why we are educating people at the dealer and distributor side, and after we pick them up. Usually there is no quarrel about that because they want to have their own people on the vendor side. We never hear no. We always ask, you can't take anybody without permission.

(General manager of a US-based computer company)

Summarizing our empirical findings relating to the rules and resources of internal labour markets of multinationals/joint ventures in Poland, we can identify both common and specific features of the two industrial sectors under review. Specific to the sectors are, above all, the rules of access – that is, the criteria and processes of recruitment. Representatives of the majority of foreign companies claim that – as a rule – the 'normal' criteria and procedures established for staffing management and expert positions in any foreign outlets are applied.

While some companies in both sectors rely on internal as well as on external 'pools', the internal labour market is more important in the food sector. This corresponds to the relatively stable career patterns of the management. That the companies in the telecommunications sector resort more frequently to external recruitment may be interpreted as a strategy for improving the basis for innovation in view of the rapidly changing technological field. Alternatively, they may be forced to use external labour markets because the types of managers and experts attracted by this sector tend to seek out frequent technological challenges rather than long-term employment positions. Finally, it can be argued that different recruitment rules according to industrial sector reflect – at least partly – the relative importance of the Polish outlets in the network of global operations of the sector. Owing to the preliminary state of activities of companies in the telecommunications sector (the opening of the Polish market is still pending) this hypothesis cannot yet be tested.

In view of these different recruitment procedures the degree of homogeneity concerning the 'cultural background' of the foreign staff in these sectors as indicated by the countries of origin (one in two is from either the US or the UK), the over-representation of middle-aged men and the prevalence of a university education in science or economics, is surprising. The degree of selectivity may be higher than is the rule in pools of foreign managers and experts because of the specific circumstances associated with accepting a position in Poland. To expand, there is – besides considerable discomfort – a high level of uncertainty, which may pose substantial risks to successful performance and, as a consequence, to the individual career. Cultural homogeneity facilitates communication among the foreign managers/experts (even of competing companies) and forges a kind of social stability.

The importance assigned to cultural resources in the recruitment of foreign managers and experts is most clearly reflected in the overrepresentation of members of the *Polonia*. Immediately after the implosion of the socialist regime, when Poland as a country, its culture and language were *terra incognita* for foreign companies, this 'inheritance' was particularly highly valued as a strategic resource. The interests of the companies were matched by strong motivations among members of the *Polonia* to return to their 'home country' and to participate actively in the transformation process.

A second common feature of almost all managers and experts in our sample is a previous history of assignments abroad. Professional experience in a foreign country is obviously an important asset for recruitment. Most of the expatriates in our sample, however, cannot be sure that their appointment in Poland will be advantageous for their career prospects in the medium term. There is at least anecdotal evidence though that, in some cases, high-level responsibilities in Poland have been given to managers who would not have been entrusted with a similar position in a Western country. For this group, at least, the delegation to Poland acts as a career push – although perhaps only temporarily.

The Pool of Freelance Foreign Experts

A third layer is the pool of freelance foreign experts. In contrast to the layer of 'political' experts and foreign managers they constitute a rather heterogeneous group. Consultants and teachers make up a substantial sub-group. Given that English is the newly established *lingua franca* of international business, the need for native English speakers is crucial. This was especially so at the beginning of the transformation process. In all former socialist countries Russian had been the obligatory first foreign language. Statistics from the Polish Ministry of Labour show that in 1994, 44 per cent of a total of 576 work permits issued to UK nationals were for training and teaching; in the first half of 1995 the corresponding figure was still 31 per cent. There is empirical evidence however that these flows of 'native speakers' are not driven only by the demand in Poland, but also gain momentum due to the effects of the current recession on British labour markets. Employment in Poland allows a considerable number of young British graduates, especially those who have a degree in the humanities or social sciences, to escape probable unemployment at home. Taking a job as interpreter or language teacher in Poland bridges the occupational gap and may even provide additional skills. As one 25-year-old English teacher in Warsaw says:

The initial contract here is for nine months and after that you can extend, what I probably will not do. We get paid the money monthly in the bank in zloty, at the moment it is about 13 million, so about 400 pounds. We couldn't live with that in Great Britain, but we can do well here. To come here you used to need a TOEFL test certificate and experience in teaching. Now that's changed, the employers want two or three years of experience before they give you a chance. At the moment I finished university just with my degree (in European cultural history), it didn't qualify me for so much. I think that is a reason why people go out here and do TOEFL. It's something that is quite easy to obtain and a lot of universities in England pushed TOEFL. A few years ago there was a recession in England, it was likely the one thing that guaranteed you to get a job in it.

Almost by definition, the professional context of this pool of foreign freelance experts is the most fluid and diverse of the three 'layers' discussed in this chapter. The rules of access to this segment of the Polish labour market are relatively 'soft', although they have been sharpened recently, for example, by adding 'work experience' as a prerequisite for getting a job. Low barriers to entry, however, mean there is little protection against competitors, which cannot help but have a negative impact on working conditions, especially on the level of salaries. Moreover, proficiency in English which provides access to the pool is a rather transitory resource. The fact that Russian has been the first and obligatory foreign language in Poland for decades has created a window of opportunities for native English speakers. However, they are contributing to an erosion of the value of this resource through their own professional activities.

While access to this 'layer' yields relatively modest resources in absolute terms, the attractiveness of such positions for foreign graduates is due to the scarcity or even lack of alternative professional positions for this (mostly young) group at home, especially in the UK. Since their specific academic certificates lack a 'market' their diplomas do not constitute a resource. This is why – in order to make a living – they have to rely on more general social skills and 'key qualifications' that they have developed indirectly through their studies. They know how to collect, interpret and use information, to build and sustain social networks and so on. Belonging to 'Generation X' creates a basis of identification and a recognition of the limited professional opportunities: Mac-jobs – even on an 'academic' level – are common.

We can only approximate the size of the freelance workforce – for example, by assessing the number of consultants attached to official support programmes on the basis of a temporary contract. According to some recent estimates, 30 per cent of all consultants in Poland work on a freelance basis. Interviews with German organizations involved in the EU programme confirm that the trend among consultants is towards more temporary work. In principle, the consultancy profession can be characterized by the fact that work experience gained through international assignments is of particular importance. Work experience in Central and Eastern Europe may accrue different value in view of the asynchronic development of transformation politics in the countries of this region. Thus maximum professional credentials derive from work in the 'pioneer' country, on the restructuring of the former GDR.

Because of the relatively low level of standardization of both rules and resources in the professional fields of freelance teachers and consultants we hesitate to claim that these are migrant institutions. There are however – to a greater or lesser degree – dense social networks developing among people in these areas, for example focused around some language schools or clubs.

Interconnections between the Migrant Institutions/Networks

Connections between the different 'layers' identified exist, but tend to be contingent upon the dynamics of the transformation process. In the early 1990s, when the transformation started, switching over from one 'layer' to another was relatively easy. The phenomenon of people who at the beginning of the transformation process were employed as interpreters or assistants in consultancies and who later set up their own businesses, has also been noted in other East European countries such as Hungary (Futo *et al.*, 1994). Having a Polish background and a Western education was sufficient to guarantee good positions. A headhunter remembers:

> Four years ago, positions were often vacant, the female bosses of today very often were once the secretaries of the general directors. The general director could not recruit really qualified personnel, the only option he [sic] had was to hire expatriates or friends or secretaries. Today there are more opportunities to find the right people because the market now offers also Polish people with adequate education.

Relations between the first and the second 'layer' certainly exist, but are rather difficult to identify empirically. None of the foreign experts in the multinational companies in our sample mentioned participation in EU programmes. One type of linkage was achieved by using personal relations among foreign experts, some of them having contracts with political agencies, some with large private companies. Affirming their commitment to the transformation process they stressed that they would transfer existing connections to other resourceful experts 'by all means'.

There is anecdotal evidence on 'passages' of experts from international or national organizations to multinationals or to the more established positions among the freelance experts. Several factors may contribute to this development. Principally, projects and very often work contracts are temporary. Contacts with foreign companies may be part of the job and/or they are made in places where foreign experts socialize. The expert moreover may have accumulated specific competence that is most valuable on the Polish labour market; so that s/he may prefer to change their job instead of being transferred to another country when the period of the contract has expired.

We came across only one instance in which a woman made the 'passage' in the opposite direction: from freelance expert into the internal labour market of a multinational. In this case it was not she who took the initiative but the company, which was looking desperately to fill a senior position with a person of a similar cultural background to the previous incumbent. The connections between the 'layers' therefore seem to be accessible in one direction only, in other words top-down. Despite this, the links between freelance consultants and companies are numerous: many are registered with more than one organization and in themselves represent connections between the 'layers'. Informal relations, which may serve as interconnecting agencies, also exist. We refer especially here to the role of the clubs, established by Polish returnees. In the case of Warsaw, another platform for exchange between the different layers is linked to the various international and national representatives such as embassies or chambers of commerce.

CONCLUSION

While the mobility of managers and experts plays an important part in the processes of internalization of political relations and economic activities in general, these groups of highly skilled personnel have an even more crucial role in the transformations of the former socialist countries. It is our central argument that capitalist regimes cannot be created simply by decree, but that the necessary transformations are dependent on fundamental and complex socio-economic changes. The 'invisible hand', Adam Smith's metaphor of the market, does not function quasi-automatically. In reality, regulations by 'markets' are the outcome of nationally and historically specific institutional settings which shape the interrelations of structures and actors. This socio-economic perspective is even more relevant if the task is to create markets in environments that were previously structured by socialist regimes. Technical and administrative measures alone are incapable of realizing this goal. Socialization processes are of paramount importance and as a consequence, the 'human factor' is indispensable: the invisible hand needs visible heads.

The mobility of managers, experts and professionals is an important feature of international labour migration. Our analysis of the flows between Western countries and Poland has demonstrated that most are highly institutionalized. By adopting the framework elaborated by Goss and Lindquist (1995) and exploring the specific rules and resources governing access to the three layers of this segment of the labour market, we found that institutionalization is articulated in different ways. Using the terminology of Goss and Lindquist we can identify these layers as migrant institutions, such as multinational companies and political organizations, providing 'sufficient capacity for time-space distanciation' (Goss and Lindquist, 1995: 336).

A large part of this highly skilled mobility is shaped – directly or indirectly – by the strategies of large companies that intend to internationalize their business in the context of globalization. The mobility of the highly skilled is structured by the rules of their internal labour markets, following mostly stable career patterns. One rule of access seems to be 'cultural homogeneity': those from the UK or the US with a degree-level educational background are over-represented and middle-aged men constitute the majority of foreign managers. To a certain degree, belonging to the *Polonia* can be interpreted as one means of access, combining a Western educational background with a knowledge of the Polish culture and language. Access to resources is linked strictly to the global market strategies of the companies and regulated by the company's centre, to which the Polish branch reports. The highly skilled labour serving the layer of political organizations also gains access to this segment through institutionalization. A high professional standard combined with political diplomacy and, often, previous experience abroad, are the main requirements in this type of institutional setting. Access to resources is dependent furthermore on the concepts and implementation of the various EU and bilateral programmes.

The third layer, the pool of freelance foreign experts, emerged as the least institutionalized. In the case of English teachers the rules of access are relatively 'soft', regulated mainly by TOEFL testing and a command of English as a native language. Some foreign teaching positions had been managed by language schools in Warsaw, which had connections to foreign multinational companies. Consultants, the second group in this layer, gained access mainly through former work experience and their established professional networks. This layer is rather fluid and institutionalization processes are in the initial stages. As a result the concept of the social network is more appropriate in this case than that of the migrant institution. This layer may however serve as a complement to the two layers mentioned above, with migrant institutions providing access to the international labour market for experts and professionals who tend to be interlinked with multinational companies or the transformation programmes of international organizations.

The concept of international migrant institutions promises to be of considerable relevance in the context of the mobility of skilled labour. The network approach offers a less precise tool for analysis in this field since it tends to place stronger emphasis on individual factors, which in our view are less relevant for the dynamics of the flows of the highly qualified. By first identifying different 'layers' characterized by specific rules and resources, we have tried to portray a more accurate picture of the migratory flows. We have shown that both the rules and the resources for access to the different migrant institutions and the links between them and the networks of freelance experts change as the transformation processes gain momentum. This finding supports the proposition that the 'migrant institution' is a useful analytical approach for understanding the dynamics of the mobility of highly skilled labour.

Future research should include the analysis of movement in an East–West direction in order to address the question of the role of international migration by highly skilled personnel in structuring the new global division of labour. Rules and resources for access may differ for flows in this direction, reflecting the role of the respective country in the international division of labour and the extent of ongoing transformation processes in Eastern Europe. Concerning the question of regional differences in migrant institutions, parallel studies in other Central East European countries are essential. Such work could also clarify speculations as to differences in the modes of incorporation of specific countries into world markets. The authors are currently undertaking a comparative empirical study in the Baltics. Additional research should also test the hypothesis that the volume of this type of migration will shrink due to substitution by other forms of communication and control in strategies of internationalization (for example, more sophisticated telecommunications and/or the 'transfer' of managers and experts on an on/off basis). It would be interesting to see whether and to what extent Central and Eastern Europe – as latecomers to the global stage – may take the lead in this respect.

NOTES

1. It is worth emphasizing that the data on Polish migration are unsatisfactory. Okólski (1996) examines international sources on Polish migration and demonstrates that – according to the various statistical sources – the picture is highly confusing.
2. Part of the empirical study was conducted in co-operation with Prof. Okólski of Warsaw University and Prof. Wisniewski of Torun University.
3. Nearly 20 per cent of all foreign investments in the first quarter of 1995 were in the food sector. Foreign investment in telecommunications was rather less (under 4 per cent of the total foreign investment), but the market is very attractive to foreign investors because of the expected deregulation in Poland (in view of association with the EU) and because of the low risks combined with high profit-expectations (based on internal statistics of the Polish Agency for Foreign Investment).
4. Salt (1989) has identified several common features of migration systems in Western Europe, the Middle East, the US and Canada, the Caribbean, the Southern Cone, South Africa and, to some extent, Eastern Europe. These similarities include: a shift to temporary migration as the norm; family reunion as a major element; more restrictive immigration policies; refugees as a major group; and an increasingly important role for institutions in controlling international migration. He also predicts that in the migration systems of the next century, changes in the international spatial division of labour will be accompanied by brain exchange and increasing mobility of highly skilled personnel.
5. A fourth category, that of academics, could be added but is not included in this chapter. For further discussion of this issue, see Rudolph (1994).
6. As a result of changes in the reporting system on direct foreign investment in 1992, there are no reliable data on this topic. An impression of the presence of Western companies and joint ventures in Poland may however be gained from the statistics of the EU-financed Polish agency for foreign investment (PAIZ). The most important investors, as indicated by

the number of companies and the volume of investments are Germany, the US, the UK and Canada. For the year 1993, PAIZ estimated that 15,000 firms were in receipt of foreign capital, while the central statistical office in Warsaw counted only 7500. These statistics pertain to companies which had existed for more than six months and which had more than five employees. During the first quarter of 1995, some 20,000 enterprises incorporating foreign capital were registered by PAIZ.

7. Between 1980 and 1989, some 271, 000 Polish people emigrated legally. The total number of long-term emigrants from Poland during this period however is estimated at 1.1–1.3 million (Okólski, 1995: 15).

8. Most of the companies in our sample began operations in 1991 (telecommunications) or 1992 (food).

REFERENCES

CIM (Centrum für Internationale Migration und Entwicklung), *Jahresbericht* (Frankfurt, 1994).

Dumon, W.A., 'Family and Migration', *International Migration*, 27 (1989) 251–70.

Fassmann H. and R. Münz, 'European East–West Migration, 1945–1992', *International Migration Review*, 28(4) (1994) 520–38.

Futo, P., D. Jones-Evans, D. Kirby, S. Kwiatowski and J. Schwalbach, 'Strategic Partnering: The Development of Technical Consultancy Services in Hungary', Paper presented at the Conference on Science, Technology and Change: New Theories, Realities and Institutions (Budapest, 1994).

Goss, J.D. and B. Lindquist, 'Conceptualizing International Labour Migration: A Structuration Perspective', *International Migration Review*, 29(2) (1995) 317–51.

Gurak, D.T. and F. Caces, 'Migration Networks and the Shaping of Migration Systems', in M.M. Kritz, L.L. Lim and H. Zlotnik (eds), *International Migration Systems* (Oxford: Clarendon Press, 1992) 149–76.

Hryniewicz, J., B. Jalowiecki and A. Myne (1992) 'The Brain Drain in Poland' (Warsaw: University of Warsaw, European Institute for Regional and Local Development, Regional and Local Studies 9, September 1992).

IOM (International Organization for Migration) *Transit Migration in Poland* (Budapest: IOM, 1994).

Knoke, D. and J.H. Kuklinski (1991) 'Network Analysis: Basic Concepts', in G. Thomson, J. Frances *et al.* (eds), *Markets, Hierarchies and Networks* (London: Sage, 1991) 173–82.

Lim, L.L., 'IUSSP Committee on International Migration, Workshop on International Migration Systems and Networks', *International Migration Review*, 21(2) (1987) 416–23.

Lomnitz, L. (1977) 'Migration and Networks in Latin America', in A. Portes and H. Browning (eds), *Current Perspectives in Lartin American Urban Research* (Austin: Institute of Latin American Studies, University of Texas) 133–50.

MacDonald, J.S. and L.D. MacDonald, 'Chain Migration, Ethnic Neighborhood Formation and Social Networks', *Milbank Memorial Fund Quarterly*, 42 (1964) 82–94.

Massey, D., 'Social Structure, Household Strategies, and the Cumulative Causation of Migration', *Population Index*, 56 (1990) 3–26.

Milardo, R.M., 'Families and Social Networks: An Overview of Theory and Methodology', in R.M. Milardo (ed.), *Families and Social Networks* (London: Sage, 1988) 13–47.

Morokvasic, M., 'Pendeln statt Auswandern. Das Beispiel der Polen', in M. Morokvasic and H. Rudolph (eds.), *Wanderungsraum Europa. Menschen und Grenzen in Bewegung* (Berlin: edition sigma, 1994) 166–87.

OECD, *Assistance Programmes for Central and Eastern Europe and the Former Soviet Union* (Paris: OECD, 1996).

Okólski, M., 'Alte und neue Muster: Aktuelle Wanderungsbewegungen in Mittel- und Osteuropa' in M. Morokvasic and H. Rudolph (eds.), *Wanderungsraum Europa. Menschen und Grenzen in Bewegung* (Berlin: edition sigma, 1994) 133–148.

Okólski, M., 'Trends in International Migration: Poland' (Warsaw University, unpublished manuscript, 1995).

Okólski, M., 'Changes in Labour Mobility in Poland under the Transition', Economic Discussion Papers No. 21, Faculty of Economic Sciences, University of Warsaw.

Pessar, P.R., 'The Role of Households in International Migration', *International Migration Review*, 16(3) (1982) 342–64.

Portes, A., 'Modes of Structural Incorporation and Present Theories of Labour Immigration', in M.M. Kritz, C.B. Keely and S.M. Tomasi (eds), *Global Trends in Migration* (New York: Center for Migration Studies, 1981) 279–97.

Portes, A., 'Economic Sociology and the Sociology of Immigration: A Conceptual Overview', in A. Portes (ed.), *The Economic Sociology of Immigration* (New York: Sage, 1995) 1–41.

Rudolph, H., 'Ex Oriente Lux? Gastwissenschaftlerinnen und Gastwissenschaftler aus Mittelosteuropa und der ehemaligen UdSSR an deutschen Forschungsinstituten', (Discussion Paper FS I 94–105 des Wissenschaftszentrums Berlin für Sozialforschung, 1994).

Rudolph, H. and F. Hillmann, 'Labour Migration between Eastern and Western Europe', *Employment Observatory East Germany*, 14 (1995) 3–7.

Salt, J., 'A Comparative Overview of International Trends and Types, 1950–80', *International Migration Review*, 15(3) (1989) 431–56.

Schminck, M., 'Household Economic Strategies: Review and Research Agenda', *Latin American Research*, 19 (1984) 87–102.

Tilly, C. and C.H. Brown, 'On Up-rooting, Kinship, and the Auspices of Migration', *International Journal of Comparative Sociology*, 8 (1967) 139–64.

Urban, R., *Report on the Polish Food Processing Industry* (Warsaw, 1995).

Waldinger, R., 'The Making of an Immigrant Niche', *International Migration Review*, 28(1) (1994) 3–30.

5 Going Home? The Implications of Forced Migration for National Identity Formation in post-Soviet Russia
Hilary Pilkington

INTRODUCTION

There is a growing academic literature in the West concerning the origins and future of the 'Russian diaspora' (see Bremmer, 1994; Kolstoe, 1995; Melvin, 1994; Shlapentokh *et al.*, 1994). This term refers to the 25 million ethnic Russians[1] who have been displaced politically in the wake of the collapse of the Soviet Union, finding themselves resident in the new geopolitical space referred to as Russia's 'near abroad'.

Whether or not Russian-speaking communities in the former Soviet republics actually constitute a diaspora is debatable, since, as Kolstoe notes, they were rarely considered as such whilst the Soviet Union was in existence and the term is only slowly gaining credence in contemporary Russian writing (Kolstoe, 1994: 1–4). Indeed it is wise to treat the term cautiously since to talk of a single Russian diaspora falsely homogenizes a disparate sociocultural group. Russian communities vary between, and even within, the former republics by socioeconomic origin, length of time in the republic, degree of integration into the host community and orientation towards return to Russia. Moreover, as Neil Melvin concludes from his study of usage of the term by Russian politicians, the 'Russian diaspora' often simultaneously connotes ethnic Russians, other minorities ethnically close to Russians, and a broad range of people culturally and linguistically linked to Russia (Melvin, 1994: 19).

A second reason for caution is the term's political connotation. To talk of a 'Russian diaspora' – or as the Russian press more often does, of 'the Russian-speaking population' (*russkoiazychnoe naselenie*), 'russophones' (*russkoiazychnie*), 'Russians' (*russkie*) or 'ethnic Russians' (*etnicheskie russkie*) – reinforces the connection of these people to Russia and thus legitimates the latter's claim to their defence. The diaspora is positioned thus as an object of Russian state concern rather than as a policy matter for either the newly independent states or the global community and, in this way, the Russian state is effectively reconnected with its wider 'nation'.

The third argument for resisting the term 'diaspora' concerns the problematic notion of 'homeland' for Russians in the 'near abroad'. In its strictest sense a diaspora refers to a people deprived of, or driven out of, its homeland. In contrast the Russian population in the 'near abroad' has its ethnic 'homeland' adjacent and apparently open for 'compatriots' to return home at any time.

This process of 'going home', in fact, has been under way since the late 1970s when the imperial pattern of the out-migration of Russians to the former republics was reversed and Russia began to receive a net inflow of migrants and Central Asia a net outflow. This pattern intensified sharply during the 1990s as ethnic conflict and economic collapse became part of the everyday realities of life in the former Soviet republics.[2] Indeed the circumstances in which return has taken place in the last decade have produced a complex and possibly unique form of involuntary or 'forced' migration. Since the beginning of the registration of returnees by the Federal Migration Service in July 1992 more than 946,000 refugees and Russian-speaking forced migrants (*russkoiazychnie vynuzhdennie pereselentsy*)[3] have been registered in the Russian Federation (Dmitriev, 1995). The latest United Nations report, however, suggests that a total of nine million people have been temporarily or permanently displaced in the former Soviet Union and it is estimated that the actual number already in Russia is between 2.5 and 6 million (Rotar', 1995). This is, therefore, a new migratory phenomenon of considerable proportions.

Defining the phenomenon may be even more difficult than quantifying it, however, since to do so raises fundamental questions about the relationship between ethnicity, territory, nation and identity. Not only does the location of the Russian diaspora necessitate a reconsideration of Russia's past (suggesting comparisons with the collapse of other European empires) but the relocation of ethnic Russians and Russian-speakers from the former republics and their experiences on return to Russia challenge simple conceptions of post-Soviet Russia's future. This chapter[4] takes these experiences as an empirical base from which to analyse some of the complexities involved in the reconfiguration of post-Soviet Russia's collective sense of self.

EMPIRICAL FLESH ON POSTMODERNIST BONES: IN SEARCH OF A CONCEPTUAL FRAMEWORK FOR FORCED MIGRATION

The natural starting point for such a project is the current concern over the 'resurgence of ethnicity' and the explosion of nationalism in Europe following the collapse of the Soviet 'Empire' (Rex, 1995: 33). As John Rex notes, although much of the academic focus has been on resurgent nationalisms of previously subordinated nations, in fact the collapse of imperial and multinational systems leads also to the emergence of irredentist – though equally 'nationalist' – movements around settlers of the former dominant nation (Rex, 1995: 28). Thus a study of returnees (the former 'colonizers') might be expected to uncover widespread support for oppositional political movements calling for greater protection of Russians in the 'near abroad', or even the reforging of the Russian nation around its ethnic representatives rather than its current administrative borders. Indeed, warnings that returnees to Russia may become the ballast for a resurgent Russian nationalism have been frequently sounded by Russian political commentators (Abdulatipov, 1994; Rotar', 1993; Safarov, 1994; Toschenko, 1994).

While there is *prima facie* evidence that such a correlation exists,[5] this chapter argues that the question of displacement and the reformation of national identity in post-Soviet Russia is broader and more complex than suggested by analyses which focus on the geopolitical and/or strategic significance of forced migration. On the empirical level the focus to date has been on drawing ethnic maps of the newly independent states and calculating intentions to migrate among the non-titular nationalities in order to allow the prediction and quantification of migration flows. On the theoretical level the question of the Russian diaspora and Russian-speaking forced migrants has been approached mainly within the historical or political science frameworks of the collapse of empire and rise of nationalism. To this extent the Russians in the 'near abroad' have been viewed as one aspect of Russia's imperial legacy and comparisons have been sought with the process of collapse of the French or British Empires.[6]

At the other end of this theoretical continuum, 'rise of nationalism' approaches have viewed the return to Russia of ethnic Russians as evidence of the continued salience of the primordial roots of nationality.[7] This is clearly not unique to the former Soviet space; Grosby argues that the very persistence of notions such as 'homeland' and 'fatherland' indicates that an important element of the modern world outlook is the linking of individual identity to a territorially bounded collective identity via a perceived biological connectedness (Grosby, 1995). Given Soviet ideology's apparent rejection of nationalism for internationalism, however, the suggestion that the civic identity fostered by communism was never able to overcome the more deeply embedded moral and cultural codes of ethnonationalism has particular significance (Schopflin, 1995). In the context of the reconfiguration of post-Soviet Russian national identity, the primordiality thesis can be seen in the use of the term 'historical homeland' (*istoricheskaia rodina*) to describe the Russia to which forced migrants are returning. This notion clearly ties national collective consciousness to a bounded territory as well as rooting the present sense of nation in its historical context.

Whilst primordial notions of national identity have a legitimate place in the theoretical debate over nation, national identity and nationalism, it is essential that their current revival is not naturalized but understood as one strand of a complex theoretical tapestry. The advancement of the primordiality thesis is being undertaken currently as a conscious challenge to modernist and postmodern emphases on the newness and political functionality of nations. The claim that 'nations' are imaginary constructs brought about through the invention of unifying myths is thus being challenged (Smith, 1995).

Postmodern conceptions of nation have been a particular target of criticism. Postmodernists are accused of overemphasizing the significance of cultural construction and ignoring the roots of nations in real social processes (urbanization, mass education, uneven capitalism) and thereby reducing the 'nation' to no more than a text for deconstruction (Smith, 1995: 9). A second criticism has been of the overemphasis of the role of 'other' over 'self' in the formation of national identity (Shils, 1995). According to Parekh, this perspective falsely reduces identity to difference when taken to the extreme (Parekh, 1995: 256).

The study of the collapse of the Soviet Union is fertile ground for the revival of primordial notions of nation; there is no clearer example of a modernist construction of a unifying (inter)national myth being swept away under the weight of the tide of nationalisms born of primordial notions of ethnic ties and historical claims to territories. Given these apparent substantive flaws in modernist understandings of nation, the only alternative to the revival of primordial theses would be to accept postmodernist accounts of the origins of national identity. Yet these are often abstract and highly theoretical, and thus appear inappropriate when applied to the very real, active and often violent field of nation-building in the post-Soviet space. It is argued here, however, that the temptation to join the backlash against postmodernist thinking should be resisted. The central pillar of postmodern explanations of nationality is that national identities are narratives produced in the process of the cultural interaction of individuals and state institutions and are thus multiple and constantly changing. This precept at least should not be abandoned. Rather, this theoretically enabling concept should be enriched and embodied by empirical research designed to reveal the concrete processes of the formation of these narratives and the full spectrum of their possible political outcomes.

This chapter seeks to provide empirical data from the period 1991–5 which will illustrate how Russian-speaking forced migrants have positioned themselves in the new Russia and/or brought new narratives which have disrupted dominant narratives of 'nation' in post-Soviet Russia.[8]

A Note on Methodology

Such an approach clearly requires not only the deconstruction of narratives of nation (for which postmodernist theorists are criticized), but a simultaneous reconstruction of the way in which forced migrants themselves identify with their 'historical native land'. This presents significant empirical problems, not least because of the experience of displacement itself. Respondents were in a state of physical and mental dislocation, unsettled and often unstable. This, combined with the fact that the focus of the research was on beliefs, perceptions and feelings rather than on social facts, meant that quantitative research methods were unsuitable. Instead, empirical data were gathered using a combination of qualitative research methods applied during fieldwork conducted among forced migrant communities between July and December 1994. Data were gathered from a total of 195 respondents, 144 of whom were settled in four rural settlements in the Orel region, Central Russia, the remaining 51 of whom were resident in the city of Ul'ianovsk in the Middle Volga region of Russia. Almost three-quarters (73 per cent) of respondents stated their nationality to be Russian and all had left the former republics (primarily the Central Asian states of Tajikistan, Uzbekistan and Kyrgyzstan as well as Kazakhstan and Azerbaijan) and resettled in Russia between 1988 and 1994. No sampling was used to select respondents since representativeness and generalizability were subordinate to validity in the project design. *Post-factum* comparisons on key demographic variables between respondents in the project and data collected by the Federal Migration Service for all registered refugees and forced migrants were undertaken however to control for any major distortions.[9] In village locations whole migrant communities were interviewed. In Ul'ianovsk, where accessing respondents was more difficult, the snowballing technique was used.

The Ul'ianovsk and Orel regions were selected on the basis of their complementarity; neither had special status as refugee/forced migrant reception areas and both had 'average' levels of reception at the commencement of the project. At the same time, the heavy depopulation of Central Russia as compared to the attractive nature of Ul'ianovsk city (given its reputation for social stability and low cost of living) meant that whilst the Orel region had a positive attitude to the reception of migrants, Ul'ianovsk was considerably more protectionist.

Three complementary methods of qualitative data gathering were used in conjunction:

- semi-structured interviews;
- questionnaires, which included open and closed questions and covered the same broad areas as interviews;[10]
- field observations, which were recorded throughout the five-month period and analysed alongside transcribed interviews.

A total of 139 interviews in the Russian language were transcribed in full and then analysed.[11] Despite the sensitive nature of the research theme there was no significant problem of non-respondence; refusals to give interviews were isolated. Two factors affecting the data are worth noting, however: there are more testimonies by women than men since women were more often at home, more willing to find time, and men were less willing to talk;[12] and the quality of interviews with the local population in rural areas was reduced by the researcher's prior association with the migrant community.

Using the testimonies of these respondents, an attempt to recreate the narratives of nation articulated by Russian-speaking forced migrants alongside some tentative suggestions as to how these might be interpreted in the context of wider theoretical debates is presented below.

'WE HAVEN'T GOT A NATIVE LAND': NARRATIVES OF NATION AMONG RUSSIAN-SPEAKING FORCED MIGRANTS

The new awareness of the 'Russian diaspora' in the 'near abroad' has revived the narrative of Russia as constituting the 'Russian people' as a whole and thus extending beyond the current borders of the Russian state. This is the increasingly dominant voice of the neo-imperialists who seek to maintain the Russian diaspora in the former republics as a way of effectively, if not actually, redrawing the borders of post-Soviet Russia. The painful social and cultural adaptation of that diaspora on return to Russia however reveals deep divisions between the Russian state and the Russian people; their reconnection is not as unproblematic as envisaged in nationalist discourse. Although there is considerable evidence of imperial consciousness among Russian-speaking forced migrants which might be channelled into support for the reconstitution of nation around ethnos rather than state, patterns of national identification among forced migrants are, in fact, more complex than this and preclude the prediction of any single political outcome.

This can be illustrated by the textual analysis of transcribed interviews with Russian-speaking forced migrants. These texts reveal a delimited set of binary categories of 'us' (*my, nash, u nas*) and 'them' (*oni, ikh, u nikh*), 'here' (*tut*) and 'there' (*tam*) as well as 'Russia', 'native land' (*rodina*) and 'Russians' (*russkie* and *rossiiane*) which indicate the boundaries of the 'imagined community' of the Russian nation as perceived by forced migrants. It is argued below that the narratives of nation which are constructed by forced migrants reveal not only colonial attitudes, as suggested by theories of collapse of empire, but a narrative of 'Russianness' distinct from, and a challenge to, both neo-imperialist and civic, federalist constructions of the post-Soviet Russian nation. The empirical data are presented in two sections, the first establishing the existence of a collective identity among Russian-speaking forced migrants and presenting the argument for interpreting this as evidence of 'imperial consciousness', the second arguing that the essence of forced migrant identity is in fact not neo-imperialism but 'cultural hybridity'.[13]

Collective Identity among Russian-speaking Forced Migrants: 'Us' and 'Them'

The peculiar 'Russianness' of forced migrants is apparent in the distinctive 'we' they forge which equates with neither ethnic nor civic Russian identities. When asked to state their nationality during the completion of questionnaires, 89 per cent of respondents in Orel region declared themselves to be 'Russian'. When the same people were asked with whom they identified, however, this national identity proved less salient. Only 25 per cent of respondents described themselves as 'Russians' (*russkie*), whilst more considered themselves to be 'Soviet' (30 per cent), the most frequently mentioned category was 'other migrants'.[14] Russian civic identity is clearly secondary to Soviet identity and in interviews with 139 respondents, only one spontaneously self-identified as a *'rossiianin'*.[15]

Forced migrants forge their collective identity through making a distinction between themselves, 'us' and 'them' (*oni*), where 'they' includes both the native population in the former republic and locals in the new place of residence in Russia (see Figure 5.1).[16] The empty top-right quadrant in the figure indicates that these are essentially negative identificatory indicators of identification. Interviews with respondents however do reveal the existence of a positive sense of 'us'.[17] Interpreting the nature of this identity, it is evident from Figure 5.1 that forced migrant identity is rooted, at least partially, in imperial consciousness; a clear cultural superiority is expressed vis-à-vis both the titular nationality of the former republic and, perhaps more surprisingly, the locals in the rural and provincial areas of Russia to which they had returned.

Forced migrants consistently described local Russians as rude, disrespectful (especially of their elders), linguistically impoverished, drunken and lazy:

> by nationality I am Russian but I consider myself Soviet...I don't consider myself a *rossiianka*...the locals...they are pure *rossiiskie* people...a Russian [*russkii*] it seems to me should be a good, kind, considerate, hospitable person, a cultured, educated person, but a *rossiiskii* – that is about getting drunk, not going to work, all that...all the bad characteristics... [119][18]

Figure 5.1 Characteristics of 'them', 'here' and 'there'

'Them' (here)	'Them' (there)	'Us'

• simple
• unhappy
• downtrodden
• drunkards
• thieves
• 'nasty'
	• kind, friendly
	• hospitable
	• respect for
	  women, elders
	  and parents
	• don't know own
	  language
	• like to be boss	

'There'	'Here'
• respect (especially for women, elders) • better educated and brought up • hospitality • good weather, fruit and vegetables all year • multi-ethnic environment • affluent life-style, big house/dacha • everything was our own • lots of friends and relatives • mix more, more leisure and rest time • friendliness and kindness	• lack of respect • swearing • cold, harsh climate • dirty • drunkenness • savage • life is hard • exploitative • lack of prospects • everyone for themselves • on our own

Notes:
1. In both areas the local population was generally referred to neutrally as *mestine* (locals). In Orel locals were also frequently referred to as 'villagers' (*derevenskie, kolkhozniki, sel'chane*) or *zdeshnie*.
2. 'Them' in the former place of residence were generally referred to by their nationality (the Kirghiz, the Uzbeks, and so on). The only common general term was *natsionaly* (or the more colloquial *natsmeny*), although the term 'Muslims' was used on occasion and the racially-loaded *chernie* by two respondents. In ascribing characteristics to the titular nationality, respondents differentiated between village and urban residents (the latter sometimes were described as 'Russified'), and between older and younger generations (the latter being seen as more aggressively oriented).
3. The following were mentioned by respondents in the Orel Region only: help one another; settle disputes with knives; divided into clans; family comes first; drink moderately, very embittered; respect bread; have strict religion; not clean/tidy. Ul'ianovsk respondents noted that 'they' were: sharp, crafty, stupid and fanatical.
4. Additional characteristics ascribed by respondents in Orel region included: easier social interaction; cleaner cities and air; more intelligentsia.
5. In addition, the following characteristics were attributed by respondents in Orel region: people talk *na ty*; no rest or leisure time; feudal social relations; lack of culture; children left unsupervised; everything is new, alien; 'nothing

here'; no respect for bread; aged population; inadequate wages; 'nothing grows'; no bath houses; no transport; 30 years behind. Ul'ianovsk respondents mentioned the following: people are inward-looking; living standards lower; provincialism; competitive attitude; expensive flats.

One recurrent theme of self-identification worthy of particular mention is that which might loosely be labelled a common 'Soviet work ethic'. This is rooted in a long-standing belief that it was the 'brightest and best' who had been sent to the non-Russian republics to raise the cultural and economic level of the backward parts of the Soviet Union. The experience of migration back to Russia, however, has provided a second focus of comparison. The self-identification as skilled, responsible and conscientious workers is thus currently expressed through comparisons with two 'others': locals in Russia who are seen as drunkards, layabouts and as having failed to improve their standard of living through hard work;[19] and representatives of the titular nationalities in the former republics who are seen as 'loving management positions', of being capable of working only in commerce and thus being incapable of doing real work, that is, producing. The former opinion is expressed here by the first respondent, the latter by the second:

local people do not understand us, we are very serious people, we work. Local residents, Ul'ianovsk residents, they... don't know how to work, that's why they don't like us, because we are too good... [150]

Who worked? Only the Russians worked. They are not capable of anything. Only to be shopkeepers or work in cafés... to water down the vodka. They are masters at short-changing... but physical work... that's not for them. [43]

The extent to which this identity is rooted in imperial consciousness, modernization ideology, social class or professional ethos is an issue requiring further consideration and may usefully become the subject of comparative research with other communities in the process of repatriation. Whatever the weight given to each of these factors, the fact that the collective 'we' of forced migrants clearly has a strong element of cultural superiority suggests that a new 'civilizing mission' could evolve as the political resolution of the displacement experienced by those returning to Russia. As one forced migrant who had settled in Orel region noted:

there is no civilization here, no order, nothing. They [local Russians] don't want to change their life *themselves*... (my emphasis). [20]

The resurgence of a defensive and regressive sense of their own Russianness amongst returnees is made more likely by the peripheral position of forced migrants in their new communities. Migrants claimed that they were labelled as outsiders by locals who referred to them as: 'newcomers' or 'strangers' (*priezhie*), 'immigrants' (*immigranty*), 'emigrants' (*emigranty*), 'migrants' (*migranty* and *pereselentsy*), 'refugees' or, according to the republic from which they came, 'Kazakhs', 'Kirghiz', and so on. This, migrants said, meant that they were effectively excluded from the common ethnic and thus civic community:

> The same Russians don't accept us as Russians... We have no rights at all here. [1]

The crudest of marginalization techniques – scapegoating – was reported by forced migrants, who complained that they were blamed for the ills of the day and even accused of 'selling out' Russia by failing to defend her interests. One respondent expressed his anger at locals' challenges to his patriotism:

> of course it jars to hear the word 'emigrants'... they simply don't know the meaning of the word... they say 'Look at them swarming here, a dozen Tajiks came out and you got scared and ran away'. I say, 'OK so I was scared by a dozen. We were only 1 per cent of the population there. But you are here in your own native land, yet you only have the courage to write in the toilet "Beat the blacks and save Russia!" You aren't capable of doing anything more'... But we weren't afraid of them there... [43]

Indeed, a parallel but equally cogent hypothesis is that a regressive nationalism could be unleashed in small rural communities rather than among forced migrants since the former feel threatened by people they often perceive as 'opportunists' who, having hit hard times, have come back to Russia with their ill-gotten gains from abroad to squeeze what they can from the local population before moving on again:

> we are not treated well, all the time we are called 'blacks'... 'foreigners'... They don't like us. Many say, 'you have taken our flats'. Very many complain, 'you have swarmed down on us, taken our jobs, our flats, because of you life is tough here now...' [178]

CULTURAL HYBRIDITY: THE ESSENCE OF 'OTHERNESS'?

The rejection of Russian civic identity together with evidence of the potential for regressive, nationalist reworkings of the experience of displacement among Russian-speaking forced migrants would appear to support the claims noted above that Russians returning from the 'near abroad' constitute potential ballast for neo-nationalist movements. The textual analysis of interviews with forced migrants, however, suggests that there is a pattern of national identification among them which challenges existing, monolithic narratives of Russianness. Four areas in which this pattern appears are outlined below and a case is made for viewing the essence of collective identity as being rooted in 'cultural hybridity' rather than in imperial consciousness.

'Other Russians'

Although we are Russians [*russkie*], we are not the same kind of Russians that live here. [1]

One reason why the top right-hand quadrant of Figure 5.1 remains blank is that in differentiating themselves from local Russians, forced migrants ascribe to 'self' those positive characteristics attributed to the peoples of the republic of former residence (top-left quadrant of Figure 5.1). Indeed, many respondents openly acknowledged this, saying that they had assimilated much from the peoples they had lived with:

We arrived like that... the East is like that. We were taught like that there. The Uzbeks, the Tajiks they are all like that. For them the main thing is the family... that is why we have got more in common with the newcomers (*priezhie*) than with the locals. There is a big difference between us and them... [20]

Given the cultural superiority expressed here, it is tempting to read the distances felt by Russians returning to Russia as a variation on the theme of 'returning colonizers', but the nature of forced migrants' self-professed 'otherness' problematizes any suggestion that 'imperial consciousness' can fully describe the identities forming among forced migrants.[20] Emil' Paiin (Head of the Inter-Ethnic Relations Department of the Russian presidential apparatus) recognizes this when he describes the Russian diaspora as an 'imperial minority'. This term recognizes its imperial past and consciousness but also its current subordinate position and the difficulties of adapting to this new situation (Payin, 1994). The 'forced', or at least state-driven, initial migration of the present Russian-speaking population to the former republics is also a factor here; Russians, it is often claimed, were equal victims of 'socialist imperialism'. Moreover, Russian-speaking forced migrants may be unique in their experience of displacement, which sees them not only displaced, as refugees and migrants are worldwide, but simultaneously confronted with the realities of the 'imagined community'. In fact one should say 'imagined communities', since the issue is further complicated by the explosion of two myths of nation: the first that of the 'Soviet people' which was revealed to be an artificial construct; the second that of 'Russia as historical homeland' which was exposed as a cultural backwater rather than a metropole.

'*U Nas Tam...*'

That returning to Russia is an experience fraught with confrontation and contestation rather than a smooth journey 'home' is evident in the peculiar distortion of us/them, here/there boundaries found amongst forced migrant respondents. Whilst one would normally expect to find among ethnic Russians in Russia the connections 'us-here' and 'them-there', Russian forced migrants frequently cross the grid in their identifications, talking about 'at home there' (*'u nas tam'*), and 'them here' (*'oni-tut'*). Although it is impossible to list all articulations of this, (which is a general speech pattern), the following statements make clear the impossibility of assuming the presence of even the fundamentals of Russian identity – common language and shared home.

> *Our* Tajiks are very hospitable, our republic is called little Switzerland, it is very beautiful. [9] (emphasis added)

> we don't even understand the Russians. When we arrived the first time, we could not understand the Russians, how they speak, the language. We could not understand. *They* don't understand us, nor we them... [31] (emphasis added)

Indeed a whole spectrum of problems of cultural adaptation was revealed through the fieldwork, suggesting that although such issues are virtually absent from the media debate on forced migration, Russian-speaking forced migrants are far from 'going home'.[21]

Empire or International?

Russian-speaking forced migrants also fail to live up to their labelling as 'colonizers'. Although they do make familiar colonial statements about the 'civilizing mission' of Russians in the former republics,[22] such statements are often tempered with a yearning for the multinational environment they have left behind and a strong belief in the negative nature of a mono-national culture. This was most evident in a recurrent theme in respondents' narratives; the claim that people in the former republic were 'kinder' (*dobree*) than in Russia. Respondents repeatedly asserted that academically proven theories demonstrated that what they saw as the 'more civilized' nature of the former republic was a direct result of the multinational nature of the society:

> A nation can't live on its own. You need some kind of mix...because each nationality differs from others somehow. One might be lower in culture, another higher. One in hospitality...Each nation takes something from another...and the result is something better, because each takes the best from the other nation...But alone, for example, the Russian nation, what can they get from one another? ...[44]

> There it was better, people there were better...probably a multinational population is better...[28]

Such statements far outweighed the alternative conclusion that one might expect migrants to draw from their experience; that the collapse of the Soviet Union proved that it was an unnatural state of affairs for representatives of any nation to live outside their territorial borders. Indeed while the *sovetskii narod* may have proved unworthy as a description of 'a new historical community of people', for Russians in the former republics it was not an empty ideological shell but a lived reality and an ethnically exclusive sense of Russianness is uncommon among forced migrants. This, it is argued here, lowers the likelihood of an extreme nationalist political outcome from their experience of displacement.

Blood, Earth and Native Land

> Maybe we were brought up like that more, we did not absorb a pure Russian culture which came from the earth but more an

international culture and because of this...relations between people and towards life are a bit different... [139]

'Soviet' identity continues to be attractive to forced migrants since it allows for the resolution of the disjuncture between ethnos and territory experienced upon displacement. This disruption is evident in migrants' statements relating to 'native land' (*rodina*) and appears to be resolved in favour of 'earth' rather than 'blood'. Of the 79 respondents in the Orel region answering the question on whether or not they considered their move to Russia as a return to their native land, only 26 (one third) said they did, while two-thirds expressly said they did not consider it a return to the *rodina*:

I was born there, lived there. Of course it is hard. You yearn ...for your native land. And that native land is there, there where you were born, in spirit you never leave... [189]

This uprooting is experienced differently, but always painfully. For some the awareness of the split between blood and earth leads to a challenging of their sense of national belonging and a recognition of their 'hybridity':

Our native land is Kazakhstan and here we are not accepted as Russians, we are not Russians. [5]

For others, however, displacement leads to a bitter sense of loss and a feeling of not belonging anywhere:

We haven't got one [*rodina*]. We are aliens there and here we are aliens...the children were born there in Uzbekistan. We haven't got a native land! [125]

Statements made by forced migrants concerning their 'native land' are complex and contradictory. Postmodern theorists would suggest that our contemporary world of diaspora, mass population movement and transcultural flows naturally problematizes the notion of native land (Gupta and Ferguson, 1992). This, however, does not fully explain the sentiments expressed by respondents. For Russian-speaking forced migrants, there was no problem in envisaging what constituted a native land, which was clearly symbolized by 'where I was born', 'where the children were born' and 'where my parents are buried'. The problem was rather a sudden disembodiment of that native land. The 'imagined community' (Russia) had been severed from the physical native land (former republic), leaving migrants displaced. This displacement – evident in the 'choosing' of one native land over the other or in a sense of having lost any native land – provides a serious challenge, however, to primordial notions of nationality; blood and earth do not necessarily have to be fused for territory to have significance.

CONCLUSION

Post-Soviet Russia is faced with a non-coincidence of state and nation which nationalists are increasingly reluctant to accept. The Russian-speaking populations in the 'near abroad' are living symbols of this split and, as a consequence, increasingly have become the focus of intense political debate. Most of this debate has concerned the situation of 'them' (Russian diaspora) 'there' (the 'near abroad'). This chapter, in contrast, has focused on what happens when 'they' come 'here' and the political implications of the existence of the 'other Russians'. The possible political outcomes of forced migration are three-fold.

First, migrant identity may prove transitory. The high negative content of migrant identity noted above means that, in some cases, it will be replaced rapidly by other social identities. This is already evident among cohesive professional groups (such as doctors and academics), who quickly re-find their niche in a new city, and among the younger generation. Those advising the president,[23] at least, confidently predict that no ethnic tension will result from the return of forced migrants, anticipating at most some minor social tension as migrants increasingly compete with locals for housing and employment.

Secondly, migrant identity may prove a progressive, democratic political force. The sociocultural profile of the forced migrant community would certainly suggest that, had they been resident in Russia, these people would have been a natural constituency for democratic forces. Under certain circumstances migrant identity may be strengthened and gather political momentum. This process was evident in two of the villages under study in Orel Region, in one of which disputes with the farm director had led to the formation of an independent organization to defend 'human rights'. Although political resistance is not generally a common characteristic of socially vulnerable sections of the community, in this sense forced migrants are a very peculiar group, since they constitute a socially disadvantaged group with extremely high sociocultural capital at their disposal. Indeed, some respondents involved in the research described here already had come to see their problems not only in terms of personal tragedy, but as evidence of the state's failure to fulfil its obligations, its willingness to sacrifice them for its own purposes and its apparent readiness to use them as 'hostages'.

The third alternative is that migrant identity may coalesce into a nationalist political stance. In this reading the experience of forced migration – feeling driven out of one's 'native land' on ethnic grounds – may give rise to a defensively aggressive sense of nation. As one returnee from Moldova noted:

> I am a Russian (*russkii*), not a *rossiianin* because... I lived on the border... On the border of the division of nations. Russians (*ros-siiane*) who live here don't understand that.... Only now are they beginning to sense that other nationalities exist, they have not understood this yet... I understood this a long time ago... and thanks to this, there on the national periphery, I became more Russian than the Russians here... [136]

The cultural superiority of Russian-speaking forced migrants may yet find future expression in the form of a new 'civilizing mission' in Russia alongside support for a greater commitment to the 'defence' of Russians in the 'near abroad'.

Although the political implications of forced migration may be far from clear as yet, studying narratives of nation among Russian-speaking forced migrants raises important questions about the 'naturalness' of the primordial notion of national identity. As Parekh argues, national identity does not refer to 'a mysterious national soul, substance or spirit' passed down through blood and earth, but to 'the way a polity is constituted' (Parekh, 1995: 263). It thus contains disparate and even contradictory elements and is constantly evolving in reaction to changing circumstances. Russia is not unique in having rival conceptions of its own collective identity and, it has been argued here, the 'otherness' of the returning Russians merely makes visible the lack of fixity which national identity displays. Forced migrants as a social group express these contradictions particularly acutely since their marginal positioning on the borderlands of nations means they inhabit that space where the boundaries between 'ourselves' and 'others' have become destabilized and unfixed (Gupta and Ferguson, 1992). This is perhaps most straightforwardly and

102   *Hilary Pilkington*

succinctly expressed by a 34-year-old returnee from Bishkek who had
settled in Orel region:

> Here we are not Russians (*russkie*), we are Kirghiz. In Kirghizia we
> were Russians, but in Russia we are not Russians... [92]

In political terms, the narrative of nation articulated by Russian-
speaking forced migrants challenges the nationalist idea of nation as
'a homogeneous cultural unit' formed on a common territory and
linked by blood ties (Parekh, 1995: 32). The cultural hybridity of
Russian-speaking forced migrants, moreover, suggests an 'other' narrative of Russianness which disrupts the unifying myth of the modern
nation. But this need not condemn Russia to the chaos of 'difference',
for, as Bhabha argues, the recognition of such hybridity may provide
the space to raise the real questions about nation, citizenship and
national belonging necessary to avoid the 'politics of polarity' and
emerge as 'the others of our selves' (Bhabha, 1994). This is more than
wishful thinking; it is a pattern of identification already visible in
forced migrant communities.

NOTES

1. There were 25.3 million ethnic Russians living in Soviet republics other
    than the Russian Federation according to the last Soviet census con-
    ducted in 1989. There were in addition approximately 11 million mem-
    bers of other ethnic groups whose primary cultural affinity was to
    Russia. These people are often subsumed into the 'Russian diaspora'
    or the 'Russian-speaking population'.
2. The ethnic conflict in Baku at the end of January 1990 produced the
    first mass inflow of internally displaced people to Russia. This flow
    consisted mainly of Armenians and Russians.
3. The term 'Russian-speaking' (*russkoiazychnii*) population refers to all
    non-titular nationalities in the former Soviet republics and is thus not
    interchangeable with 'ethnic Russians'. Indeed it is a matter of dispute
    that this term is often used to refer to non-Slavic minorities such as the
    Uzbeks in Kazakhstan whose cultural affinity is closer to the titular
    nationality than to Russia. 'Forced migrants' (*vynuzhdennie perese-
    lentsy*) is a legal term emanating from current Russian legislation
    ('Law on Refugees' and 'Law on Forced Migrants', both of 19 Febru-
    ary 1993) which distinguishes between 'refugees' (*bezhentsy*) and 'forced
    migrants' on the basis of citizenship. 'Refugees' are those without
    Russian citizenship seeking temporary residence in Russia but intending

to return to their former place of residence. 'Forced migrants' are displaced persons who hold Russian citizenship and who are seeking permanent resettlement in their 'historical homeland'. To obtain either refugee or forced migrant status applicants must be able to prove that they or their family have suffered violence or the threat of violence.

4. Earlier versions of this chapter were presented to the BASEES Annual Conference, Fitzwilliam College, Cambridge, 30 March–2 April 1996 and to the ERCOMER conference, Utrecht, 18–20 April 1996. I would like to thank participants at both these conferences, in particular Dr John Russell and Prof. Kees Groenendijk, for their extremely helpful comments and suggestions. The ideas advanced here remain tentative and arise from an exploratory research project concerning wider issues related to the sociocultural adaptation of Russian-speaking forced migrants upon their return to Russia from the former republics of the USSR during and after the collapse of the Soviet Union as a single political space. The research was supported financially by the Economic and Social Research Council under the Research Grant scheme (Award R000221306) 'Going home: a sociocultural study of Russian-speaking forced migrants', June 1994–August 1995.

5. There was much talk of a strong pro-Zhirinovsky vote among Russian citizens abroad in the December 1993 elections and first analyses of voting patterns in the 1995 Duma elections suggest that the Congress of Russian Communities – a moderate nationalist grouping – took a much larger proportion of the vote among Russians in the 'near abroad' than it did overall, coming second only to the Communist Party (see Parrish, 1995).

6. The political implications of the return of Russian-speaking forced migrants might be compared, for example, to that of the *pieds-noirs* from Algeria.

7. Such understandings of the origins of national identity focus on 'the sensitivity of human beings to the primordial facts of descent and territorial location...' (Shils, 1995).

8. The broader project also considered the discursive construction of the post-Soviet Russian 'nation' and how this has positioned Russian-speaking forced migrants by analysing media and academic discourses as well as the legislative and institutional framework within which refugees and forced migrants are positioned.

9. The only significant discrepancies were higher educational levels and a high proportion of ethnic Tatars among Ul'ianovsk respondents, reflecting the snowball sampling method used here.

10. This included: socio-demographic data; material situation and help received; motivations for leaving; evaluations of reception by the receiver community; and national identification.

11. The analysis of interviews from the two regional bases was conducted separately since differences of experience between refugees and forced migrants having settled in rural and urban locations was a key comparative dimension of the project. In the data presented here however, only attitudes and experiences cited by both urban and rural respondents are included. During analysis particular attention was paid

to the gendered nature of the experience of displacement. For a detailed discussion of the gender dimension of the project, see Pilkington (forthcoming).

12. This was because, they claimed, their wives 'talked better', because they were drunk or because they were never at home.

13. The notion of 'cultural hybridity' is advanced particularly well in the work of Homi Bhabha and Stuart Hall. Both Bhabha and Hall dispute the totality and fixity of 'national imagined communities' by considering the 'counter-narratives' of those who exist on the margins of nations and who disrupt or erase traditional national boundaries (Anthias and Yuval-Davis, 1992: 38). Cultural hybridity suggests an identity which 'lives with and through, not despite difference' and construes national identity as a complex and constantly dynamic politics rather than an 'essence' (Hall, 1990: 234). Voutira is working along similar lines when she argues that cultural identity is a dynamic concept 'determined each time in terms of the opposition between the relevant "we–they" groups' (Voutira, 1991: 402).

14. The findings here are not accounted for by any 'hierarchy' of identification being activated since respondents were not restricted to only one answer. It should be noted, however, that identification as a community of migrants was more pronounced among respondents from Orel region than Ul'ianovsk. This can be attributed to the more anonymous urban social relations in Ul'ianovsk and to the greater hostility encountered from the established community in Orel. In Ul'ianovsk forced migrants were more likely to relate to networks along ethnic lines (Armenian and Tatar communities, for example) or based on their city of origin (Dushanbe, Baku).

15. During interviews it became clear that the term *rossiianin* had almost no meaning for forced migrants and was used consistently to refer only to local Russians when differentiating them from themselves.

16. Although differences were noted between respondents in the Orel region and in Ul'ianovsk, there appear to be sufficient commonalities in the labelling of the 'other' to suggest that the significant 'other' is 'Russia' in general and not merely rural residents.

17. This identification is, of course, partially circumstantial. Collective identity, for example, is rooted in shared current problems (housing, loss of relatives, uprooting), empathy for each other's situation and as a result, a greater sense of collectivity develops as other migrants come to play for each other the role of the family, kin and friendship networks they have left behind.

18. In the interests of anonymity, respondents are referred to only by the identification number assigned to them in the database of biographical details.

19. One respondent suggested that the difference between *rossiiane* and *russkie* (that is, between local and migrant Russians) was that the former skived work in order to watch soap operas!

20. A similar sense of 'other Russians' was located by Lebedeva in her study of long-established migrant communities in the Transcaucasus; respondents in a number of different communities repeatedly referred to

distinct differences between 'Russians here' and Russians in Russia (Lebedeva, 1993: 59).

21. The reason for this absence is of course that the recognition of cultural difference between Russians in the Russian Federation and those in the 'near abroad' would necessitate the acceptance of the non-coincidence of Russian state and nation.

22. In answering open-ended survey questions on 'What did Russians do for the [native population]?', respondents frequently suggested that the Russians had brought 'civilization' and 'culture' to the republic, even to the extent of having taught the local population 'to go to the toilet standing up'.

23. Mukomel', chief analyst of the Analytical Centre of the Russian Federation Presidential Apparatus, Moscow, was interviewed by the author on 20 July 1995.

REFERENCES

Abdulatipov, R., 'Russian Minorities: The Political Dimension', in V. Shlapentokh, M. Sendich and E. Payin (eds), *The New Russian Diaspora: Russian Minorities in the Former Soviet Republics* (New York/London: M.E. Sharpe, 1994) 37–44.

Anthias, F. and N. Yuval-Davis, *Racialized Boundaries* (London: Routledge, 1992).

Bhabha, H., *The Location of Culture* (London/New York: Routledge, 1994).

Bremmer, I., 'The Politics of Ethnicity: Russians in the New Ukraine', *Europe-Asia Studies*, 46(2) (1994), 261–83.

Dmitriev, C., 'More Refugees Flee to Russia from CIS countries', *OMRI Daily Digest*, 238(1) (8 December 1995).

Grosby, S., 'Territoriality: The Transcendental, Primordial Feature of Modern Societies', *Nations and Nationalism*, 1(2) (1995), 143–62.

Gupta, A. and J. Ferguson, 'Beyond "Culture": Space, Identity and the Politics of Difference', *Cultural Anthropology*, 7(1) (1992) 6–23.

Hall, S., 'Cultural Identity and Diaspora', in J. Rutherford (ed.), *Identity, Community, Culture, Difference* (London: Lawrence and Wishart, 1990).

Kolstoe, P., *Russians in the Former Soviet Republics* (London: Hurst, 1995).

Lebedeva, N., *Sotsial'naia psikhologiia ethnicheskikh migratsii* (Moscow: RAN Institut Etnologii I antropologii im N.N. Miklukh-Maklaia, 1993).

Melvin, N., 'Forging the New Russian Nation', Royal Institute of International Affairs (RIIA) Discussion Paper 50 (RIIA, 1994).

Melvin, N., *Russians beyond Russia's Borders* (London: Pinter/RIIA).

Parekh, B., 'Ethnocentricity of the Nationalist Discourse', *Nations and Nationalism*, 1(1) (1995) 25–52.

Parekh, B., 'The Concept of National Identity', *New Community*, 21(2) (1995) 255–68.

Parrish, S., 'Russians Abroad Also Turn out to Vote', *OMRI Special Report: Russian Election Survey*, 15 (1995).

Payin, E., 'The Disintegration of the Empire and the Fate of the "Imperial Minority"', in V. Shlapentokh, M. Sendich and E. Payin (eds), *The New Russian Diaspora: Russian Minorities in the Former Soviet Republics* (New York/London: M.E. Sharpe, 1994) 21–36.

Pilkington, H., ' "For the Sake of the Children…" Gender and Migration in the Former Soviet Union', in M. Buckley (ed.), *Post-Soviet Women: From the Baltics to Central Asia* (Cambridge: Cambridge University Press, forthcoming 1997).

Rex, J., 'Ethnic Identity and the Nation State: The Political Sociology of Multi-cultural Societies', *Social Identities*, 1(1) (1995) 21–34.

Rotar', I., 'Drugie russkie: O tragedii sredneaziatskikh emigrantov', *Nezavisimaia Gazeta* (2 June 1993).

Rotar', I., 'Russkikh pereselentsev pytaiutsia ispol'zovat' kak politicheskuiu silu', *Nezavisimaia Gazeta* (7 June 1995).

Safarov, R., 'Reformator Solzhenitsyn I musul'manskii vopros', *Nezavisimaia Gazeta* (26 August 1994).

Schopflin, G., 'Nationhood, communism and state legitimation', *Nations and Nationalism*, 1(1), (1995) 81–91.

Sergeev, A., 'Nado otdelit' politicheskikh bezhentsev ot ekonomicheskikh', *Inostranets*, 18 (1995).

Shils, E., 'Nation, Nationality, Nationalism and Civil Society', *Nations and Nationalism*, 1(1) (1995) 93–118.

Shlapentokh, V., M. Sendich and E. Payin (eds), *The New Russian Diaspora: Russian Minorities in the Former Soviet Republics* (New York/London: M.E. Sharpe, 1994).

Smith, A., 'Gastronomy or Geology? The Role of Nationalism in the Reconstruction of Nations', *Nations and Nationalism*, 1(1) (1995) 3–23.

Toschenko, Zh., 'Potentsial'no opasnie tochki', *Nezavisimaia Gazeta* (1 March 1995).

Voutira, E., 'Pontic Greeks Today: Migrants or Refugees?', *Journal of Refugee Studies*, 4(4) (1991) 400–20.

Part II
Social Constructions of the
New Migration

6 Representing New Identities: 'Whiteness' as Contested Identity in Young People's Accounts
Ann Phoenix

INTRODUCTION

Studies of 'race', racism, ethnicity, identities and migration histor- ically have tended to focus on black people and those from other minority ethnic groups. Over the last decade, however, there has been increasing recognition, largely inspired by debates within feminist scholarship, that 'whiteness' is as much a social construction as is 'blackness'. As such, it has always constituted a central part of the context within which black and other minority peoples are racialized (C. Hall, 1992; Ware, 1992). The absence of focus on 'whiteness' coupled with implicit constructions of white people as 'the norm' (Phoenix, 1987) serves to maintain the privileged position of 'white- ness', but also to obscure the ways in which it is implicated in power relations (Pajaczkowska and Young, 1992; Trepagnier, 1994; Wong, 1994).

Those who have contributed to the burgeoning literature on 'white- ness' generally agree that 'race', racism and ethnicity are part of the lives of white people (Frankenberg, 1993). In other words, white people's lives are racialized. Attempts to understand racism thus require a focus on the white majority as well as on black or other minority experiences (Back, 1993; van Dijk, 1987; Hooks, 1992; Troyna and Hatcher, 1992; Wetherell and Potter, 1992). The relative absence of work on 'whiteness' in comparison with the numerous pieces of research that focus on 'blackness' however, may well con- tribute to making 'whiteness' as an identity position silent and hence less tangible than 'black identity'. As a result of this, it can be very difficult to analyse 'whiteness' or for white people (other than those associated with opposition to racism or with white nationalist organ- izations or standpoints) to reflect on what it means to be white.

Yet, although many white people find it difficult to reflect on what it means to be white, there are a variety of forms of 'whiteness', in the same way that 'blackness' is a multiple and differentiated category (Jeater, 1992). Patterns of migration within, and into, the 'New Europe' make the ways in which 'whiteness' is differentiated more evident than previously (even if not more recognized by 'insiders'). Thus, for example, movements of people from the former Yugoslavia to other European countries have brought new groups of white people into contact with both white and black people in the countries in which they have sought refugee status or asylum. Changes in the former Yugoslavia and the former Soviet Union have created new ethnic and national identities for many white Europeans and have served to clarify the ways in which there are European hierarchies of nation, ethnicity, religion and 'whiteness'. The emergence of 'Europism' (Essed, 1995) has promoted images of white (as well as black), majority (as well as minority) ethnic group 'others' (Lutz, 1997). There have, of course, long been hierarchies of 'whiteness' in Europe, with Jewish people, Irish people, gypsies, and so on all having experienced racialized discrimination (Burman, 1994; Hickman and Walter, 1995). In the context of various newly emerging social identities in Europe, however, more white people have been shifted into devalued categories of 'whiteness'.

These social changes in Europe help to demonstrate the ways in which the racialization and ethnicization (of 'whiteness', 'blackness' and other ethnicities) are historical processes which are socially constructed and geographically situated. 'Whiteness' and 'blackness' are lived out in relation to each other as well as being internally differentiated. At the same time, 'whiteness' continues to be invisible as a racialized position for many of those for whom these social changes are less immediate and who, as a result, have not had cause to question their racialized or ethnic positions in their own countries or in Europe more generally. In this context, it has become still more important to attempt to understand whether, and if so, how, 'whiteness' as an identity position is part of the lives of people in specific regions and countries of Europe and how it is lived in relation to 'blackness'.

This chapter presents examples from a study of the social identities of young Londoners which explored 'whiteness' as a social identity. It is argued that many of the white young people interviewed found it difficult to talk about what being white meant to them and, in contrast to the black young people interviewed, few presented themselves as having 'white identities'. Those white young people who had ancestry other than white English generally had more to say about ethnicity and being white than those who were white and English. Thus, Irish, Jewish or Scottish white young people were more likely than white, English young people to say that they had thought about issues related to ethnicity and to being white. Most of the white young people however consistently played down the significance of colour while, contradictorily, frequently producing accounts which indicated that their lives were racialized. Such accounts demonstrate the complexity of essentialism. Many of the young people appeared to be refuting essentialist thinking by insisting on the individualism of 'people just being people, whatever colour they are'. At the same time, they gave accounts which were broadly essentialist, of black people as 'other'.

THE STUDY

This chapter is based on data from a study of the social identities of young people in London.[1] It discusses the extent to which 'whiteness' as a social identity has a place in young people's lives. In order to highlight some of the issues raised, the chapter also presents on occasion accounts of 'blackness'. The study thus was not of 'whiteness' *per se*, but of young people's social identities more generally. The young people were interviewed about a variety of aspects of their identities, including gender, social class, 'race', ethnicity, and nationality.

A total of 248 14–18-year-old Londoners attending 58 different schools (29 state and 29 private) were interviewed for approximately one and a half hours each, using a semi-structured interview technique. The sample included 152 young women and 96 young men. Of the young people 101 were white, of UK origin, 89 were black, of African Caribbean descent, and 58 were of 'mixed parentage' (with one black parent of African or African Caribbean descent and one white parent of European descent). The groups of young people in the study mostly were not immigrants. For all the young people however, processes of migration meant that their social relations, and their thinking about their identities, occurred in a context of ethnic, 'racial' and cultural plurality since all lived in a cosmopolitan city (London). In addition, most of the black and mixed parentage young people had at least one parent or grandparent who were themselves migrants, as did a minority of the white young people.

Both quantitative and qualitative analysis were carried out on the data collected. The quantitative analyses relied predominantly on the chi-square statistic, while the qualitative analyses concentrated on narrative analysis to explore the ways in which the young people constructed narratives in response to the questions put to them.

RACIALIZED IDENTITIES: AN ISSUE IN BLACK *AND* WHITE

While it is often believed that racialized identities are relevant only to black people, they are increasingly being recognized as equally relevant to white people (Frankenberg, 1993). Growing up in what has been called 'multiracist Britain' (Cohen, 1988), 'race' and racism featured in the lives of the white young people in this study in various ways, albeit often differently from the experiences reported by the black and mixed parentage young people.

As a result of the different social positions which they occupied, the white young people's racialized identities were both experienced and expressed differently. For example, young white people spontaneously expressed more uncertainty about which colour terms to use than did black or mixed parentage young people. Twenty-nine per cent of the white sample expressed such uncertainty, compared with 15 per cent of each of the other two colour groups. They were also more likely to use the term 'coloured' than were black or mixed parentage young people (62 per cent; 30 per cent and 43 per cent respectively) and to confine use of the term 'black' to people of African and African Caribbean descent rather than, for example, to include people of South Asian descent (72 per cent of white young people compared with 52 per cent and 53 per cent of black and mixed parentage young people respectively). Relatively few of the total sample defined people of mixed parentage as black (24 per cent of black young people spontaneously said this, compared with 5 per cent of the other two groups). In looking at some of the young people's answers, it is evident that young white people are uncertain about how to answer questions about 'race' and racism because they have given less thought to such issues and are fearful of giving the 'wrong' answer. At the same time, they are more likely to report that they are never conscious of their colour and less likely to report that they have ever wanted to change their colour.

Since much of the literature on racial identity suggests that some young black children wish to be white, we asked all the young people if they had ever wished to be another colour. Because white young people had much less experience of racism, this colour group was the least likely often to have wished to be another colour in the past. Thus, while 12 per cent of black young people and 23 per cent of young people of mixed parentage said that they had often wished to be a different colour in the past, only two white young people reported this. In terms of *ever* having wanted to be a different colour, 28 per cent of black young people, 51 per cent of mixed parentage young people and 14 per cent of white young people said that they had, at some time, wished to be a different colour. The high proportion of young people of mixed parentage saying this was generally because (according to their reports) they felt that they would prefer to be either black or white rather than 'in between' what they perceived to be binary opposite colours.

More of the young people, whatever their colour, reported that they had wanted to be a different colour in the past than currently. The most marked reduction, however, was for black young people, none of whom said that, currently, they often wanted to be a different colour and only two of whom said that they currently sometimes wished that they were not black. Although the numbers involved are small, they demonstrate racialized differences between young people. Young black people who had wanted to be white tended to say that they had wanted to be white earlier in life in order to avoid racial discrimination or name calling; in order not to 'be different'; or to have the same hair as their white peers. The 14 per cent of young white people who (had) wanted to change colour tended to do so later in life for reasons of style, youth culture or attractiveness, which they equated with looking like many people of mixed parentage.

Pleased and Proud to be White?

One of the arguments often made against transracial adoption (which is generally the adoption of black children and children of mixed parentage by white parents) is that black young people growing up in white households will not be proud and pleased to be black. Presumably, those who advance these arguments assume either that white young people will necessarily be proud to be white since they are not subject to the racial discrimination and devaluation to which black young people are subject, or that, for the same reasons, it is not necessary for them to be proud to be white. Since issues of 'race' and racism are generally not assumed to be relevant to white young people however, they generally are not investigated, but left implicit. We asked the young people in our study whether they were pleased and proud to be the colour they were. Fewer young white people (60 per cent) said that they were pleased, compared with 95 per cent of black young people and 81 per cent of young people of mixed parentage. With regard to pride in their colour the percentages were 92, 77 and 34 for black, mixed parentage and white respectively. Black young people were much more likely than the other groups to report that they had been told to be proud by their parents (66 per cent of black, 40 per cent of mixed parentage and 6 per cent of white young people). Thus while being pleased to be their own colour was less colour differentiated than taking pride in colour, with the majority of young people saying that they were pleased to be their colour, young white people were the least likely to say that they were pleased.

Most of those white young people who eschewed pleasure or pride in their colour gave accounts which indicated that it was unwarranted to take pleasure in, or be proud of, a characteristic over which they had no influence. Their accounts mainly suggested that they were pleased to be themselves and consistently played down the significance of colour. At first glance, the pattern of the young white people's responses appears to fit into an egalitarian ideology (commonly advocated by most of the young people in the study). Unlike the black and mixed parentage young people we interviewed, they presented individualistic arguments when asked to talk about their racialized identities. In the following quotation, the young woman suggests that it is not possible to be proud of being any colour, but that it is possible to be proud of oneself as an individual:

Q. On balance, are you pleased that you are white?
A. Don't think it bothers me, don't really think about it that much.
Q. Would you say you are proud of being white?
A. Don't think you could really be proud of being any colour, proud of being myself, not proud of being white.

(white young woman)

The notion that colour is largely irrelevant and that all colours are basically the same was sometimes expressed even by the minority who, like the young man quoted below, said that they felt proud to be white:

Q. On balance, are you pleased to be white?
A. I shouldn't really mind what colour I am but, yes, I am quite

pleased with my colour.
Q. Are you proud of being white?
A. Yes.
Q. Did your parents ever tell you should be proud of being white?
A. No, I don't really think they had to tell me. I realize whatever colour you are, you should be proud to be yourself and it doesn't really matter what colour you are.

(white young man)

The Salience of 'Whiteness'

The overall differences observed in our study between white, black and mixed parentage young people in their experiences of 'race' and racism, in the terms they used and in whether or not they had ever wanted to change their colour, might well be expected given previous research and the pervasiveness of racism in Britain. Yet the questions of whether or not such differences are reproduced when young people are asked to reflect on being their own colour and to what extent 'whiteness' constitutes an absent discourse for white young people remain.

To approach these questions, we also asked the young people whether they were ever conscious of their colour. Black and mixed parentage young people were most likely to say that they were sometimes conscious of their colour (68 per cent of black; 63 per cent of mixed parentage and 45 per cent of white young people). Only one white young person said that they were always conscious of their colour in comparison with 12 black young people and five of mixed parentage.

It is hardly surprising that white young people were the least likely ever to be aware of their own colour, with over half of them (55 per cent) saying that it almost never impinged on their consciousness (in relation to approximately a third of black and mixed parentage young people). The mixed parentage and black young people were moreover much more likely to report themselves to be aware of colour than were white young people.

Recognition of Difference

It would appear from these accounts that 'whiteness' does not constitute part of young white people's identities. Asked directly the questions that black young people and those of mixed parentage are frequently asked in studies of racialized identities, most indicate that, if they are pleased to be white, it is because they are pleased to be themselves. Colour, they argue, does not matter to them and, hence, they give it little thought. Yet while 'whiteness' was a silent/absent discourse for the young Londoners we interviewed, they were positioned, and also positioned themselves, as 'white'. It was an implicit part of their identities in that many positioned themselves in contradistinction to black people. This positioning emerged not when they were asked about their individual feelings about being white, but when they were asked: about the circumstances in which they became conscious of their colour (if they ever did); their feelings about black people collectively; whether or not they considered that their lives would be different if they were not white; and racism. The accounts many gave in response to such questions contradicted both the egalitarian ideologies and the individualism of their earlier accounts. For, in talking of black people as a collectivity, they gave largely essentialist accounts, viewing all black people as if they were the same. They seemed to believe that black people necessarily behave in particular ways *because* they are black. This view was partly because, out of school, few white young people mixed with black people, and this informal segregation allowed the perpetuation of stereotypic views.

Common social constructions of black people are such that many of the stereotypes attached to young blacks of African Caribbean origin are gender-specific. The content of these stereotypes is related mainly to violence and lawlessness and is associated with young black men rather than young black women. These stereotypes were reproduced in many young people's (of all colours) spontaneous discourses about black people. In the accounts which follow, young people talk about black or 'coloured' people either really being, or erroneously being seen to be, violent and threatening. Many, however, were actually referring to black young men. Many white young people gave accounts which, like the two presented below, showed that they constructed black young people as 'other'.

In a way I feel sorry for them [black people] like the way how they're treated, but in other ways not so sorry. Like sometimes you hear about a lot of black people starting trouble and that.
                                             (white British young man)

Q. Have you ever not done something you wanted to do because of your colour?

A. ... There are places I would avoid because I know that there are coloured people there ... and generally a lot of my friends have had bad experiences with people like this. They have knives and things ... You get white people who are just the same ... I don't think it's because of what colour they are particularly.

(white girl)

From the accounts given by young black people (both women and men), it is possible to see that, for black young men, there are deleterious consequences of this pervasive social construction of black male youth. Young black men were generally upset about the ways in which they were stereotyped and many young black men and women (as well as some of their white friends) told stories about eliciting reactions as if they were dangerous, criminal and/or violent. The answer from the young man quoted below was in response to a question about whether he had ever been discriminated against. He was upset at being treated as a frightening thief as he went about his daily business.

... There was an old white lady ... She walked past me and she goes, 'Oh don't mug me! I haven't got nothing in my bag' ...

(black young man)

'Whiteness' as a Social Relation

While saying that colour was largely irrelevant, then, many of the young white people experienced 'whiteness' as a social relation in that they were afraid of black people on the street. In their perpetuation of the racist stereotype of black people as dangerous and frightening, their discourses were suggestive of racialized differences between black and white people. Thus, while they reported that they did not necessarily perceive themselves consciously as white, they did experience racialized social relations, predicated on the differences between their 'whiteness' and the 'blackness' of 'others'.

Some young people, however, also understood that 'whiteness' made social sense only in relation to 'blackness'. For example, one of the reasons that some white young people reported that they were pleased to be white was because they recognized that 'whiteness' conferred some advantages. They sometimes spoke of it as making life easier, as in the quote below:

Q. On balance, are you pleased to be white?
A. I think so, yes. It probably makes life easier.

(white girl)

This also helps to explain why 66 per cent of the white young people said that they were not proud to be white, and why some were equivocal and others negative about taking pride in 'whiteness'. They recognized that being white signifies a social location and, as such, has a history of interconnections with other colours. Reticence about claiming 'whiteness' as something about which to be proud was related to their awareness that, around the world, white people have often oppressed black people. For some young white people, there were thus inherent contradictions in being proud of 'whiteness'. These contradictions differentiated them from black and mixed parentage young people, who expressed no such qualms about being proud to be black or of mixed parentage.

POSITIONED DIFFERENTLY: DIFFERENTIATED BY NATION

Another way in which the young people's responses were differentiated related to how they perceived membership of the English nation and the British state. Michael Billig (1995) has coined the term 'banal nationalism' to indicate that everyday nationalism and the processes by which it is reproduced are not innocent and insignificant. The findings of our study of social identities indicated that 'banal nationalism', expressed through national identities, was racialized.

Overall, half the young people's accounts reproduced pervasive 'little England' discourses, which construct the English as white. Some produced discourses that combined colour, descent and upbringing. A minority of the young people said that residence was sufficient for inclusion as English. Rather more considered that being born in England would confer Englishness than that residence would. This answer was not significantly differentiated by colour of respondent. Few people mentioned that the parents would have to have been born in England for their children to be white, although this factor emerged in answer to other questions. With regard to most of these answers, young people of mixed parentage were more similar to black than to white young people. Few (4 per cent) mentioned social class as an element of this discourse. They thus produced elements of a 'primordial' view of ethnicity which predicates the symbolic boundaries of 'Englishness' on fixed, rather than flexible, notions of colour and descent (Smith, 1984). 'Race' was therefore intertwined with nation in many of the young people's constructions of national identities.

In this context, it seems surprising that young white people produced responses which were less exclusionary than those of black or mixed parentage young people. There were significant differences (by respondents' colour) in the opinions given about whether English people are necessarily white, or whether the term includes anybody who lives in England. In both cases, young white people were more likely than young mixed parentage or black young people to give answers which were less exclusionary. For example, white young people were the group least likely to say that the English were white (38 per cent, compared with 61 per cent of black young people and mixed parentage young people).

The most likely explanation for this relates to the ways in which the complex concept of 'Englishness' is constructed and interpreted through everyday experiences. Our study included more areas than those reported here. It was evident from the accounts received that many black and mixed parentage young people had experienced racism. This may well have led them to construct themselves as excluded from the nation. White young people were better able to maintain their egalitarian ideology in response to these questions because they are not constructed as outsiders or subject to racism in the same way. This is apparent from some of the answers given in response to questions about whether they considered themselves English or British. Their answers appeared to be ideal and theoretical, while the black and mixed parentage young people's answers were more practical, arising from racialized experience. It is for these same reasons that many young white people said that being white was irrelevant to their lives.

Despite these differences, being asked about national identities was not necessarily easier for white than for black young people. There sometimes seemed to be some embarrassment for white young people about defining themselves too readily as English in case this appeared 'racist' or jingoistic. The following example illustrates this 'dilemmatic' notion of ideology (Billig *et al.*, 1988). The dilemma concerns expressing their views while not appearing racist, as is apparent in the account below:

Q. ... And what sort of people do you think of as being English?
A. Um (pause)
Q. ... Do you think of English people as being white?
A. Yes, probably yes I do ... I know I shouldn't but I probably do.
Q. Why do you think you shouldn't?

Ann Phoenix

A. Because I think that's probably racist.
Q. Why...?
A. Um because I think it's discriminating. It's saying that people who are not white are not like fully a part of this country...which is wrong. It's kind of a subconscious thing...like the stereotyped Englishman.

(white young man)

The equation of 'race', nation and culture therefore poses dilemmas for some young white people. This leads them to use rhetorical devices that are 'two-sided', in which 'two contrary themes are expressed simultaneously...' (Billig *et al.*, 1988: 109). In the above instance, the young man suggests that he recognizes that it is racist and exclusionary to equate Englishness and 'whiteness'. He thus expresses reluctance to espouse the idea and indeed, does not do so until expressly asked. It may be, of course, that other young people refused to give answers they thought would be considered racist. In their response to questions about how they found the interview some white young people expressed anxieties about putting forward their views without appearing racist.

Discomfort on the part of white young people can be warded off by viewing ethnicity and nationality as optional and voluntary rather than as related to subject positions. From this perspective young white people perceived black people as having more choice than white people about opting into or out of 'Englishness'.

They *can* call themselves English, but some of them choose to call themselves West Indian. They can still do that.

(white young man)

The 'optional' view expressed by the white young man quoted above led some white young people to construct black people as benefiting from instrumental aspects of nationality in a way white people could not. They may, perhaps, have felt envious of black people's (assumed) wider horizons in having knowledge of and/or being rooted in at least two countries and cultures. Ethnic and national differences could thus provide a focus of resentment. This was a finding described in the Burnage report of the inquiry into the murder of a young Asian boy by a white boy in their school playground (Macdonald *et al.*, 1989). Macdonald and his colleagues found that many of the white working-class boys considered that they did not have a culture and that whites were disadvantaged by the presence of black people and other minority ethnic groups whom they perceived to have cultures and identities. This is a finding echoed by Cohen (1987), who argued that his taped interview with 10- and 11-year-old-boys 'illustrates the main normative elements to be found in working class racism – ... its constant refrain of relative deprivation "the blacks are doing better than us"' (Cohen, 1987: 31).

It is, of course, not being suggested that all young people are positioned in the same way with regard to 'whiteness'. Young white people of Irish descent and young Jewish people in Britain often themselves had experienced racism and so were differentiated from the white majority. In addition, young white people had varied narratives about black people and racism. All were, however, positioned in relation to black and other minority people and to racism in complex ways (Burman, 1994; Hickman and Walter, 1995).

IN CONCLUSION

One of the striking features of the study reported here was the reluctance of many white young people to think of themselves as 'white' or to view 'whiteness' as having any social meaning. Their accounts were of 'whiteness' as natural and involuntary rather than constructed, socially significant and open to question. Disavowal of 'whiteness' often went hand in hand with disavowal of the symbols of nation. Many white young people considered it unacceptable to be proud of the British flag on the grounds that, as a symbol, it had been appropriated by the racist Far Right. In consequence, some felt ashamed to claim 'Britishness' or 'Englishness' and vacated national identity. As with 'blackness', 'whiteness' was dynamic and differentiated, for example, by ethnicity, social class and gender.

This chapter has argued that such findings can be understood only in the context of the young people's lives. On the one hand, their lives are racialized in such a way that 'whiteness' in itself accrues some privileges. On the other hand, in late twentieth century Britain, multiculturalist and anti-racist educational strategies have made racism unacceptable and, to some extent, have encouraged 'colour-blind' approaches which, paradoxically, do not take sufficient account of racialized power differences between young people. These policies have not necessarily made any difference to the ways in which young people from different racialized groups construct each other. As a result, some white young people had stereotypic and static, racialized notions of black people as dangerous and violent (male) 'others'. Many of the white young Londoners interviewed felt particularly tentative and uncertain when asked to discuss issues of 'race'. Not surprisingly then, processes of racialization continue to be part of a contested terrain where 'blackness' is constructed as a signifier of identity but where many white young people deny that 'whiteness' has any meanings and do not consider it to confer any identity.

Paradoxically, the necessity for 'whiteness' to be an explicit identity position is obviated by the fact that many black and mixed parentage young people overtly position themselves as having racialized identities. Young white people can thus consider themselves 'raceless' while continuing to accrue the privileges associated with 'whiteness'. It is thus possible to see how silence about 'whiteness' implicitly serves to maintain the *status quo* of power relations between black people and white people, minorities and majorities.

It is important to locate these findings in the specific geographical context in which the study was undertaken: London. Arguably, the taken-for-granted of 'whiteness' results partly from the fact that, in comparison with those European whites who have experienced dislocation and the redrawing of their national boundaries, the white young Londoners interviewed for this study have experienced relatively little which has caused them to rethink their ethnic or racialized identities. This, in itself, illustrates that what Stuart Hall (1989/96) has called 'diaspora-ization' is important to the understanding of racialized identities. Studies of 'whiteness' are crucial to this project.

NOTES

1.   This study was conducted jointly with Barbara Tizard at the Thomas Coram Research Unit, University of London.

REFERENCES

Back, L., 'Youth, Race and Nation within a Predominantly White Working-class Neighbourhood in South London', *New Community*, 19(2) (1993), 217–233.
Billig, M., *Banal Nationalism* (London: Sage, 1995).

Billig, M., S. Condor, D. Edwards, M. Gane, D. Middleton, and A. Radley, *Ideological Dilemmas: A Social Psychology of Everyday Thinking* (London: Sage, 1988).

Burman, E., 'Experience, Identities and Alliances: Jewish Feminism and Feminist Psychology', *Feminism and Psychology*, 4(1) (1994), 155–78.

Cohen, P., 'The Perversions of Inheritance', in P. Cohen and S. Harwant Bains (eds), *Multi-racist Britain* (Basingstoke: Macmillan, 1988).

Cohen, P., 'Reducing Prejudice in Classroom and Community: Report on the First Year', PSEC/CME Cultural Studies Project (1987).

van Dijk, T., *Communicating Racism: Ethnic Prejudice in Thought and Talk* (London: Sage, 1987).

Essed, P., 'Gender, Migration and Cross-ethnic Coalition Buliding', in H. Lutz, A. Phoenix and N. Yuval-Davis (eds), *Crossfires: Nationalism, Racism and Gender in Europe* (London: Pluto, Press 1995) 48–64.

Frankenberg, R., *White Women, Race Matters: The Social Construction of Whiteness* (London: Routledge, 1993).

Hall, C., *White, Male and Middle Class* (Cambridge: Polity Press, 1992).

Hall, S., 'New Ethnicities', reproduced in D.Morley and K.-H.Chen (eds), *Stuart Hall: Critical Dialogues in Cultural Studies* (London: Routledge, 1996).

Hickman, M., and W. Bronwen, 'Deconstructing Whiteness: Irish Women in Britain', *Feminist Review*, 50 (1995) 5–19.

Hooks, B., *Black Looks: Race and Representation* (Boston, MA: South End Press, 1992).

Jeater, D., 'Roast Beef and Reggae Music: The Passing of Whiteness', *New Formations*, 18 (1992) 107–21.

Lutz, H., 'The Limits of Europeanness: Immigrant Women in Fortress Europe', *Feminist Review* (in press, 1997).

Macdonald, I., R. Bhavnani, L. Khan and G. John, *Murder in the Playground* (London: Longsight Press, 1989).

Pajaczkowska, C., and L.Young, 'Racism, Representation, Psychoanalysis', in J. Donald and A. Rattansi (eds) *'Race', Culture and Difference* (London: Sage, 1992) 198–219.

Phoenix, A., 'Theories of Gender and Black Families', in G. Weiner and M. Arnot (eds), *Gender under Scrutiny* (London: Hutchinson, 1987) 50–63.

Smith, A., 'Ethnic Myths and Ethnic Revivals', *Archives Européenes de Sociologie*, 24(3) (1984), 283–303.

Trepagnier, B., 'The Politics of White and Black Bodies', *Feminism and Psychology*, 4(1) (1994), 199–205.

Troyna, B., and R. Hatcher, *Racism in Children's Lives: A Study of Mainly-white Primary Schools* (London: Routledge, 1992).

Ware, V., *Beyond the Pale: White Women, Racism and History* (London: Verso, 1992)

Wetherell, M., and J. Potter, *Mapping the Language of Racism: Discourse and the Legitimation of Exploitation* (London: Harvester Wheatsheaf, 1992)

Wong, L.M., 'Di(s)-secting and Dis(s)-closing "Whiteness": Two Tales about Psychology', in B. Bhavnani and A. Phoenix (eds), *Shifting Identities, Shifting Racisms: A Feminism and Psychology Reader* (London: Sage, 1994) 133–53.

7 Catholic and State Constructions of Domestic Workers: The Case of Cape Verdean Women in Rome in the 1970s
Jacqueline Andall

INTRODUCTION

In the 1980s academic interpretations of the 'new migration' to Italy tended to accentuate the significance of 'push' or supply-led factors in sending countries in their explanations of the presence of migrant workers. Some more recent studies have begun to challenge these interpretations and have demonstrated that migrant workers fulfil demand in specific economic niches (Ambrosini, 1995; Pinto 1992). One area in which the 'supply-push' thesis alone is clearly inapplicable is the domestic service sector. Studies dealing with migrants' insertion into the labour market have described the domestic work sphere unequivocally as a sector in which there is considerable demand for migrant women's labour (Favaro and Bordogna, 1991; Pugliese, 1990).

In this chapter I examine some of the factors which contributed to a particular construction of migrant women's social identity in the 1970s. I suggest that female migrants to Italy were subject to a double invisibility as women and as workers. National discourses of gender did not address women's specific situation as *female* migrants; rather, women were categorized only as migrants. This positioning contributed to their invisibility as workers because of the location of many of them in a marginalized and feminized sphere of the economy – the domestic work sector.

Women from the Cape Verde Islands began their migration to Italy long before academic and public interest in immigration developed in the 1980s. Cape Verdean women have been present in Italy since the 1960s, with numbers steadily increasing during the 1970s. At this time, however, the question of immigration was still focused on Italian migration (internal, external and return migration) and as a consequence, the conditions of migrant women achieved limited public visibility. None the less, both the institutional and informal organization of migrant women's labour force participation during this decade were instrumental in constructing migrant women's social identities in a particular fashion. In the postwar period Italian women had been ideologically confined to a traditional wife and mother role. The emergence of an active feminist movement in the 1970s challenged this model and younger women began to develop new social identities (Bimbi, 1993*b*). Participation in the labour market was seen to be integral to the feminist project, but this led to an unresolved tension regarding reproductive labour in Italy, contributing to a rising demand for domestic workers.

The domestic work sphere in Italy historically has constituted a marginalized category of employment in comparison with other employment sectors. This marginality can be attributed to the nature of the legal regulation of domestic work in Italy and its generally low status as a form of employment. As a result of these factors, Italian women have been reluctant to engage in live-in domestic work, thus creating a demand for migrant workers. In this chapter, I contend that the contemporary features of migrant women's employment in Italy reflect not only the historical organization of the domestic work sphere, but also the historical construction of migrant women's presence as migrant workers. Since this early stage of migrant women's presence in Italy has contributed significantly to a particular contemporary model of female migrant identity, it is important to review this historical context as a means to gaining a deeper understanding of the current labour market situation.

Three principal areas are addressed in this chapter: the sociohistorical background to domestic work; government regulation of migrant domestic labour in the 1970s; and Cape Verdean women's experiences during this period. I argue that the interlocking social identities of migrant women as women, migrant workers and members of ethnic minority communities were negated in this period and that there was a hierarchical structuring of these roles which privileged migrant women's labour function. The Italian example lends support to the findings of studies carried out in other contexts which have shown how the domestic labour of African and Asian migrant women is increasingly utilized by middle-class women as a strategy to facilitate their own salaried employment (Chang, 1994; Nakano Glenn, 1992) and how this perpetuates asymmetrical race and class relationships between women (Bakan and Stasiulis, 1995).

CATHOLIC INFLUENCE IN THE DOMESTIC WORK SECTOR

An examination of the sociohistorical development of the domestic work sphere in Italy is crucial for an understanding of migrant women's disadvantaged position in the labour market. This development must be understood in the context of the extreme political polarization which emerged in Italy during the immediate postwar period. The dominance of two ideologically opposed political frameworks – Catholicism and Communism – had an effect not only on the organization of trade union activity but also on the philosophy guiding the trade union sub-cultures of Catholicism and Communism. The domestic work sphere was an arena in which the Catholic sector dominated and was consequently subject to Catholic social teaching in the arena of labour relations.

The Catholic labour perspective was based on the conciliation of capital and labour (Bedani, 1995). The aim was to avoid conflict and to achieve a harmonious employer/employee relationship. The formation of the influential Christian organization ACLI (*Associazioni cristiane dei lavoratori italiani*)[1] in the immediate postwar period reflected Catholic social and political discomfort at the existence of a unitary trade union body in which it was feared that the Communists and Socialists would dominate. In terms of the association's ambitions within the work arena, there were two areas of relevance to Italy's domestic workers. One was ACLI's aim to protect the practice of the faith and Catholic morality within the workplace. The second was the aim to assist workers in recognizing and formulating solutions to their problems based on Christian criteria (see Pasini, 1974).

ACLI-COLF[2] operated within ACLI. It emerged in the postwar period as the only national body to concern itself specifically with domestic workers. This had particular implications for the type of mobilization which took place regarding domestic work. The nature of ACLI-COLF mobilization was highly influenced by both Catholic ideology pertaining to the family and by Catholic ideology regarding the resolution of labour conflict. These combined to ensure a subordinate position for the domestic worker in relation to the employer.

Migrant women would thus be absorbed ultimately into a sector which was organizationally weak and in which the workers' needs historically had been subordinated to those of the employer. The influence of Catholic ideology pertaining to the family could clearly be seen in ACLI-COLF's teaching. Catholicism ascribes to women a fundamental role within the home as mothers and wives and waged labour was seen to constitute a threat to this role. It was for this reason that ACLI-COLF was concerned to present domestic work as a preferable alternative to other types of paid work. The promotion of domestic work as intrinsically different from other categories of work was inextricably bound up with Catholic perceptions of women's relationship to the home and the family. At the national congress of ACLI-COLF in 1958 the president Clara Storchi stated, 'We have said that the family is the ideal working environment for a woman and we maintain this'.[3] Although there was some recognition that certain characteristics of factory work (proper contracts, secure wages and a fixed working time schedule) explained women's preference for this type of work, the association argued that domestic workers should find value in the subordination and invisibility of their work because it was work carried out for others and more importantly because it gave support to the Italian family unit. Catholic notions of privation, sacrifice and altruism were thus clearly being promoted.

The appointment of Father Erminio Crippa in 1956 to provide for the moral and spiritual welfare of the domestic work sector led to a number of publications which projected on to domestic workers both an appropriate mode of perceiving the nature of their work and an appropriate model of behaviour. His publications clearly reflect Catholic ideology regarding the resolution of labour conflict. One 1959 publication entitled 'Your professional morality' stressed the need for domestic workers to view their work as an act of love towards God and as an act of charity towards their neighbour.[4] In a 1961 publication, there was an attempt to promote a vision of the employers' home as 'a little church' where domestic workers should conceive of their profession 'as collaboration with the family and a means to love God wholeheartedly' (Crippa, 1961: 10). In 1956 Pope Pius XII stated that domestic workers should view their employers as fathers. In this manner, the Catholic sphere eschewed any class-based analysis of domestic work. Blatant appeals to women's assumed 'natural' maternal instincts were made to encourage the domestic worker to view her role in this vein:

Don't you feel similar to a mother? Sometimes, don't you give her a hand and don't you act as a substitute when she is not there? Isn't your life a little like hers, full of sacrifices and lack of sleep, and don't you multiply yourself according to necessity and don't you split yourself a hundred ways to help everyone, making everyone feel that you are there totally for them?

(Crippa, 1961: 16)

There was additionally an attempt to present domestic work as intrinsically better than other categories of work:

Don't dream of being a secretary in an office: she only carries out one aspect of your profession! At home, you know the vocabulary of everyone ... you know the secrets of everyone; at the market, you remember everyone's tastes ...

(Crippa, 1961: 16)

Although by the 1950s ACLI-COLF recognized a growing trend amongst Italian domestic workers to opt for hourly-paid work, it felt that certain categories of families still required the services of live-in workers. These included families with children or with elderly or sick relatives and professional women who needed to entrust the running of their homes and the care of their children to someone else. It also included those families whose need for live-in workers was essentially a status-driven demand. This support for live-in work was moreover conditioned by Catholic preoccupations with morality. There was some concern that part-time work and independent living arrangements would expose domestic workers to moral danger. Consequently, the solution proposed by the association revolved around an improvement of the live-in relationship. The basis of this improvement would lie in the reciprocal respect and duties of both the employee and the employer.

Consonant with a Catholic labour perspective, collaboration between the employer and the employee was thus considered to be an essential aspect of good labour relations. The nature of this collaboration was unambiguously delineated. For domestic workers it centred on perceiving the employer's family as a family rather than as an employer. Domestic workers were expected to accept their subservient role. Indeed, Father Crippa advised that in the event of a disagreement between employer and employee, regardless of who was to blame, the onus was on the worker to break the ice with a smile, greeting or some form of service. The employer was expected to treat the domestic worker as a member of the family community. Obstacles to this mutual collaboration on the part of the employer would consist of an excessive focus on the employment aspect of the job, the non-protection of the employee's health and the equation of the domestic worker's subordination with inferiority. For the employee, obstacles to collaboration would arise if she did not love her work or if she felt that she was exploited and misunderstood.[5]

The position of ACLI-COLF is thus quite explicit regarding the subordination of the domestic worker to the employer. This perspective is seen to reflect not a belief that the domestic worker is inferior but that she is differentially situated within the employer/employee relationship. In this instance, the primacy of domestic workers' role in assisting a family unit was clearly of paramount importance given Catholic concerns with regard to the institution of the family. This concern was in fact utilized to justify the subordination of the domestic worker.

At this stage, the strategy of ACLI-COLF was related to a national constituency of domestic workers. Italian women from industrially depressed and rural areas within Italy had engaged in internal migration processes throughout the postwar period to seek employment as domestic workers. The ACLI-COLF strategy had nevertheless shaped the domestic work sector into which migrant women would be integrated. It adopted a distinctly more radical approach in the early 1970s, influenced by broader changes occurring in the trade union movement, which included the leftward shift of Catholic activists.[6] Until the 1970s however, a clerical approach to labour relations had been promoted explicitly by the only national body to deal specifically with domestic workers. Its legacy would persist for some time and in any case it had conferred considerable advantage on employers. Although ACLI-COLF's subsequent radicalism in the 1970s coincided with the increased presence of female migrant workers in Italy, its analyses were dominated by a class perspective. It therefore interpreted the presence of migrant domestic workers as a strategy of the employers to fracture class solidarity. Throughout the 1970s, the association was principally concerned with improving its relationship with the worker's movement and this meant that limited attention was paid to migrant women. It was in fact the more conservative API-COLF which began to investigate the specific conditions of migrant women, with Erminio Crippa publishing a book on their experiences in 1979.

It was not just Catholic domination of this labour market sphere which contributed to the weakness of the sector, however.

The fundamental structural problem of the domestic work sector was its categorization in the Italian civil code as atypical work. This signified that it was the employing family which was expected to protect the rights of the worker. The atypical status of domestic work thus presupposed a harmonious relationship between employer and employee in which the benign paternalism of the family would suffice as protection for the domestic worker. In 1969 this article was abolished as a result of its contravention of Article 3 of the Italian Constitution which stated that all citizens were equal before the law. This was a critical ruling since it paved the way for national collective bargaining for the sector. This would eventually begin to offer domestic workers greater protection via the collectively bargained national contracts. The legal regulation of domestic work coupled with Catholic notions regarding the resolution of labour conflict had previously signified a weak position for the domestic worker. The low status associated with domestic work also meant that where possible Italian women would seek alternative employment. This led to a strong demand for migrant domestic workers in the 1970s.

GOVERNMENT REGULATION OF MIGRANT DOMESTIC WORKERS

National legislation regarding migrant workers was not introduced in Italy until 1986. The regulation of overseas domestic workers during the 1970s thus occurred via government circulars issued by both the Ministry of Labour (*Ministero del Lavoro*) and the Ministry for Overseas Affairs (*Ministero degli Affari Esteri*). These circulars indicated both a desire to protect the position of Italian workers and to construct the labour function of migrant women as their pre-eminent role. In 1972, the Ministry for Labour acknowledged the increasing use of overseas labour for domestic work, attributing this to a desire amongst employers to avoid paying insurance contributions. There was clearly some concern that this would mean that foreign labour would be more attractive than Italian labour. Government circulars therefore unequivocally prioritized the employment of Italian nationals over and above that of foreign nationals. A ministerial circular issued in 1973 and applicable to migrant workers in general was indicative of this. It maintained that work permit authorizations for migrant workers should be issued in economic spheres where there was availability within the domestic labour pool. The circular stated that the use of foreign labour should be rigorously controlled and advocated maximum use of the domestic labour market. Further circulars specifically regulating domestic work were issued in 1973 and 1975. They reiterated the view that foreign labour was being utilized because it was considered to be economically beneficial to employers. Indeed, the 1975 circular was intended to prevent the illegal employment of foreign domestic workers. The Ministry of Labour believed that employers were deliberately finding ways to avoid utilizing the correct recruitment channels as delineated in ministerial dictates. It is clear that despite ministerial concerns to restrict the employment of foreign nationals as domestic workers and to encourage the employment of Italian nationals, a specific demand for migrant women's labour was apparent. The undocumented employment of female migrant workers, where economic benefits could be accrued by the imposition of exploitative and illegal working practices, was one factor which lay at the basis of this preference. This preference can also be attributed however to modifications in the organization of domestic work. By the 1970s Italian domestic workers were increasingly reluctant to work as live-in domestic workers and had begun to work largely on an hourly-paid basis. This left a specific gap in the market for live-in domestic work which migrant women would be forced (institutionally) and encouraged (informally) to fill.

At government level, the desire to restrict the incoming migration of foreign domestic workers is clearly discernible. In 1979, a Ministry of Labour circular acknowledged the extent of the demand for foreign domestic workers, but then established an inter-ministerial group to 'eliminate, or at least contain the phenomenon of the uncontrolled presence of foreign workers, regulating the influx according to the real necessities of the national market for domestic work' (Circular no. 140/90/79). The position of the ministry seems to have been conditioned by a belief that a potential pool of Italian nationals could be mobilized to engage in this sector of employment and thus eliminate the necessity for migrant workers.

Despite this ministerial concern to restrict the employment of foreign labour, the ministerial regulation of foreign domestic labour probably contributed to the attractiveness of migrant domestic workers for the Italian employer. Although Italian and foreign domestic workers were subject to the same legislation regarding domestic work itself, the position of migrant women was somewhat different because of the nature of government regulation of their situation as migrants. Indeed, the regulation of foreign domestic workers was envisaged in such a way as to construct the labour function of migrant women as a dominant role. By 1972 a Ministry of Labour circular already had stipulated that migrant domestic workers could only be employed for full-time work. Thus, the option of hourly-paid domestic work was a legal impossibility for potential recruits. In reality, only the latter option of hourly-paid work enables women to articulate their multiple social identities. The fact that this was not legally possible emphasizes that it was the labour function and the labour function alone of migrant women which was conceptualized as beneficial to Italian society.

The 1979 circular irrevocably tied the prospective migrant domestic worker's presence in Italy to her employment function. In the event of a breakdown in the employment contract, the domestic worker would have to return immediately to her country of origin and would not be able to seek employment in Italy for another three years. This reflects a vision of foreign domestic workers as contractual migrant labour. It also clearly placed the migrant domestic worker in a vulnerable position in relation to her employer, particularly in situations of extreme exploitation or abuse. In those instances where the foreign domestic worker otherwise would have been inclined to change employer, this had to be weighed up against the prospect of an effective three year repatriation period.

Government regulation of migrant domestic workers thus negated the interlocking identities of migrant women and accentuated only their labour function. This totally inverted national discourses of gender regarding appropriate roles for women. The tension with regard to Italian women had centred on how their increasing entry into the paid labour market removed them from an 'essential' family role. The construction of migrant women's labour function as their primary role implied that such gendered considerations were not applicable to them.

METHODOLOGY

The results discussed in the following section constitute part of a wider study. In the early 1990s, 28 semi-structured interviews were conducted with black women migrants from the Cape Verde Islands, Eritrea, Ethiopia and Somalia. Fifteen of the interviewees were from the Cape Verde Islands and of these, 11 had migrated to Rome in the 1970s. All the Cape Verdean women had originally been employed as live-in domestic workers and only one did not have any children. Further information regarding the experiences of Cape Verdean women in the 1970s was obtained via informal discussions held with women at the religious *Tra Noi* Association in Rome, a long-standing meeting place for Cape Verdean women, and also at the community's public meeting place at *Piazza Fiume* in Rome. One of the disadvantages of this retrospective methodology is clearly related to the manner in which interviewees may represent their earlier experiences. Generally, however, I found that the women were verbally quite precise over details such as how long they had worked for particular families, why they had changed employers and how long it had taken them to find alternative employment. In any case, the lack of attention given to migrant women in the 1970s meant that recourse to an oral history constituted the principal means through which one could gain access to women's experiences during this period.

While the Cape Verdean community is small in comparison to some other ethnic minority communities in Rome, it nevertheless represents an interesting and important community. First, in the context of Italy's 'new migration', Cape Verdean migration represents one of the oldest communities. Secondly, Cape Verdean migration was predominantly a female single-sex migration. It constitutes an original female migrant model in Italy and one which has led to specific difficulties for Cape Verdean live-in domestic workers. Finally, Cape Verdean migration was initiated by Capuchin friars based in the Islands who began to recruit domestic staff for employers connected to Catholic parishes in Rome (OMCVI, 1989). This marked the beginning of Catholic involvement in the sector of immigration and can be seen to account partially for the prominent role that the Catholic voluntary sector would eventually play regarding immigration.

Whilst the results presented here refer to Cape Verdean women, they are generalizable to those ethnic groups which approximate the Cape Verdean model of migration. The Filipino community in particular evolved from a predominantly female single-sex migration in the 1970s.[7] New models of female migrant identity have emerged in Italy over time. The models referred to in the Italian migration literature refer to female-headed households, family migration units and women who migrate through family reunification policies as wives (Favaro and Bordonga, 1991; De Filippo, 1994). The importance of documenting the original model which prevailed in the 1970s lies in its potential to further our understanding of the significance of gender within migratory processes, particularly where this model constitutes not only a primary migration but also a predominantly single-sex phenomenon.

CAPE VERDEAN WOMEN IN ROME (*LAZIO* REGION)

Catholic influence within the domestic work sector and government regulation of migrant women's recruitment were not the only factors to contribute to the construction of migrant women as marginal subjects. Female single-sex migration was an additional factor. The primary migration of young, single Cape Verdean women was due to the gendered labour market opportunities for migrants in the region. There is little reliable data regarding the presence of migrant workers in the 1970s. Statistics from the Rome provincial office regarding work permits, however, highlight the extent of female migrant labour force participation. In 1978, the overwhelming majority (65.2 per cent) of employment permits were issued to nationals from developing countries. It is particularly interesting to note the dominance of domestic work as a category of employment for foreign workers. In 1978, 90 per cent of the work permits issued by the Rome office to nationals from the developing world were for domestic work (ECAP-CGIL, 1980). This can be seen to account for the single-sex migration of Cape Verdean women. A gender imbalance within the Cape Verdean community still persists, with 1990 data demonstrating that 83 per cent of the Cape Verdean community in the *Lazio* region is female.

Interviews with Cape Verdean women demonstrated that several had encountered some difficulties in obtaining a legal work contract in the 1970s. Some Cape Verdean women did migrate to Italy with a regular contract. Matilde, for example, migrated to Rome in 1978, aged 18. She had her contract arranged for her by her sister who was already living in Italy. However, employment was readily available in the undocumented sector of domestic work. Maria Joanna entered Italy on a tourist visa in 1969 and she subsequently worked illegally for three years. It is clear that many employers preferred the flexibility of not stipulating an employment contract. In the case of Maria Joanna, despite the fact that she had entered on a tourist visa, her employment had already been arranged while she was resident in Portugal – her first country of migration. Indeed, her employer came to collect her at the airport but did not legalize her position. The quest to legalize their status was thus often behind the employment mobility of Cape Verdean women. The possibility of such mobility indicates that there was substantial demand within the domestic service sector. One respondent worked for a total of six years as an illegal worker. During this period she changed families three times, each time with the expectation that her employers would legalize her status.

Lack of legal status was not however the only motive for a change in employment. Women would also change employers for more personal reasons. Rosa, for example, had worked for nine months with one family but had left their employment because her day off was on Wednesday. This meant that she could not meet with other members of her family resident in the region, who, like most domestics, were free on Thursday afternoon and Sundays. Clara also changed her first job so that she could be nearer to her sister. She changed employers despite the fact that she described the family for whom she then worked as 'an excellent family'. These examples demonstrate that despite the primary function of migrant women having been constructed as that of a worker, the proximity to other family members was of some importance to these female migrant workers. The willingness of migrant women to change employer in order to facilitate family contact points to the development of strategies to combat the subordination of their multiple social identities to a dominant work function.

Cape Verdean women in the 1970s were employed exclusively as live-in domestic workers. This period thus marked the beginning of a distinct racialization of the live-in sphere. This sector would gradually come to be dominated by migrant women while Italian women remaining in the sector increasingly engaged in hourly-paid work. The demand for Cape Verdean women's labour as live-in workers was high. As one respondent stated:

> In the 1970s it was the employers who asked us if we wanted to work for them. They used to stop you in the middle of the street to ask you if you had a friend or a sister. Or else sometimes your employers would ask you on behalf of their friends. Now we have to ask for work and we are sometimes even unemployed.

Cape Verdean women were employed both in cases where the mother of the employing family was engaged in paid work or where her function was that of a full time housewife. This indicated that Cape Verdean women's labour was being used not only to resolve the issue of child-care for employed Italian women but also to fulfil the status requirements of wealthy Italian families. The women I interviewed all described domestic work as difficult and taxing work. But more pertinently, all of the women highlighted the difficulty of being on call for virtually 24 hours a day. Some felt that they had been particularly exploited when they first arrived because they were not familiar with their working rights and thus worked many more hours than they were legally obliged to work. One respondent stated that not only were the working hours long, but that her employers' primary interest in her labour meant that they attempted mentally, if not practically, to restrict other aspects of her social identity. Thus, her female employer did not want her to have a boyfriend and frequently told her that she should not get married. The power of the employer was thus also frequently expressed via control over domestic workers' free time.

My qualitative data could only provide information about the employers through the perspectives and work experiences of domestic workers themselves. While it is impossible to point to any uniformity, it is fair to say that the demand for migrant women's labour in the 1970s did not guarantee a congenial working environment. Where employment conditions were favourable however, Cape Verdean women exhibited remarkably high levels of employment stability. For example, two of the respondents had worked for the same family for 20 and 18 years respectively.

The organization of female migrant labour as live-in domestic workers effectively suppressed the multiple social identities of Cape Verdean women. In particular, live-in domestic work severely exacerbated the problems of combining reproductive and productive labour. The logistical problems that maternity posed for live-in domestic workers restricted migrant women's fertility by forcing them to postpone, either indefinitely or in the short term, their decisions regarding procreation. The principal options available to live-in domestic workers with children in the 1970s were residential homes, fostering, leaving children in the country of origin or sending them back, acquiring hourly-paid work and independent living accommodation.

The experiences of Clara with regard to her negotiation of the maternal process exemplify the difficulties of maternity. She migrated to Italy in 1971 aged 22, leaving behind her three young children (aged five, two and one) to be cared for by her mother. Even when she was finally in a position to bring one of her three children to Italy from the Cape Verde Islands, having worked as a domestic for ten years, she was obliged to place her daughter in a residential home for four years because she could not find hourly-paid work and appropriate accommodation. Antonia migrated in 1977, leaving a son of two in Cape

Verde. Ten years later she took him to Lisbon to be looked after by friends. At the time, she felt unable to bring him to Italy because she did not have access to independent living accommodation and could not keep him with her at her employers. The situation in Portugal became problematic and she eventually had no option but to bring her son to live in Italy where he was immediately placed in a residential home. As she stated, 'We can never be together, not even in the summer or at Easter.' The transition to hourly-paid work and independent accommodation is the remedy normally pursued in such a situation. Yet from an employment perspective this can lead to a different set of problems, the most serious of which is increased competition from Italian hourly-paid domestic workers. This leads to vulnerability in employment which has serious implications for households headed by single women.

The combination of Cape Verdean women's desire for maternity and the organization of their labour as live-in domestic workers in the 1970s thus led to specific problems. Single parent working mothers with young children constituted an unfamiliar phenomenon in Italy. The relative cohesiveness of the Italian family in the European context has been well documented and statistics have shown that there are relatively few Italian single parent families with young children (Bimbi, 1993*a*; Ginsborg, 1994). This has meant an absence of structures to accommodate the specific needs of single parent migrant working women with children. Extended family networks have been used widely by Italian women to enable participation in the labour market (Del Boca, 1988; Paci 1983; Saraceno, 1987). The uniformity of migrant women's employment function in the 1970s meant that access to family- or friendship-based networks drastically reduced the possibility of informal assistance for the care of their children. The gendered labour market opportunities available to migrant workers in Rome also had some impact on family organization. Cape Verdean men were more likely to migrate to other European countries such as Portugal or the Netherlands for employment. In Rome, they encountered a much less secure labour market environment, working in restaurants or as builders, but also employed jointly with their partners as domestic workers.

During the 1970s, the Catholic voluntary sector was a prominent protagonist within the sphere of immigration. In Rome, the reception centres and organizations offering assistance were almost exclusively religion-based. The Catholic sector thus assumed an important role in relation to migrant women in the 1970s. Not only had it played a crucial recruitment role in initiating the migration of Cape Verdean women, but this involvement subsequently led to its organization of the social environment of Cape Verdean women.

The religious association *Tra Noi* in Rome constituted an important social and religious focal point for Cape Verdean women and was also a means through which the Catholic sector could spread its influence. The Catholic sector had developed in addition an organizational network which functioned as a useful resource for those women attempting to reconcile live-in domestic work with the maternal process. Its network of residential homes and mother and baby hostels was an important source of assistance and the Catholic organization *Caritas* also provided financial help for women whose children were placed in such homes. This set a precedent in relation to the family organization of single female primary migrants which has been perpetuated to this day. In the 1970s, Catholic ideology pertaining to the family remained strong. But the organization of the Catholic sector's family support for migrant women effectively meant protection for the Italian family and a parallel but different organization of the family unit for migrant women.

Given the very visible and active profile of the Italian feminist movement in the 1970s, one might have anticipated some involvement from this sector. In many ways, however, feminism's principal mobilizing issues and theoretical concerns were not easy to reconcile with the needs of Cape Verdean women. Feminism was seen to be at its peak during the mobilization for the legalization of abortion which occurred in 1978. Thus feminists became noted for their commitment to the right to choose not to be mothers. The needs of Cape Verdean women and the theoretical evolution of Italian feminism therefore stood at different stages with regard to maternity in the 1970s. Cape Verdean women were struggling to find the space for a maternal identity while Italian feminists were still locked into an ambiguous, if not overtly negative appraisal of the mothering role. Cape Verdean women's specific constraints consequently remained largely invisible to Italian feminists during the 1970s.

CONCLUSION

Research into the migration of Cape Verdean women to Rome in the 1970s demonstrates the existence of explicit gendered labour market opportunities, particularly in the 'site-specific' sector of domestic work. Furthermore, the limited public response to Cape Verdean women's presence in the 1970s, when compared with the hostile and restrictive approach to male migration in the 1980s, suggests that this difference in reception was determined by migrants' gendered employment location within public and private arenas. Brah (1991: 171) has argued that we need accounts of 'why certain categories of women perform particular kinds of paid work'. The literature on domestic work has pointed to a racialization of the domestic work sector (see Cock, 1980; Romero, 1992). Nakano Glenn (1992: 31) has in fact spoken of a new 'racial division of reproductive labour' which constitutes 'a source of both hierarchy and interdependence' between black and white women. Evidence of these trends can be identified in the Italian context if one compares not only the differences in employment experiences between Cape Verdean and Italian women domestic workers, but also if one interprets the employment of Cape Verdean women in relation to the new roles being assumed by Italian women.

The temptation to view the presence of migrant workers as a straightforward process of continuity from Italian domestic workers to migrant domestic workers should be avoided. Italian live-in workers generally envisaged domestic work as a temporary occupation until marriage, although there were many who did not marry and who continued working until retirement. None the less some recognition of their gendered social identities was apparent via the ideological equation of their paid labour role with a maternal role and the ultimate subordination of this paid work function to their family function.[8] The importance of Catholic morality at this time also meant that single Italian women were unlikely to embark on single parenthood in the same way that Cape Verdean women did in the 1970s.

Cape Verdean women's external migrant status was not entirely comparable to the earlier internal migrant status of many Italian domestic workers. Cape Verdean women were vulnerable as undocumented migrant workers given the possibility of repatriation. Domestic work moreover constituted a long-term rather than a temporary occupation for Cape Verdean women. This meant that demand for their labour within the live-in sphere was especially problematic in relation to child-rearing. By the 1970s, the archaic organization of the live-in sphere was clearly unattractive to Italian women, particularly given the gains that workers had made in other employment sectors (see Bedani, 1995). The racialization of the live-in sphere via the use of migrant labour meant that an old system could be perpetuated with a new supply of labour. The advent of a new model of the female migrant was embodied in the characteristics of Cape Verdean migration. This marked a distinct break in continuity between Italian and migrant women's experience of domestic work, as Italian women moved into the hourly-paid sector or other sectors of employment.

As has been shown above, the gendered aspect of Cape Verdean women's social identities was principally apparent via their involvement in a feminized sector of the economy. None the less, the organization of their labour entailed a negation of the maternal role and consequently their exclusion from mainstream discourses of gender. The contemporary problems which migrant women in Italy face are thus partially attributable to a historical definition of their principal function as workers. This has meant that their main task has been to facilitate the transformation of Italian women's social identities. The hierarchy and interdependence which currently characterizes the relationship between migrant women and Italian women have led to parallel but diverse constructions of female identity models within Italy.

NOTES

1. This organization was intended to promote the study, development and application of Catholic social teaching in the world of labour.
2. This group was initially known as the *Gruppi ACLI domestiche*. The term COLF is an abbreviation of *collaboratrice familaire* – family collaborator.
3. Clara Storchi, *'Il lavoro domestico, vera professione', III Congresso Nazionale domestiche ACLI*, April 1958. All translations from Italian used in this chapter are the author's own.
4. ACLI-COLF also saw the professional development of the sector as requiring urgent attention. See ACLI (1960).
5. *'Il lavoro domestico, collaborazione con la famiglia', IV Congresso Nazionales, Gruppi ACLI domestiche*, 1961.
6. The conservative wing which had dominated until that time regrouped under the name of API-COLF and continued to pursue the former strategy of the association.
7. See Kornspiern's (1990) study of Filipina domestic workers in Rome.
8. An ACLI-COLF document written by Crippa in 1959 categorically stated that should the domestic worker's parents need assistance she should abandon her employment and return to them. This indicated a clear prioritization of Italian women's family role over and above their

work role, with an implicit assumption that their wage was supplementary rather than central.

REFERENCES

ACLI, *I Gruppi ACLI Domestiche* (Rome: Edizioni ACLI, 1960).
Ambrosini, M., 'Immigrati e lavoro in Lombardia. Verso il superamento di un doppio pregiudizio', *Studi Emigrazione*, 32 (119) (1995) 491–503.
Bakan, A.B., and D.K. Stasiulis, 'Making the Match: Domestic Placement Agencies and the Racialization of Women's Household Work', *Signs*, 20(21) (1995) 303–35.
Bedani, G., *Politics and Ideology in the Italian Workers' Movement* (Oxford: Berg, 1995).
Bimbi, F., 'Gender, "Gift Relationship" and Welfare State Cultures in Italy', in J. Lewis (ed.), *Women and Social Policies in Europe* (Aldershot: Edward Elgar Press, 1993*a*) 138–70.
Bimbi, F., 'Three Generations of Women: Transformations of Female Identity Models in Italy', in M. Cicioni and N. Prunster (eds), *Visions and Revisions. Women in Italian Culture* (Oxford: Berg, 1993*b*) 149–66.
Brah, A., 'Questions of Difference and International Feminism', in J. Aaron and S. Walby (eds), *Out of the Margins: Women's Studies in the Nineties* (London: The Falmer Press, 1991) 168–76.
Chang, G., 'Undocumented Latinas: The New "Employable" Mothers', in E. Glenn, G. Chang and L. Forcey (eds), *Mothering: Ideology, Experience and Agency* (London: Routledge, 1994) 259–85.
Cock, J., *Maids and Madams: A Study in the Politics of Exploitation* (Johannesburg: Rav An Press, 1980).
Crippa, E., *La tua morale professionale* (Torino: Casa Serena, 1959).
Crippa, E., *Le Sante del nostro lavoro* (Torino: Casa Serena, 1961).
Crippa, E., *Lavoro amaro: le estere in Italia* (Rome: API-COLF, 1979).
De Filippo, E., 'Le lavoratrici "giorno e notte"', in G. Vicarelli (ed.), *Le mani invisibili. La vita e il lavoro delle donne immigrate* (Rome: Ediesse, 1994) 65–72.
Del Boca, D., 'Women in a Changing Workplace. The Case of Italy', in J. Jenson, E. Hagen and E. Reddy (eds), *Feminization of the Labour Force. Paradoxes and Promises* (Cambridge: Polity Press, 1988) 120–35.
ECAP-CGIL 'Considerazioni sul problema dei lavoratori stranieri nella regione Lazio' (Rome: ECAP-CGIL, 1980).
Favaro, G., and M. Bordogna, *Donne dal mondo. Strategie migratorie al femminile* (Milan: Guerini, 1991).
Ginsborg, P., 'La famiglia italiana oltre il privato per superare l'isolamento', in P. Ginsborg (ed.), *Stato dell'Italia*. (Milan: Il Saggiatore, 1994) 284–90.
Kornspiern, A., 'L'immigrazione femminile: uno studio sulle lavoratrici domestiche filippine a Roma', in A.M. Nassisi (ed.), *Il lavoro femminile in Italia tra produzione e riproduzione* (Rome: Instituto Gramsci, 1990) 153–70.
Nakano Glenn, E., 'From Servitude to Service Work: Historical Continuities in the Racial Division of Paid Reproductive Labour', *Signs*, 8(1) (1992) 1–43.

OMCVI (Organizacao da Mulheres Caboverdeanas em Italia), *Capo Verde: Una storia lunga dieci isole* (Milan: D'Anselmi Editore, 1989).

Paci, M., 'Struttura e funzioni della famiglia nello sviluppo industriale "periferico" ',in M. Paci (ed.), *Famiglia e mercato del lavoro in un'economia periferica* (Milan: Franco Angeli, 1983) 9–70.

Pasini, G., *Le ACLI dalle origini* (Rome: Edizioni Coines, 1974).

Pinto, P., 'L'inserimento di lavoratori stranieri in imprese italiane: il caso di Bologna', Il *Corriere Calabrese*, 2(1) (1992) 33–9.

Pugliese, E., 'Dove lavorano e che lavoro fanno gli immigrati', in D. Demetrio, G. Favaro, U. Melotti and L. Ziglio (eds), *Lontano da dove* (Milan: Franco Angeli, 1990) 238–41.

Romero, M., *Maid in the USA* (London: Routledge, 1992).

Saraceno, C., 'Division of Family Labour and Gender Identity', in A. Showstack Sassoon (ed.), *Women and the State* (London: Hutchinson, 1987) 191–206.

8 Observing Migration: The Construction of Statistics in a National Monitoring System
Paolo Barbesino

INTRODUCTION

This chapter focuses on the structure and operation of a statistical system collecting data on international migration in Italy. An ethno-statistical approach which studies statistics as the outcome of a social process is deployed, using the concepts of impartiality, symmetry and reflexivity, originally developed in social studies of science. A constructivist analysis is adopted in order to map the agencies involved, to scrutinize the set of monitoring devices and to investigate how the latter are implemented in the ordinary practices of the former. This approach provides useful insights into the way in which the discourse on migration is framed within a single national context, and provides some opportunities for comparative analysis. This chapter also looks at how the particular monitoring system under study was established and the kind of transformations it has undergone, thus adding to our understanding of the historical transformation of the discourse on migration. While processes of interpretation and negotiation between different actors are crucial in establishing what is to be counted, official statistics play a significant role in shaping the agenda of policy makers, social scientists and public opinion and thus are critical not just in the development of theoretical discourses on migration but also in the development of migration policy.

STATISTICS AS CULTURAL ARTEFACTS

Social scientists today are in a paradoxical situation. The more they have succeeded in turning the kind of knowledge which natural or 'hard' sciences produce into a suitable object of social inquiry, the less they seem to apply reflexively this same attitude to the knowledge claims they themselves make. In other words, while social scientists have consistently challenged the assumption that science describes the real world as it is, they are increasingly less likely to question their own capacity to describe society. As a result of this paradox, an uncritical attitude persists which has often led to the consideration of the entire set of social science theory and methodology, as well as the statistical techniques sustaining it, as immune to any further investigation. Statistical data support the law-like generalizations of theories. These in turn play a crucial role in empirical research in that they provide a cumulative and specific cognitive background which allows new statistical data to be generated. Even when statistical tools have proved inadequate, their inadequacy has often been explained in terms of a reduced representative capability, rather than a failure to approximate reality.

Other than a few attempts following Karl Mannheim's sociology of knowledge, only Marxist social scientists have challenged this common understanding. For some time, unmasking the implicit preconceptions of social knowledge and revealing the ideological bias of statistical data in fact became quite a fashionable activity. This challenge however rested on the assumption that access to social reality was ultimately possible. A critical approach could therefore easily confirm that a bias-free statistics can describe the 'strong and solid' nature of 'things' (Desrosières, 1993). From this standpoint, a distinction is drawn between that part of the statistical discourse which depends upon truth and science, and that which might depend on something else, so that this perspective always entertains 'a virtual relation with something which would be the truth' (Foucault, 1977: 12).

This suggests that social knowledge and ideology be conceived of as if they were subordinate to something operating as an economic or material structure or determinant. Applied to a secondary analysis of statistics, this argument emphasizes that official figures may suffer from bias and distortion, and that bureaucracies' practical concerns may prevent data from being formulated according to social science standards (Hammersley and Atkinson, 1995: 168–9). The task for social scientists thus was either to help official sources to produce more adequate statistical data or to get rid of them altogether.

As a result of these alternative goals, different strands of research have emerged. Originally, the main focus was on the creation of commensurable datasets, hence encouraging a systematic analysis of sources, methodologies, concepts and definitions. A second, related area gave rise to improved, harmonized and comparative statistics. A third strand of research enhanced the quality of data using statistical methods. Most recently, increasing attention has been paid to meta-data which allow the user to attain a more accurate understanding and manipulation of statistics.

One may wonder, however, whether the boundaries of this type of research have not, in some respects, been reached. Constructivist-oriented social studies of science have shown that scientific knowledge cannot be conceived of as the self-tuning of methods and theories on an underlying reality. Rather, it must be understood as a process whereby this very reality is constructed by means of observation. The assumptions which made an ideological critique of statistics possible, therefore, can no longer be maintained. Instead, the import-ant thing is to investigate how effects of truth are brought about historically within discourses which are themselves neither true nor false (Foucault, 1977). Yet however intriguing this approach may be conceptually, it seems to be difficult to apply in practice. This is particularly the case in studies of statistical classification and coding procedures which seem to rely on conjectures and speculations. Indeed, few social scientists would take the key requirements of symmetry and impartiality inherent in a constructivist-oriented socio-logy of knowledge so seriously as to pay any real attention to what sounds odd and unfamiliar at face-value (Bloor, 1991; Desrosières, 1993).

The classification of animals suggested in a 'certain Chinese encyclo-paedia' to which Michel Foucault refers in *The Order of Things* is a case in point. According to this classification, animals are divided into:

a) belonging to the Emperor, b) embálmed, c) tame, d) sucking pigs, e) sirens, f) fabulous, g) stray dogs, h) included in the present classification, i) frenzied, h) innumerable, k) drawn with a very fine camelhair brush, l) *et cetera*, m) having just broken the water pitcher, n) that from a long way off like flies.

Foucault recalls that when he first read this classification laughter shattered all the familiar landmarks of his thought, breaking up 'all the ordered surfaces and all the planes with which we are accustomed to tame the wild profusion of existing things' (Foucault, 1970: XV). Similar laughter may be caused by a Census classifying people accord-ing to their star sign, or putting more emphasis on whether they are left- or right-handed than on their education.

In classification, the divide between the familiar and unfamiliar is simply a result of the interpretation of social reality. The nature of classification is local and contingent, and its consistency is based on the possibility of being stabilized. For an interpretation to make sense of reality, events have to be translated, models for understanding developed, meaning drawn out and conceptual schemes assembled. Ambiguity must be dealt with by coercing useful answers (Daft and Weick, 1984: 286–7). Cognitive dissonances should be kept latent, whether they arise internally in the process of interpretation or externally question the consistency of such a process. People may still be sorted by sex although the idea that gender rather than sex matters is becoming increasingly accepted. Multiple personalities may still be conflated in one body and counted as a single unit, despite the psychiatric evidence that each fully developed social person cohabiting in a single biological organism has its own patterns of participation in social interactions, its own gender, and may even display typical body hexis and a particular style of speaking and moving (Lemke, 1994: 91). Inconsistencies should be ruled out systematically, but this can only make sense within the process of interpretation and negotiation occurring in the creation of knowledge (Knorr-Cetina, 1993: 258–9). An example from migration studies may help to better understand this point. In a paper presented recently to a plenary session of the Italian Statistical Society, on Foreigners in Italian Society, one author commented on the impacts of the 1992 citizenship law:

> in the future it will become impossible to determine the size of the foreign immigrant population and their descendants in the country by referring to their nationality, for such a category does not enable us to distinguish and to monitor the ever increasing numbers of people who *have become* or who *are held to be* Italians.
>
> (Strozza 1995: 3, emphasis added)

This statement enacts a paradox. It is suggested that people who *have become* or who *are held to be* Italians under the law on citizenship should not be counted as Italians. Yet the only way to make a decision as to whom has to be counted as Italian is to examine whether or not someone *has become* or *is held to be* Italian under the citizenship law. Such a paradox cannot be unfolded by appealing to any set of clear rules. On the contrary, it can only be ruled out through interpretation and negotiation.

One solution is to redefine and categorize the foreign population to produce new tabulations of statistical data. This is the case in Norway, for instance, where children who are Norwegian citizens are counted as foreigners if their parents were foreign-born. A second solution is to collect information on 'ethnicity', as in Britain for example, where the 1991 Census included an 'ethnic question' whose articulation combines concepts of ethnicity, nationality and citizenship in a way which can be understood only by considering the particular demographic situation of the British population (M.R.D. Johnson, 1993). A third solution is to restore the time-honoured classification by 'colour' as in the first Census in the United States in 1791, thus transforming a statistical concern into a highly sophisticated if questionable chromatic exercise.

In establishing classification standards and setting coding procedures, practices of ontological gerrymandering are constantly deployed. This allows the preservation of boundaries between conceptual and theoretical assumptions which are meant to be ostensibly problematic and others whose status as 'truth' is not to be questioned. A differential susceptibility of phenomena to ontological uncertainty is thereby produced and reproduced over time so that it remains possible to portray some areas as ripe for ontological doubt and others as immune to it (Woolgar and Pawluch, 1985: 216).

In conventional research on crime, delinquency and law, for instance, a basic assumption is made which conceives of compliance and deviance as having an autonomous ontological significance and of the 'measuring rod' as consisting of some set of rules whose meaning is also ontologically and epistemologically clear (Cicourel, 1967: 331). In medical statistics, a standard list of causes of death was defined during the eighteenth century and is still currently used. Although the list is constantly revised, in several countries it has long been 'illegal to die of anything except causes on the official list. ... It is for instance illegal to die of age' (Hacking, 1991: 182–3).

Research on the labour market has had to work out a definition of unemployment which could be conceived of only under particular circumstances. The category of the unemployed was introduced as recently as the nineteenth century to complement the more traditional notion of the poor by relating it to the idea of a salary tying and subordinating the worker to the employer (Desrosières, 1993: 311–17). Similarly, in migration studies the idea of individual migrants moving in time and space and concepts of citizenship, country of origin and nationality are usually taken as unproblematic. Under the construct of 'undocumented migrant' moreover, different definitions merge without necessarily bearing any similarity with one another.

'Unrecorded migrant' is often taken to be synonymous with 'illegal migrant', when in fact the two are not equivalent. Recorded migrants may somehow be in an illegal situation just as unrecorded migrants may be present legally in a country. In addition, there is often an overlap between categories of migrants who are temporary, in irregular employment and those who are unrecorded, therefore giving rise to double-estimates which are very difficult to detect.

Ontological gerrymandering pertains not only to the basic procedures of gathering and sorting statistical data but also exerts a far-reaching impact on the language in which social problems are framed. Statistics impose by giving rise to administrative rulings but also by determining classifications within which individuals have to conceive of themselves and of the lines of conduct which are open to them (Hacking, 1991: 194). At the level at which social problems are discussed, the entire set of decisions which structure the representation of reality is invisible and everything is widely misperceived as transparent (Fairclough, 1992: 211). In turn, the thematization of social problems by policy makers, social scientists and public opinion has an impact on the way new data are gathered and sorted, giving rise to a dissemination of knowledge in which different sets of statements with different statuses emerge, merge and re-emerge in and through a plurality of discourses. As a result, a discursively circular form of discourse within discourse emerges so that the origins of given interpretative decisions can barely be traced (Walker, 1988: 55).

Official statistics play a crucial role in this process, although their position remains ambivalent. Statistics lie at the crossroads of different agendas and the status of their knowledge is constantly torn between a descriptive and a prescriptive standpoint. Since its inception, the administrative production of statistical knowledge has displayed the characteristic of combining standards of scientific adequacy with the administrative concerns of the state. The social sciences too are caught in this ambivalence. Since they either rely heavily on official statistics or produce alternative data-sets which have to comply with pre-set standards of adequacy in order to become useful, an important empirical question is how contradictions and inconsistencies are avoided or reduced in social sciences and administrative practices.

Statistical monitoring systems are structures involving both administrative agencies and research institutions, and thus represent the field where intellectual technologies, such as the use of tables, graphs, reports and forms, are at work to elicit, record, memorize and transfer information. They therefore constitute an indispensable mechanism whereby specific aspects of governed reality are shaped as knowable entities amenable to governing (Dean, 1994: 187–8). Such systems reflect a particular form of government which developed only within the modern nation-state, with population rather than estates or property comprising the object of state rule. This form of government, which Michel Foucault terms 'governmentality', is composed of an ensemble of institutions, procedures, analyses, calculations, reflections and tactics, and is paralleled by the invention, operationalization and institutionalization of specific knowledges, disciplines and technologies, which themselves form the conditions for an extension of the governing capacity (Foucault, 1991: 102–3; T. Johnson, 1993: 140–1). Historically, its areas of concern have been poverty, illness, unemployment, emigration and later immigration. In order to be observed however, these phenomena first had to be defined by setting their boundaries.

This suggests that statistics should not be taken at face value and ultimately questions the degree of their adequacy in the light of an ontological understanding of social reality. Rather, they should be seen as cultural artefacts taking shape within localized and contingent orders of representation that make it possible for different configurations of sources, definitions and concepts to emerge. Such a secondary qualitative approach, following Gephart, can be defined as 'ethnostatistics' and is concerned with the actual behaviour, and the informal sub-culture or local knowledge and activities, of producers and users of statistics. The formal and technical knowledge codified in statistics is in fact integrated and extended by a body of informal knowledge. An understanding of this knowledge can help explain why objects and phenomena are described statistically in particular ways (Bloor, Goldberg and Emslie, 1991; Gephart, 1988: 10).

AN ETHNOSTATISTICAL APPROACH

Statistics, like all artefacts, are a human product. They may be the product of an individual, for example, someone who tries to keep track of the monthly budget on an annual basis, or of a group, such as sports journalists who release figures about the football league. In modern society, statistics quite often are the product of large systems involving different agencies. The configuration of these systems may vary according to the kind of data produced and may change over time. Some agencies may gather data only as a by-product of their main activity, for example administrative agencies or corporations, while for others, such as the National Statistical Bureau and some research centres, the production of statistics is their main institutional task. Different agencies often have different ideas as to what has to be counted and how (Hacking, 1990: 34). Since they communicate with one another to some degree however, these agencies constitute a system.

A basic distinction may be made in the study of systems producing statistical data between system integration and system articulation. 'Integration' refers to the systematic continuity in collecting data as well as to the capacity for interconnection between different databases and the linkages between agencies. Analysis of integration focuses on gathering procedures, the organizational dynamics of single agencies, and the interorganizational dynamics shaping the overall configuration of the monitoring system. To assess the performance of a system, the problems of a lack of synchronicity in the gathering of data by different agencies and heterogeneity in the structure and quality of data have to be considered. In Western liberal democracies integration is usually achieved by a formal exchange of information among different agencies and by the provision of different databases with adequate linkages under the assumption that no information should be inadvertently disclosed about identifiable individuals and households. This also requires that guidelines be issued in order to set the timing of monitoring activities and to define compatible and standardized procedures at both the national and local level. But integration can also be achieved in the absence of such a framework when some agencies are in the position to gain access to information collected by other units in the system, while others are not. Privileged positions have a far-reaching impact on the way in which issues are socially constructed and conversely represent an outcome of this very construction.

'Articulation' refers both to the total extent of monitored variables and to the degree of internal differentiation of each variable. It can be considered either at the level of a single agency or at the level of the system as a whole. An analysis of articulation aims to map the variables monitored and to assess the degree of precision and accuracy of the implemented devices. In order to avoid any ontological assumptions, and to comply with the key requirements of impartiality and symmetry, precision and accuracy must be measured by a cognitive frame which accords with the set variables rather than with the epistemic standards of the external observer. A medical questionnaire from the early 1980s, for instance, may contain the question: 'Do you suffer from any of the following?' and allow the following answers: a) arthritis, b) asthma, c) athlete's foot, d) back pain, e) congestion, f) dandruff, g) diabetes, h) hayfever, i) hearing difficulty, j) heartburn, k) migraines, l) snoring'.[1] Assessing the level of articulation would mean comparing the range of items included with those which were actually conceivable in the particular historical configuration of early 1980s medicine. It would be mistaken to conclude that articulation is low because items are missing which were only conceivable within later developments of medicine. In this example, however, articulation is relatively low, since within the cognitive frame of early 1980s medicine a much wider range of variables could easily have been listed and for some of those actually included in the answer it may be appropriate to question whether or not they were consistent with this given frame in that particular historical configuration.

A low degree of articulation within a single data-set can be compensated at a system level provided that a sufficient degree of integration is attained. Articulation is therefore a measure of the number of dimensions in which statistical representation is enacted under localized conditions. In that they produce a connection between representation and a transcendental reality which is supposed to reside outside representing agents, these dimensions exert a crucial impact on the way a social problem is framed (Woolgar, 1989: 202).

In order to conduct an ethnostatistical analysis of a national system producing statistical data, all the agencies involved in monitoring activities must be sorted. It is essential to distinguish between the territorial and functional segmentation of agencies and administrative agencies must be distinguished carefully from non-administrative statistical sources, whether or not they belong to the state. In this way the configuration of the system can be mapped, and its structure can be defined by distinguishing between agencies which collect raw data and those which tabulate and publish them. Potential networks of formal communication between different units and agencies can also help to find out whether and how information flows within the system. Information consists of raw or tabulated data for end-use, but it can also involve guidelines and suggestions as to how to gather and process new data. Further ethnographic fieldwork may allow the detection of networks of informal communication among agencies which may help the system cope with low levels of integration.

A further step is to collect the set of monitoring devices used in day-to-day activities (for example forms, questionnaires, individual records). The variables included and the way in which they are shaped should also be considered over time. A monitoring device currently in use is often the result of several amendments that can sometimes appear even at a first glance. New alphabetically ordered items may, for instance, have been added to former ones without reordering the set. Discrepancies in terminology may appear. Methods of collection – which may be direct or indirect, centralized or computerized – should also be analysed. At this stage, the structure of computer software has to be considered, along with the procedures by which data are transferred from paper form, since discrepancies in information often occur when transferring data to computer-aided storage and processing. Sometimes this causes a loss of information which can remain unnoticed even by those performing the task. The computerized record may contain more information than the paper form if supplementary data are collected by other means. Eventually one has to analyse the published statistics and the accompanying rhetoric.

As well as a qualitative methodology such as that described above, originally developed within social studies of science, interviews with experts can be useful. Interviews should target those people who are in charge of deciding methodological options and defining data-collecting procedures. This type of interview is particularly difficult to handle for the interviewer, however, since they have a common background knowledge and shared understandings with the respondents (Platt, 1981), when the main aim of such interviews is to explore to what degree the respondent can convey information with which s/he is familiar but which may seem (intentionally) unfamiliar to the interviewer.

THE STATE MONITORING SYSTEM IN ITALY

The concepts discussed above were tested in an empirical research project that I conducted in Italy. From late 1994 and throughout 1995 I conducted an ethnostatistical study of the structure and functioning of the Italian statistical system disseminating data on migration. My analysis of this system's integration and articulation provides useful insights into the way in which the discourse on migration is framed in Italy and how it has changed since its emergence in the late 1980s.

In Italy, 11 agencies currently are responsible for producing 14 major types of data on immigration. The most relevant of these are administrative bodies (the Ministry of the Interior, the Ministry of Labour, the Ministry of Justice), the National Statistical Bureau and an NGO. The configuration of this particular system is thus one in which agencies of different institutional status interact, although integration is far from being attained consistently. Indeed, integration has itself only recently become an issue on the agenda. In the absence of an overall monitoring policy, interorganizational communication occurs mainly through informal networks in which civil servants, social scientists, and social workers interact. This occurs both among different units within a single agency and between different agencies, regardless of whether or not they are functionally or territorially segmented. To date, few stable linkages among different databases have been established. Agencies in charge of implementing public security policies none the less have privileged access to data collected by other units, thus giving rise to asymmetric patterns in information flows.

Proposals to counterbalance this trend by providing leave to remain permits with an alphanumeric code to be reported in any case involving a foreign individual have been rejected. For foreign citizens, unlike Italian citizens, the linking of information through the national social security and fiscal code is still rarely implemented. This leads to an increasing lack of synchronicity between different statistics. Data referring to diverse but partly overlapping dimensions are not made available within the same timespan. Some agencies process and release data with more than a year's delay, even when no apparent technical difficulty seems to justify this. Rather than being systematic and periodical, checking procedures mostly respond to the internal organizational dynamics of administrative and state agencies. Any chance of analysing structural features and developmental trends in migration fully therefore is seriously affected. Official data moreover need to be approved by senior officers before publication, although this does not prevent unofficial data from circulating or from being passed to the media.

While most administrative and state agencies release statistics, the National Statistical Bureau is still far from acting as the agency in charge of publishing all available data in a single report (ISTAT, 1993). Within the Statistical Bureau the transfer of relevant information on international migration often occurs through informal communication. No *ad hoc* unit has been established and collaboration between different experts occurs only on an occasional basis. Any attempt to assess the global number of immigrants, for example, has taken place only as a by-product of calculations to assess the GNP of a given year which require a calculation of the hidden segment of the labour market in which undocumented immigrants are employed. Statistics on migration often are produced exclusively as part of the overall monitoring activities of the population in the country and by using uncustomized monitoring devices. As a consequence, articulation is seriously affected. This helps explain why, though the 1991 Census form for foreigners contained instructions in six languages other than Italian, the relevance of data on the language in which the form was completed was perceived only after beginning the data-entry. This meant that no field for language was inserted in the database, therefore causing a loss of information in the transfer of data from the paper form.

Since the early 1990s an annual report on immigration in Italy has been released by an NGO which supplies policy makers, social scientists and the media with statistics mostly produced by administrative and state agencies. In turn policy makers, social scientists and the media rely heavily upon this report to shape the discourse on migration. As a result, an unofficial report becomes a highly influential and almost official publication. But in order to maintain relatively unrestricted access to the latest available first-hand data and to preserve good informal relations with institutions, the report does not engage in any in-depth secondary qualitative analysis of the database construction in administrative and state agencies.

The current configuration and structure of the monitoring system is the result of the different timescales on which international migration became an issue on the agenda of the different agencies involved. The divide between visibility and invisibility clearly emerges as a result of the frame within which each agency conducts its own observation. The Ministry of the Interior has been releasing official statistics on refugees since 1954 and on legal immigration since 1968. In the late 1960s the Ministry of Justice began to collect data on criminality among foreign people. These statistics refer to the total number of crimes, custodies and convictions, and therefore no information can be derived as to recidivism.

The structure of these data has far-reaching consequences for the increasingly shared belief that deviant migrants are the main source of social problems and malaise (Palidda, 1994). The National Statistical Bureau (Istat), which since 1986 has been publishing data on foreign people residing in the country, introduced citizenship into its records of births, deaths and marriages two years earlier, in 1984. But it was only in the early 1990s that efforts were made to establish a national monitoring system in the wake of the new Italian migration policy arising from law 39/1990 (Natale, 1990). An expert at the Statistical Bureau described the situation thus:

> Before 1990 we were well aware that there were lots of people around. We saw them on buses and trains or walking in the street. Sometimes visiting friends at their place we came across a foreigner serving there. But then when we went back to work we were unable to find any trace of all these people. It was a rather uncomfortable situation indeed.

An influential senior officer at the Ministry of the Interior commented:

> During the early 1980s police-headquarters had been continuously reporting to us about the burgeoning growth of immigrants in the country. We informed policy makers and asked them for responses in terms of policy. But we were left devoid of any real device to monitor what was happening around us. In a sense we have been for long relying upon informal communication. All records on immigrants were hand-written or typewritten. Only later we stored them in our computer system.

Yet no data were available on the labour market before 1990 or on social security before 1991 (published in 1994), though the Ministry of Labour conducted an *ad hoc* survey on regularizations in 1986. In the same year the Statistical Bureau introduced a question on citizenship on most of the forms used in the national health system. No statistics were produced for health policy purposes, however. Thus far the item on citizenship remains the only one monitored by the NHS, despite the fact that NGOs providing medical assistance to those not entitled to the public service have warned that issues such as ethnicity and religion are relevant to improving the quality of healing. Systematic data on schooling on a national basis are still missing, whereas some local administrations carry out local area studies using different classification standards.

The increased sensitivity towards immigration prompted an improvement in the monitoring capacity of different agencies. In 1992 the law establishing the National Statistical System promoted higher levels of integration and articulation. Yet the current situation can still be described in terms of crisis (Campani, 1993). As one policy expert stated:

We were always thinking that immigration would be a temporary process. Public and private needs arising from rapid migration were not foreseen, even though the forecast predicted a rapid increase in migration. This is because, still, in this country, *a foreign person is seen either as a worker and/or as a threat to public order.* The perception remains that after we address these two problems of foreigner as worker and foreigner as threat, that will be sufficient. We build policies to address an extraordinary situation. However, we need to change our starting point, to see migration not as an extraordinary occurrence, but rather as an ordinary fact of life in Italy. (emphasis added)

The monitoring system is thus shaped by and functions according to an understanding that emphasizes the need to frame different dimensions of migration in mechanisms of security. Often this is evident in the very name and position within administrative agencies of units in charge of dealing with foreign individuals, counting them, and releasing statistics. At the Ministry of the Interior, for example, the Foreign Citizens' Office is a branch of the Public Security Department; at the City Council in Milan, the Foreign Citizens' Office was a branch of the Department of Hygiene, Health and Marginality until early 1996.

Such an orientation towards security strengthens the crucial role played by statistics on permits of stay. Claims by politicians and public opinion as to a likely invasion are supported by appealing to such figures. These are usually released twice a year by the Ministry of the Interior in the form of aggregated tables, but in fact only parts of the information gathered is tabulated. Permits of stay are issued by police headquarters. Before approval, applications are stored in computers at a local level. Since late 1991, as part of a top-down standardization of procedures, an electronic network connecting local police headquarters to the national database has been introduced, though there have been local differences in the timing of implementation. This system does not however allow any connection between different police headquarters. To issue or extend a permit of stay, data have to be transferred to the national database where checking procedures are implemented automatically. If an application is accepted, data are stored.

Analysts usually emphasize that the data do not include young people who, not holding an individual permit of stay, are listed on their parents' or relatives' document. They also note that duplications as well as a small number of expired permits may be included in the released data. These features can be understood fully once one recognizes that the structure of the Ministry of the Interior's database has been shaped to meet security requirements aimed at keeping track of the actual position of each foreign person before the law. In interviews, senior officers and technicians at the Ministry of the Interior have been particularly careful not to disclose any significant detail about the structure of their database.

Statistics refer to the total number of permits of stay with active records in the database. This implies not only that a certain number of permits referring to the same person may be included in the database at a given date, but also that expired but not yet write-protected records may be counted. The decision to write-protect a record is made by local police headquarters according to different rationales, though it has to be implemented at the national database level. Indeed after the expiry of a permit of stay police officers may decide not to write-protect a record in order either to allow its holder to apply safely for an extension or to keep track of information pertaining to the holder leaving the country. The time before write-protection is set only at the local level. Different police-headquarters have different timing for implementing this option, and sometimes write-protection has been implemented within a two-year timeframe.

All available information about an individual is immediately to hand in the national database, including the number of permit renewals, different ways of spelling their name and, in some cases, any aliases used. Criminal information is also supplied. If the database is asked about the total number of stored records it will simply provide the number of records referring to permits of stay which are either still valid or expired but not write-protected. These data by no means automatically refer to the actual number of people legally entitled to stay in the country, let alone to the number of foreign individuals currently in the country.

In the cognitive frame of the Ministry of the Interior the national database is first and foremost conceived of as a device for supplying information on individuals. As a result, according to an influential civil servant at the Ministry:

The overall reliability of our database is unquestioned. In our records one can read the story of an individual in the country. The only problems we have are when a foreign person leaves the country or dies. For the time being our main concern will be to increase the level of security.

Double computation is therefore not a major issue on the agenda. Recently, the National Statistical Bureau has in fact released statistics on the number of permits of stay which are free from counts of duplicate and expired permits (ISTAT, 1995). But, despite providing the Bureau with individual records in computerized form, when questioned about this the Ministry replied that they were not aware of this practice.

Statistics on the labour market issued every three months by the Ministry of Labour are Italy's second most important data source on immigration. In interviews, senior officers said that new types of labour migrants are emerging which are manifested in flows of tourist workers, suitcase traders and many forms of temporary employment, including illegal employment. Yet statistical tools have not been upgraded to cope with the new situation. Official data exclusively refer to unemployed and recently employed workers. The former are arranged so as to count the stock of unemployed workers applying for a job at employment bureaux. The latter refer to the number of placements per term and therefore count positions. The way in which data are aggregated does not allow any cross-tabulation, and no evidence on historical trends can be supplied, since data on the employment history of individuals are not monitored.

Data are collected locally and aggregated to be sent later to the Ministry, mostly on paper sheets following a standardized form. At the Ministry no *ad hoc* unit has been established. At the office in charge of monitoring overall trends in the Italian labour market, two people collect the forms and enter data in a standard spreadsheet. Checking procedures are limited to assessing at face value the consistency of new data with previous series, and no transfer of raw data occurs. To date, no national database has been established, though several local offices store data in computer systems. The software is provided by the Ministry but on a local level the programme has been customized to fit local needs. Computer records contain an extensive range of information on individual workers. Hand-written or typewritten records containing less information are also compiled. Data are collected drawing on this archive. Sometimes there are misunderstandings between the Ministry and local units as to how to fill in tables correctly, and quite often these misunderstandings are barely perceived by the actors involved.

The Ministry of Labour and the Ministry of the Interior use different lists of 'nationality' categories. In its current version, the standardized form issued by the Ministry of Labour allows data entry of as many as 26 different nationalities, others being grouped under the heading 'Other countries'. The form itself is the result of three different amendments through which new nationalities have been added on the basis of feedback from local units. A first list is alphabetically ordered, two later sets of items have been added without being sorted. Comparing this ranking with that supplied by the Ministry of the Interior, one can see that nationalities which in the latter are within the top 30 (such as those referring to Romania, CIS, Peru, Colombia, and Dominican Republic) are not monitored by the former. On the contrary, quantitatively less important nationalities in terms of permits of stay (such as those referring to Algeria, Turkey, Japan, Chile, Lebanon, Mauritius and Nigeria) show in the list. In the published tables, these statistics list only 23 nationalities. Such a list is extremely poor when compared with guidelines issued by the National Statistical Bureau and used by other Ministries, which to date list as many as 134 countries.

The articulation of the statistics on labour can be understood fully by considering the frame in which issues of migration are shaped within the Ministry of Labour. In an interview a senior officer depicted it by saying:

> If you are a good worker in the workplace you will not have problems .... A policy which is particularly geared towards foreigners, in my opinion, should not be geared towards special laws. *The less you distinguish, the less you discriminate.* (emphasis added)

This idea was confirmed when the same officer commented on the educational policies promoted by the Ministry of Education on the basis of a detailed monitoring of foreign pupils in schools: 'In terms of multicultural education, I think there is far *too much emphasis on difference*' (emphasis added). As a guiding principle, de-emphasizing difference results in a reduced articulation in the monitoring of the labour market because the only distinction which is deemed to be worth considering is that between 'good' and 'bad' workers.

CONCLUSIONS

Ethno-statistical research helps us to understand how statistics are constructed within single agencies, so that some things are made visible, others invisible. Once applied to the overall structure and functioning of a monitoring system, this approach offers valuable insights into the interplay of a plurality of agencies and different frames in shaping the discourse on migration within a given national context. In Italy, it is only in recent years that migration has been constructed discursively, 'not as an extraordinary occurrence, but rather as an ordinary fact of life' (quote from interview with policy maker, extracted above). Statistical devices have been worked out gradually to observe the characteristics, needs and expectations of migrants. At this level, non-governmental actors play a crucial role in increasing the articulation of the monitoring system. Information of use to those concerned with service delivery issues, particularly in the area of welfare, is nevertheless only occasionally monitored, and its meaning is often misperceived. Whereas refugees are asked about religion and ethnicity, for instance, the latter is still often confused with nationality, as exemplified in the following statement by a senior officer involved in the promotion of multicultural educational policies:

> *I very much appreciated you asking me the question of terminology . . . it is important that we understand one another.* From a cultural point of view, there is a modern interpretation towards migrants which involves the mutual enrichment of cultures. An educational agency should have this as its goal . . . .Our laws and circular letters accept integration and interaction; foreign pupils and students, even illegal ones, must be encouraged to learn their original language and culture, and we also promote common activities. We face many practical problems however. *We have 134 dispersed ethnic communities.* (emphasis added)

No doubt, the issue of how to include within monitoring devices items relevant for social workers has come under much discussion. This discussion, however, occurs through informal networks of communication rather than by reaching actual agreements between state agencies and NGOs. Thus the attainment of an effective integration remains a major concern.

In this respect, an ethno-statistical approach focusing on a single national case may be of some help in exposing inconsistencies, highlighting suboptimal procedures, and suggesting alternative solutions. From a comparative perspective, the study of the actual configuration of national monitoring systems in the European Union and the differences in their practices and functioning (Salt and Singleton, 1994; Singleton, 1995) may help explain the different degrees of visibility of migration issues as well as the different forms taken by their thematization in national discourses. This is an essential preliminary task in assessing the degree of convergence among migration policies and their representation in the EU member-states.

NOTE

1. This example is borrowed from an undated questionnaire of the British Centre for Consumer Interest.

REFERENCES

Bloor, D., *Knowledge and Social Imagery* (Chicago: The University of Chicago Press, 2nd edition, 1991).
Bloor, M., D. Goldberg and J. Emslie, 'Ethnostatistics and the AIDS Epidemic', *British Journal of Sociology*, 42(1) (1991) 131–8.
Campani, G., 'Immigration and Racism in Southern Europe: The Italian Case', *Ethnic and Racial Studies*, 16(3) (1993) 507–35.
Cicourel, A., *The Social Organization of Juvenile Justice* (London: Heinemann, 1967).
Daft, R.L. and K.E. Weick, 'Toward a Model of Organizations as Interpretation Systems', *Academy of Management Review*, 9(2) (1984) 284–95.
Dean, M., *Critical and Effective Histories. Foucault's Methods and Historical Sociology* (London: Routledge, 1994).
Desrosières, A., *La Politique des grands nombres. Histoire de la raison statistique* (Paris: Éditions la Decouverte, 1993).
Fairclough, N., 'Discourse and Text: Linguistic and Intertextual Analysis within Discourse Analysis', *Discourse & Society*, 3(2) (1992) 193–217.
Foucault, M., *The Order of Things* (New York: Vintage Books, 1970).
Foucault, M., *Metafisica del potere* (Torino: Einaudi, 1977).
Foucault, M., 'Governmentality', in G. Burchell, C. Gordon and P. Miller (eds), *The Foucault Effect: Studies in Governmental Rationality* (Hemel Hempstead: Harvester Wheatsheaf, 1991) 87–104.
Gephart, G.P., *Ethnostatistics* (London: Sage, 1988).
Hacking, I., *The Taming of Chance* (Cambridge: Cambridge University Press, 1990).
Hacking, I., 'How should we do the History of Statistics?', in G. Burchell, C. Gordon and P. Miller (eds), *The Foucault Effect: Studies in Governmental Rationality* (Hemel Hempstead: Harvester Wheatsheaf, 1991) 181–95.
Hammersley, M., and P. Atkinson, *Ethnography: Principles in Practice* (London: Routledge, 1995).

ISTAT, 'La presenza straniera in Italia', *Notiziario Istat* 14(11) (1993).
ISTAT, *Rapporto annuale* (Rome: ISTAT, 1995).
Johnson, M. R. D., 'A Question of Ethnic origin in the 1991 Census', *New Community*, 19(2) (1993) 281–9.
Johnson, T., 'Expertise and the State', in M. Gane and T. Johnson (eds), *Foucault's New Domains* (London: Routledge, 1993) 139–52.
Knorr-Cetina, K., 'Liminal and Referent Epistemologies in Contemporary Science: An Ethnography of the Empirical in Two Studies', *Teoria sociologica*, 2 (1993) 258–82.
Lemke, J. L., *Textual Politics: Discourse and Social Dynamics* (London: Taylor & Francis, 1995).
Natale, M., 'L'immigrazione straniera in Italia: consistenza, caratteristiche, prospettive', *Polis*, 5(1) (1990) 5–40.
Palidda, S., *Devianza e criminalità tra gli immigrati*, (Milan: ISMU Working Paper, 1994).
Platt, J., 'On Interviewing One's Peers', *British Journal of Sociology*, 32(1) (1981) 75–91.
Salt, J., and A. Singleton, 'Report on the Extension of the Historical Series of Statistics on International Migration Held in the MIGRAT Database', report to the Migration Statistics Working Party Eurostat, Luxembourg, November 1994.
Singleton, A., 'International Migration in Europe. Data Sources and Data Availability. Recent Developments, Problems and Possibilities', Paper presented at the EAPS/IUSSP European Population Conference, Milan, 4–8 September 1995.
Strozza, S., 'Possibilità di quantificazione della presenza straniera in Italia: il punto della situazione', paper presented at the Italian Statistical Society, 1995.
Walker, T., 'Whose Discourse?', in S. Woolgar (ed.), *Knowledge and Reflexivity: New Frontiers in the Sociology of Knowledge* (London: Sage, 1988) 55–79.
Woolgar, S., 'Representation, Cognition and Self: What Hope for an Integration of Psychology and Sociology?', in S. Fuller (ed.), *The Cognitive Turn* (Dordrecht: Kluwer, 1989) 201–24.
Woolgar, S., and D. Pawluch, 'Ontological Gerrymandering: The Anatomy of Social Problems Explanations', *Social Problems*, 32 (1985) 214–27.

9 Redefining the Refugee: The UK Media Portrayal of Asylum Seekers
Ron Kaye

INTRODUCTION

In the UK, as in other parts of Europe, there is a growing trend of greater restrictionism towards refugees and asylum seekers through both legal statute and the political process. It has been argued elsewhere (Kaye, 1994) that these changes have been able to take place partly because the public perception of refugees has been altered and devalued. This has occurred through a narrowing by public policy makers of the definitions of refugee status, and a blurring of the distinctions between refugees and immigrants, on the one hand, and ethnic minorities on the other. Earlier work has focused on the role of political parties in this process. There has, however, been little serious analysis of the role of the media in the public perception of refugees (Brosius and Eps, 1995; Coleman, 1995; Tomasi, 1993). This chapter presents an analysis of the media portrayal of refugees and its relationship to the policy process, focusing on broadsheet newspapers. The present study builds on an earlier pilot study of the same topic. (Kaye, 1995)

The structure of the chapter is as follows. First, the influence of the media is examined from a general perspective, with a more detailed consideration of two particular concepts used in the study, namely agenda-setting and news-framing. Secondly, the language which is the particular focus of analysis in this chapter is briefly discussed. Thirdly, there follows a description of the methodology and a presentation of empirical data on UK broadsheet newspaper coverage of refugees, alongside an analysis of the emergent patterns and their significance. Finally, the results and their implications for the representation of refugees and asylum seekers in other forms of media and in the European context are critically discussed.

THE INFLUENCE OF THE MEDIA

In the field of media analysis and in its relationship with the polity the mass media is seen as an influential means through which communications are mediated between the political élite and the electorate in advanced liberal democratic nations. The role of the mass media as a disseminator of information makes it a key political actor with a vital role in the framework of national and international affairs. Yet the function of the media has been interpreted in at least two different ways. First, it has been attributed a watchdog function, acting as a check on the political élite. Alternatively, it has been cast in a more invidious role, as the means through which governmental regimes, the power of élite groups and dominant ideologies are perpetuated. There is thus a dichotomy between media-centred interpretations and society-centred views. The former position tends to stress the independent role of the media as an influence as against the more dependent role assumed by the latter. It is clear, however, that some elements of both roles are discernible. While there is evidence of a centrality of newspaper control, the press also have the potential to exercise independent power. Despite the increasing domination of the press by a number of groupings moreover, there is still a sufficiently wide base to argue that there is a diversity of reporting on most major issues of a contestable nature.

Views among media analysts on the role of the media in influencing public opinion have gone through four broad stages of development (Ansolabehere *et al.*, 1993; McQuail, 1993; Norris, 1995). Initially, the media was thought to be highly influential, and early analysts, impressed by the rapid growth of mass communications in the pre-World War II period, stressed that the public could easily be swayed by media techniques. In the context of such beliefs, systematic research using survey and experimental methods began in the 1920s and 1930s. This transition to empirical enquiry led to a second phase of thinking about media effect. Postwar studies, analysing the first systematic survey evidence, reacted to the initial overplaying of the role of the media by stressing theories of minimal consequence which considerably de-emphasized the significance of the media's influence. This stage persisted until the early 1960s, when its end was marked by disillusionment with the outcome of this type of media research.

The third phase of theory and research involved those who were reluctant to dismiss the possibility that the media might indeed have important social effects and be an instrument through which social and political power is exercised. It also marked a shift towards a focus on long-term changes and towards the analysis of collective phenomena such as climates of opinion, structure of belief and ideologies. In addition this research benefited from a growing interest in how media organizations processed and shaped information before it was delivered to audiences. The fourth and most recent approach dates back to the late 1970s. This emerging model has a number of propositions. First, it is argued that extant studies demonstrate the limited but specific effects of the media in setting the policy agenda. Secondly, it is proposed that the media constructs social formations and indeed history itself by framing images of reality in a predictable and patterned way, and in addition that people in an audience construct for themselves their own view of social reality and their own place in it. These propositions have been labelled 'agenda-setting' and 'news-framing' respectively. Together, they provide the theoretical basis of the present chapter and are thus discussed here in more detail.

Agenda-setting is the process of determining which issues are seen as priorities for policy development and political action. There are differing views on how the power of the media in setting the political agenda is exercised. One view is that issues go through a number of stages: first they are publicized by the mass media, then they arouse public opinion and only then are they addressed by policy makers (Mayer, 1991). A second view argues that the process is usually reversed, with issues originating from policy makers.

Most media analysts have adopted the first position; in other words, the role of the media in this process is primary. One example frequently presented in support of this view is that of Enoch Powell and immigration in the 1970s (Seymour-Ure, 1974). In this case a speech given to a small audience by a well-known politician with strong views on the subject (but who was at that point certainly not a policy maker) was picked up and widely publicized by the media. Thereafter it was firmly on the political agenda even though it went against the preferences of the majority of policy makers. A contrasting view, and one supported by most political scientists, is that this is a rare example and that the process is more commonly reversed, with issues originating from policy makers, the government and political parties, and then being reflected in the media. From this perspective, the relationship between media coverage, public opinion and government action is seen as far more complex.

The news-framing model argues that news is not simply the media's report of an objective reality. This model adopts the perspective that the news is a frame through which reality is socially constructed (Tuchman, 1978). News content research has shown that much news is presented within frameworks of meaning which derive from the way news is gathered and processed. News is framed thematically for easier understanding and it is reasonable to suppose that audiences employ some of the same frames in their processing of incoming news. Such frames thus influence the newspaper reader as they not only convey what is important (in other words, what makes the news) but also transmit positive or negative cues which help shape the public characterization of events.

Although agenda-setting and news-framing are conceptualized as separate processes, they can also be seen to be strongly linked. In relation to refugee agenda-setting, for example, the agenda is not a unitary phenomenon but one which consists of many linked subsets of agendas. The phase of agenda-setting which involves defining the agenda is conceptually very close to the process of news-framing, in which the role of the media in agenda- setting is considered. In this way the frame through which the news is portrayed is in itself part of the agenda. In a previous study it was noted that the way in which political parties portrayed refugees was a significant and influential aspect of refugee agenda-setting, with at some stages the Conservative Party defining the refugee agenda in terms of immigration and Labour depicting it in terms of racism/anti-racism (Kaye, 1994). There is sufficient difference between these concepts, however, to consider them as separate processes, at least for the purposes of preliminary analysis.

In the study upon which this chapter is based, two broad approaches to investigating the role of the media in agenda-setting and news-framing in relation to the specific issue of their portrayal of refugees and asylum seekers were considered. The first was the content analysis approach. As McQuail (1993) argues, however, this approach involves deciding in advance of the analysis the categories to be utilized. This entails a risk of meaning being imposed on the material rather than emerging from it, and there is a danger of distortion through pre-selection of categories. The second approach was that of a form of discourse analysis, namely structuralism, with its close analysis of text to reveal implicit meaning. The main problem with this approach is its opposition to any form of quantitative analysis. The analysis of implicit rather than explicit content can moreover be highly subjective and dependent on the researcher's own conceptual frameworks. In addition, there are clear limitations on the degree to which generalizations can be drawn from findings derived from this type of research.

The approach adopted in this study takes elements from both approaches, and combines both qualitative and quantitative methods. In analysing the use of language, rather than simply overt opinion, it reflects the structuralist approach. Yet it achieves this through a quantitative analysis of the use of specific terms which have explicit, and in fact pejorative meanings. It also attempts to relate the analysis of media coverage to concurrent external events linked to the refugee agenda. Specifically, it considers broadsheet newspaper coverage in terms of the manipulation of language in commenting upon the status of refugees and asylum seekers. This is considered in more detail in the following section.

LANGUAGE

The focus of this study is how, through the use of specific language, the status of refugees and asylum seekers has been questioned and doubt has been cast upon their 'genuineness' in terms of the UNHCR definition as interpreted by the UK authorities. The terms studied here are: 'bogus' and 'phoney' refugees or asylum seekers; 'economic migrants'; and 'economic refugees'. While these phrases vary in the degree to which they are pejorative, they have the same implication, namely that the individuals referred to are not in reality refugees, and that their desire to enter the UK is in fact due to a desire to better themselves economically. The frequent use of such language has already been reported in an earlier study on political parties and the refugee agenda (Kaye, 1994). The choice of the particular language to be studied was influenced by this previous investigation. In addition, the use of the terms selected here has been widely commented upon, for example by Le Lohe (1992).

Usage of the terms identified above and raising doubts about the 'genuineness' of refugees were noted in both tabloid and broadsheet newspapers and the political élites of the two major parties were seen to make frequent use of these same terms. It was evident, for example, that the Conservative government had, at strategic moments, used such language when introducing restrictive legislation in 1991–2, during the 1992 election campaign when they 'played the race card' on the issue, and again in 1995–6 (Kaye, 1994; Refugee Council, 1996). It is perhaps more surprising that, in the course of attacking the government's policies over refugees and asylum seekers, the Labour opposition made use of similar language, albeit for purportedly different purposes (Kaye, 1994).

In this chapter it is argued that the frequent use of such terms as 'bogus', 'phoney' or 'economic migrant' socializes the readers to think that the use of such terms is normal political discourse, and it also gives credence to the notion that 'bogus' refugees and asylum seekers represent a problem, without in any way questioning the assumptions upon which such debatable assertions are based.

THE STUDY

The present study investigates the ways in which three UK broadsheet newspapers have, over time, framed refugee issues. The particular news-frame studied relates to the questioning of the status of refugees, in other words questioning whether they have been genuinely driven from their home country by persecution, or whether they are more economically motivated. This is approached through an analysis of the language used by the newspapers in relation to this topic.[1] The study further addresses the question of the relative primacy of newspapers and policy makers in setting and framing the refugee agenda. This is a development of a more limited pilot study which used data from *The Independent* newspaper only (Kaye, 1995). The present study expands the range of newspapers to three of the main UK broadsheets, and takes a slightly extended timeframe. As a result of the pilot study some areas of analysis were also modified.

FOCUS OF STUDY

Timeframe

The timespan is from October 1990 to October 1995, encompassing years particularly crucial for the development of UK refugee policy. First, it covers the period during which there was a rapid increase in the number of asylum seekers, followed by a decline and then a further rise. Secondly, it spans the introduction, passage and eventual implementation of the 1993 Asylum and Immigration Appeals Act. Third, it includes the 1992 British general election, during which refugees and asylum issues became very much part of the political agenda. Finally, it captures the beginning of the latest trend of governmental concerns in this policy area, which led to the introduction of new restrictive legislation in November 1995, although the culmination of these developments is outside the current research timeframe.

Newspapers

Three broadsheet newspapers were studied to span the political spectrum – *The Times*, which is generally seen as a conservative newspaper, *The Guardian*, noted for its more liberal views, and *The Independent*, which, as its name suggests, claims freedom from political influence or affiliation.

Theme

As noted above, the focus of the study concerns the ways in which language that challenges the status of refugees is used by newspapers, casting doubt on the 'genuineness' of many asylum applications. This focus emerged from insights gained in the earlier pilot study. CD ROMs of the three newspapers from 1 October 1990 to 30 September 1995 were searched for references to refugees or asylum seekers. Approximately 15,000 such references were found. These references were then further searched to exclude mentions of refugees and asylum seekers in countries other than the UK, and to find the key words that related to doubts about the status of refugees. These expressions were:

- Phoney or bogus refugee(s) or asylum seeker(s)
- Economic migrant(s) (when referring to refugees or asylum seekers)
- Economic refugee(s).

When constructing the searches, however, it was recognized that expressions with identical meanings can come in slightly different forms, for example, 'a bogus application for asylum' which would not be picked up in a search using the string 'bogus asylum seeker'. The searches were therefore finally constructed using the following strings:

- 'Phoney' *and* 'refugee(s)'
- 'Bogus' *and* 'refugees(s)'
- 'Phoney' *and* 'asylum seeker(s)'
- 'Bogus' *and* 'asylum seeker(s)'

- 'Economic migrant(s)'
- 'Economic refugee(s)'

While some irrelevant examples were picked up in the searches using the terms 'bogus' and 'phoney' in this way, the numbers of irrelevancies were not high and it was possible simply to discard them after inspection. A similar approach to finding a more comprehensive selection of articles by using the strings 'economic' *and* 'migrants' however came up with an unmanageably large number of irrelevant articles on immigration. It was therefore decided to use the strings 'economic migrant(s)/or refugees' for the search, although it is recognized that there may be some omissions of a few relevant articles as a result of this decision.

The articles found were then checked for relevance to UK asylum issues, and rechecked for inclusion of the key words and strings. This process resulted in a total of 193 relevant articles. These were then coded according to the data sheet in Appendix 9.1. The articles were then analysed to reveal their form, that is, whether they were an editorial, letter or article, and the overall frequency of the use of each expression. The way in which the language itself was framed, that is, to what extent the writer was making use of the language in their own writing, and to what extent they were reflecting or reporting its use by politicians or others was assessed. In addition, it was noted whether or not there was any commentary in the newspapers on the actual use of the language. The pattern of the appearance of these references over time, and the relationship between the pattern found and other events was analysed. In relation to all the above avenues of enquiry, the question of whether there were differences in the ways in which the three newspapers used the language, and the way in which this reflected their political leanings was considered. While some of the questions above are largely factual in nature, others were designed to tap into the key issues approached at the beginning of the chapter. Specifically, how far does the media set the agenda and to what extent does it simply reflect the agendas of politicians and others and what is the role of the media in framing these issues?

RESULTS

It can be argued that the significance of some types of newspaper item is greater than others, both in terms of their relationship to the newspaper's attitude and of their potential influence on the reader. The content of letters is likely to be a less significant indication of the newspaper's approach to a subject than that of either an article or report, or, more obviously, an editorial which explicitly states the newspaper's views. The frequency of different types of item is noted in Table 9.1.

Table 9.1 Type of item

Type of item	Guardian	Independent	Times	Total
Report	30	36	26	92
Editorial	2	6	2	10
Letter	9	17	1	27
Article	19	28	17	64
Total	60	87	46	193

The selected expressions were most commonly used in reports of events (including speeches) and in articles. There was also some appearance in letters but little in editorials. The relative infrequency of the appearance of refugee issues in editorials suggests either that they had a low priority in the policy agenda of the newspapers, or that the language being analysed here did not appear very often in this type of news item. If the latter scenario were true, this may be hypothesized to reflect a more careful and thoughtful use of language in editorials. The testing of this hypothesis is outside the scope of the chapter but could be an interesting subject of further research.

Table 9.2 shows the frequency of use of each set of expressions. For the purposes of this analysis, the data on the terms 'bogus' and 'phoney' which are judged to have identical meanings are aggregated. This table also shows the frequency of use of the terms as a percentage of the total use. It should be noted that more than one term was used in some articles.

The terms 'bogus' or 'phoney', which can be considered more directly insulting and potentially harmful to the public perception of refugees than the other terms, were used in 58 per cent of the articles analysed. While *The Guardian* and *The Times* made less use of the terms overall, *The Guardian*'s use tended to concentrate on the words 'bogus' or 'phoney'. Table 9.3 shows the frequency of criticism of the use of the expressions.

Table 9.2   Use of different expressions

Expression	Guardian		Independent		Times		Total	
	n	%	n	%	n	%	n	%
Bogus, or phoney refugees or asylum seekers	49	74	45	45	34	55	128	58
Economic migrants (applied to refugees)	15	24	44	44	13	21	72	33
Economic refugees	1	2	11	11	15	24	19	9
All expressions	65	100	100	100	62	100	219	100

Table 9.3   Criticism of the use of expressions

Category of criticism	Guardian	Independent	Times	Total
Writer criticises use of expressions	20	23	9	52
Writer reports criticism by others of uses of expressions	4	12	0	16
Total criticism of expressions (% of total use)	24 (37%)	35 (35%)	9 (15%)	68 (35%)

The pattern of criticism of the use of the terms is worthy of note, particularly when taken in conjunction with the overall frequency of use shown in Table 9.2. On 35 per cent of occasions the language was used in the context of criticizing its use by others or of reporting such criticism. There are however differences between the newspapers in this respect. Whilst, as seen in Table 9.2, *The Guardian* made disproportionate use of the more pejorative terms, Table 9.3 shows that for more than a third of the time, both *The Guardian* and *The Independent* used the terms in the context of criticizing their use or reporting criticism of use by others. This is consistent with their liberal and 'independent' stances respectively and with the fact that both were critical of government policy on refugee policy. On the other hand, while *The Times* made less use of all the terms than the other two newspapers, it also made comparatively little criticism of the use of such terms and reported no critical commentary. This is consistent with the general perception of *The Times* as a more obviously 'conservative' broadsheet.

One key question posed in this study concerns the relative primacy of the media (in this case broadsheet newspapers) in setting agendas and framing news about refugees and asylum seekers. The articles were therefore coded as to whether the writer of the article made direct use of the expressions, or whether the use was in quoting another person. The original user of the expression was also recorded. In coding the articles a distinction was made between original use by a politician or government official and use by others. Table 9.4 shows the extent to which the writer of the article originated the use of the term, and that to which the article referred to or used quotes by others.

Table 9.4   Original use of language

Original use	Guardian	Independent	Times	Total
Writer uses expressions	18	29	25	72
Writer reports use by UK politician or government official.	39	47	28	114
Writer reports use by persons other than UK politician or government official	8	18	1	27

On less than a third of occasions overall was the writer initiating the use of the expression. In the majority of cases the usage was a report or a quotation of the use by someone else – most commonly a UK politician or government official. This would suggest that at least in this sample, the newspapers are not taking the lead in setting the agenda. The newspapers are largely accepting the agenda as defined by politicians and government officials, and framing the news accordingly. The pattern is somewhat different for *The Times*, however, in which in approximately half the items the writer used the expressions directly rather than quoting. The frequency of the use of any of the chosen expressions over the years studied is shown in Table 9.5.

It can be seen from this table that 1991 was the peak year for the use of these expressions, with references dropping rapidly by 1993, but beginning to rise again slowly in 1995. *The Independent*, consistent with its overall higher frequency of use, had a markedly higher use in 1991 than the other two newspapers. In analysing the use over time in more detail, some patterns emerge which may explain variations in frequency. Table 9.6 shows the quarterly frequency of use and notes the timing of certain key events involving refugee issues.

Table 9.5 Pattern over time

Year	Guardian	Independent	Times	Total
1990 (3rd quarter)	3	3	2	8
1991	24	52	15	91
1992	20	23	17	60
1993	6	5	1	12
1994	3	2	2	7
1995 (1st 3 quarters)	4	2	9	15
Total	60	87	46	193

Table 9.6 Relationship of pattern to external events

Quarter	Guardian	Independent	Times	Total	External events
90/3	3	3	2	8	• Large increase in number of refugees reported. Government concerns noted. • Government announces review of asylum procedures. • Numbers of asylum seekers rise from 15,000 to 25,000 during 1990 (a fourfold increase over 1988)
91/1	0	6	4	10	• Cabinet committee discussion on asylum seekers. Government considers emergency measures to reduce numbers claiming asylum.
91/2	6	9	1	16	• Announcement of fourfold increase in number of officials processing asylum applications.
91/3	4	9	7	20	• Government announces tighter controls on asylum seekers. Critical reaction by MPs and by refugee and human rights organisations
91/4	14	28	3	45	• Asylum issues discussed at the two major party conferences. • The Asylum Bill introduced into parliament and debated. • Criticism by opposition parties and a variety of refugee and human rights groups.
1991 total	24	52	15	91	• General: Numbers of asylum seekers rise to 42,000

Table 9.6 Contd.

Qua-rter	Guar-dian	Indep-endent	Times	Total	External events
92/1	6	9	3	18	• Continuation of Asylum Bill through Parliament. Some amendments made due to criticisms. • Internal dissension within UKIAS. Its refugee unit removed from its control. • Government runs out of time on Asylum Bill, because of amendments to bill and the general election. • Immigration/racism/asylum are issues on the general election agenda.
92/2	5	4	6	15	• General election in April. • An announcement of the Bill to be reintroduced after Conservative Party victory at election.
92/3	3	2	2	7	
92/4	6	8	6	20	• Introduction of new Asylum and Immigration Appeals Bill. • Bosnian refugees become an issue.
1992 total	20	23	17	60	• General: Number of asylum seekers fall to approx 24,000 before passage of Asylum Bill.
93/1	3	2	0	5	• Bill proceeds through parliament
93/2	3	2	0	5	• Bill proceeds to final stages in parliament.
93/3	0	0	0	0	
93/4	0	1	1	2	• Bill becomes law in July.
1993 total	6	5	1	12	• General: Number of asylum seekers falls again to approx. 20,000. • More interest in the European dimension, particularly the changes in German asylum law.
94/1	2	1	0	3	• First impact of new Asylum Bill is the high rate of refusal for ELR and more in detention. • Hunger strikes in detention centres for asylum seekers.
94/2	0	0	0	0	• More disturbances in detentions centres for asylum seekers.
94/3	1	1	2	4	
94/4	0	0	0	0	
1994 total	3	2	2	7	• General: Number of asylum seekers rises to approx. 32,000.

Table 9.6 Contd.

Qua-rter	Guar-dian	Indep-endent	Times	Total	External events
95/1	2	1	5	8	• After studying consultants' recommendations on operation of 1993 Asylum Act government announced new proposals to accelerate asylum procedures. • Reports in press of new tougher government measures being considered.
95/2	1	0	3	4	• Schengen agreement to abolish border controls becomes operational in seven EU states.
95/3	1	1	1	3	• Home Secretary's comments in parliament on impending clampdown of 'abuse of social security benefits' by asylum seekers. • Number of asylum seekers • Rises to approx. 31,000 by end of September. For all of 1995 rises to approx 40, 000

Up until early 1991, there was only a modest number of references to the status and motives of refugees. Thereafter there was an increase, reaching a peak in the later months of 1991, and then declining over the next few years. This rise occurred at the time of the government decision to limit the flows. It peaked during the initial stages of the first attempt to introduce an asylum bill. There was a notable dip during the election campaign of 1992, possibly when other political agendas were more prominent, but the frequency increased, though to a somewhat lesser extent, up until the time when the legislation was reintroduced in October–December 1992, declining thereafter until the end of 1994. In 1995 the references begin to increase again, reflecting the increasing numbers of applications and government warnings that measures would be taken to limit these numbers

The relationship between the use of language casting doubt on the status of refugees and the effect of this use on readers' attitudes is a very complex one. It cannot be assumed that particular language will have a predictable effect. In the pilot study for this research, attempts were made therefore to measure the impression of refugees the article made on the reader (Kaye, 1995). Attempts were also made to measure the writer's attitude to refugees as perceived by the reader. This study used a three-point scale (positive, negative, neutral or mixed) for both these measures, with each article assessed by five independent raters[2] on both reader's impression and writer's attitude. It was interesting to note, however, the range of ratings by different respondents, particularly with respect to the reader's impressions of refugees.

Further attempts were made in the present study to separate more clearly the writer's attitude from the reader's impression. Two independent raters were asked to rate the writer's attitude using a much more carefully constructed rating scale, which tried to achieve a more objective rating by use of a detailed specification for each point on the scale. In the event it proved impossible to achieve inter-rater agreement on ratings even using this apparently more objective measure. On questioning the raters following this trial, it became clear that they were making judgements of writers' attitudes based on a complex and varied set of personal criteria which involved the writer's selection of material, the rater's own attitudes, as well as what the writer actually said to demonstrate his/her own sympathies or otherwise with refugees.

While the data from this part of the study are not of sufficient reliability to draw any conclusions about the degree of sympathy or hostility to refugees in the articles selected and the impact of this on the reader, the complexity of determinants of the ratings, and the different perceptions of even a relatively homogeneous group of respondents is in itself interesting. In investigating the impact of the media on the public perception of refugees, it is important not to lose sight of the influence of existing conceptual frameworks and expectations on the part of the reader. People demonstrate this not only through their choice of newspaper, but also in their own selective perception of the material presented.

DISCUSSION

The findings reported above are consistent with the finding of the earlier pilot study (Kaye, 1995). The data from this study support the view that, on this particular issue, the newspapers framed the news in line with the defined agenda of politicians and government officials. This finding, taken with the pattern of reporting over time in relation to the sequence of external events, suggests an orchestrated government campaign to downgrade the public perception of refugees before introducing legislation in 1990–1 and 1992–3 to control the numbers entering the UK (see Table 9.6). This pattern appeared to be repeating itself in 1995. It is therefore argued that, in the case of refugees and asylum seekers, there is insufficient evidence to show that the media significantly sets the agenda. On the contrary it is suggested that, on the evidence presented, public concerns are more likely to be shaped by political élites, with the media playing a largely intermediary role.

The fact that at least two of the less 'conservative' newspapers frequently challenged the way in which politicians and government officials used pejorative language about refugees would initially suggest that these newspapers were playing a key role in framing the news in a manner contrary to the model presented to them by politicians. When considered in more depth, however, it can be seen that, in the course of this debate, the newspapers were in reality following the lead of politicians in reflecting the construct 'genuine–phoney' in their writing. The fact that an article criticizes a politician for claiming that a refugee is making a bogus application for asylum and is largely economically motivated in itself reinforces the message that the validity of claims for asylum is an significant issue. It is therefore argued that the frequency of use over time of these expressions by newspapers is potentially more significant in influencing public opinion than whether articles are in themselves sympathetic to refugees or critical of politicians for denigrating them. The news is framed in terms of the 'genuineness' of refugees being a newsworthy question, demanding frequent comment, report and discussion, and this may in itself have the effect of socializing the reader into using this construct when thinking about refugees. This goes some way towards explaining the confusion in the minds of readers who were found to have difficulty in distinguishing the intentions of the writers.

This research is among the first to look at this important subject in a systematic manner. To give a full account of the impact of the media on public opinion and the political agenda in relation to refugees and asylum seekers, however, it is necessary to expand future research on this issue in a number of ways.

First, this study covered only 'serious' broadsheet newspapers. While this section of the media is important in that broadsheet newspapers are more likely to conduct more in-depth analysis and to pursue a subject in a more consistent manner, the growing influence of tabloid newspapers nevertheless should not be underestimated. Tabloid newspapers are more inclined to move away from a topic after a relatively short time, and also to concentrate on 'human interest' stories rather than issues as such. An exception to this however, is the phenomenon of a tabloid newspaper effectively running a 'campaign' on a specific issue. While traditionally it has been thought that broadsheets are more likely to be read by 'opinion formers' among the public, policy makers themselves may be more influenced by tabloid press coverage than previously thought, if only because of their sensitivity to its potential impact on voters' attitudes. The higher circulation figures of the tabloid press also make it more likely that they have a potentially more immediate impact on public opinion. It is also apparent, even through cursory analysis, that the tabloids have taken up strong negative positions in relation to refugees and asylum seekers, and there is already evidence to indicate that their inclusion in future research might lead to modifications of the conclusions of the current paper (see Coleman, 1995).

Secondly, widening the scope of the research to cover both radio and television would also be useful, although this poses more technical difficulties, particularly in analysing the relative impact of language and images. While most people today tend to receive most of their news knowledge from television, and while politicians have been forced to adopt new styles of political rhetoric for the new medium, there has been no evidence as yet to suggest that television has been a major factor in agenda-setting or news-framing on this issue, in that most television news coverage tends to be fragmented and devoid of much thematic content. In addition the control mechanisms that govern the operations of terrestrial television in the UK limit the scope of too obvious a bias in the reporting of news and current affairs, as compared with press coverage where no such direct controls operate. Despite this, given the importance of television it is important in the future to consider whether television has been a significant influence on public opinion, in setting the agenda or in framing the content of the debate by the use of its news and commentary programmes.

Thirdly, the present study focuses on the use of language which explicitly, and often pejoratively, casts doubt upon the status of refugees and asylum seekers. There are however other ways in which public opinion might be swayed towards a negative perception of refugees. In a previous study of the role of political parties in refugee agenda-setting, the more subtle impact of politicians constantly linking discussion of refugees and asylum seekers with broader issues of immigration was noted, with the undoubted result that the two groups have become almost indistinguishable in terms of public perception. Even without systematic study it can be seen that much media coverage when referring to refugees and asylum seekers often uses terms such as 'migrant' or 'immigrant' (Le Lohe, 1992). Given the generally negative public attitude to immigration, it can be argued that this is likely to have a negative impact on public opinion. Similarly, a range of less explicit language and themes, and other phrases and euphemisms, may be present in media representations and may also have an impact. Investigation of these less explicit and more subtle representations of refugees and asylum seekers would demand a different approach, for example studying in more depth a narrower number of items, possibly linked to a particular set of events or shorter timescale.

Further, given that trends very similar to those in the UK are occurring in refugee and asylum policy and practice in Europe, it is clear even from the limited research that has already been undertaken in this area that stereotyping of refugee and asylum seekers is occurring in many parts of the European media. It is therefore important in analysing these trends across Europe to tease out the similarities and differences in their treatment by the media.

Finally, there is the question of whether there are some means by which to redress the balance of the relative negativity in which refugees and asylum seekers are depicted. Media campaigns similar to that highlighting the success of immigrants and ethnic minorities in the UK, organized by the Commission for Racial Equality (CRE) in 1996, possibly could be mounted on behalf of refugees and asylum seekers (CRE, 1996). An understanding of the role of the media is crucial in considering how to approach such campaigns.

As has been argued, however, the evidence of the influence of the media on both short- and long-term public opinion in this area is uncertain. More compelling is the role of political élites in giving a lead in influencing public opinion. The evidence suggests that, while the issue of refugees and asylum seekers remains contestable in the political arena, and therefore susceptible to the vagaries of political competition, the scapegoating of refugees and asylum seekers by politicians, aided and abetted either consciously or unconsciously by parts of the media, will continue. The probable outcome is likely to be that the plight of refugees and asylum seekers will continue to be devalued and undermined, unless governments can be persuaded of the potentially positive contribution that refugees and asylum seekers can make. Without first convincing the political élite, the impact of media campaigns to change public opinion in their favour is likely to be limited.

Appendix 9.1   Data sheet

Newspaper
Guardian
Independent
Times

Date

Article Code Number (*serial no. for year*)
Expression Used (*tick any number*)
Bogus, or phoney refugee(s) or asylum seekers   1
Economic migrant(s)   2
Economic refugee(s)   3

Type of Article (*tick one*)
Report   1
Editorial   2
Letter   3
Article   4

Original Usage of Expressions (*tick any number*)
Writer uses expression   1
Writer reports use of term by UK politician (or government official) 2
Writer reports use of term by other   3
Reflects critically on use of term   4
Reports criticisms of term by others   5

NOTES

1. The author would like to acknowledge the advice and assistance of Valerie Kaye in the analysis of the data.
2. Members of staff and postgraduates in the Department of Social Sciences, Glasgow Caledonian University.

REFERENCES

Ansolabehere, S., S. Behr and and S. Iyengar, *The Media Game: American Politics in the Television Age* (New York: Macmillan, 1993).
Brosius, H.-B. and P. Eps, 'Prototyping though Key Events: News Selection in the Case of Violence against Aliens and Asylum Seekers in Germany', *European Journal of Communication*, 10 (3) (1995) 391–412.

Coleman, P., 'Survey of Asylum Coverage in the National Daily Press', *The Runnymede Bulletin* 291 (1995) 6–7.

Commission For Racial Equality, *Roots of the Future* (London: Commission for Racial Equality, 1996).

Iyengar, S. and D. Kinder, *News that Matters: Television and American Opinion* (Chicago: University of Chicago Press, 1987).

Kaye, R., 'Defining the Agenda: British Refugee Policy and the Role of Parties', *Journal of Refugee Studies* 7 (2/3) (1994) 144–59.

Kaye, R., 'Refugees and the UK Media: A Pilot Study of Newspaper Portrayal of Refugees', Paper presented to COST A2 Refugees in Europe – Research Issues Fourth Meeting, Amsterdam, 25–28 May 1995.

Le Lohe, M., 'Political Issues', *New Community* 18 (3) (1992) 469–74.

Mayer, R., 'Gone Yesterday Here Today: Consumer Issues in the Agenda Setting Process', *Journal of Social Issues* 47 (1) (1991) 21–39.

McQail, D., *Mass Communication Theory* (London: Sage Publications, 1993, 3rd edition).

McCombs, M., and D. Shaw, 'The Evolution of Agenda Setting Research', *Journal of Communication* 43 (2) 58–67.

Norris, P., 'Political Communications in Election Campaigns: Reconsidering Media Effects', Proceedings of the Political Studies Association Conference, University of York, 1995, 593–608.

Refugee Council, *The State of Asylum: A Critique of Asylum Policy in the UK* (London: The Refugee Council, 1996).

Seymour-Ure, C., *The Political Impact of Mass Media* (London: Sage Publications, 1974).

Tomasi, S., 'Today's Refugees and the Media', *Migration World* 20 (5) (1993) 21–3.

Tuchman, G., *Making News: A Study in the Social Construction of Reality* (New York: The Free Press, 1978).

Part III
The New Migration as a Social Reality

10 Out of the Frying Pan and into the Fire: A Case Study of Illegality amongst Asylum Seekers
Khalid Koser

INTRODUCTION

The regulation of international migration in Europe and elsewhere has created the possibility for unauthorized immigration (Miller, 1995). The control of what is more commonly referred to as illegal immigration has become a central issue of politics and public policy in the advanced industrial democracies over the last decade. Although it is very hard to quantify the scale of illegal immigration, there has been a growing convergence between these countries in terms of the tightening of policy to control these migration flows, and in terms of increasingly negative public reactions to them (Cornelius *et al.*, 1994).

This chapter, however, suggests that Europe's new illegal immigrants include asylum seekers and refugees. It has become clear that most European governments have opted to extend restrictive immigration policies to cover asylum seekers too (Escalona and Black, 1995). This is despite sound reasons grounded in international law why asylum seekers should be assessed within an alternative paradigm to that used for other migrants (Hathaway, 1994), and despite fears that such restrictions impinge upon *bona fide* refugees as much as they do upon other asylum seekers (Collinson, 1993). Drawing upon a case study amongst Iranian asylum seekers in the Netherlands, this chapter shows how asylum seekers, just like many other migrants, are being forced into illegality to overcome restrictions upon legal means of entry.

One of the central implications of their illegality for the asylum seekers in this case study is demonstrated to be increased vulnerability. It is suggested that far from targeting assistance upon refugees, current asylum policies are instead exacerbating the need of all asylum seekers for protection by engendering their transformation into illegal immigrants. In this way, the case study also carries broader implications for the definition and conception of, and for responses to, the phenomenon of illegal immigration in Europe today.

DEFINING ILLEGAL MIGRATION

When applied to migration, the term 'illegal' has been used to cover a variety of situations normally concerning conditions of entry, residence and employment. It has been used in the context of the entry strategies of migrants to describe people who enter a country without a passport or those who have a passport but enter clandestinely, avoiding control (Couper and Santamaria, 1984). It has also been applied in the case of foreigners who overstay short-term visas; or to those who work despite visa restrictions upon their employment (Miller, 1995). It has also been used on occasion to describe foreigners who are perceived as a threat to state security or who commit a crime, or legally resident foreigners who work in illegal activities.

Turning to the question of the definition of illegal migrants, an important distinction can be identified. While many illegal migrants consciously violate laws or restrictions, there are at the same time situations where illegal migrants can be produced overnight by changes in policies or by the complexities of maintaining legal residency. One example of such a process was when thousands of Palestinians were made illegal and expelled from Kuwait after the defeat of Iraq in the Gulf War. Similarly, some of the estimated 25 million Russians presently living outside the borders of the post-USSR Russian Federation risk becoming illegal migrants if they decline to become citizens of a Soviet successor state or otherwise cannot adjust their status to conform with altered political circumstances (Miller, 1995).

Illegal migration nevertheless continues to be surrounded by negative connotations, and political attention has focused almost exclusively on the issue of control (Miller, 1994). This observation is true also of illegal migration as a subject of academic inquiry (Cornelius *et al.*, 1994), and the enrichment of migration studies generally by the opening-up of analyses to questions relating to the experience of migration for the individuals concerned has rarely occurred in the specific case of illegal migration (Dumon, 1983). There are, however, indications that beyond its political implications, illegality has very important implications of a different nature for migrants. One example from the European context covers the increasing incidence of the illegal trafficking of migrants (IOM, 1995). At the most horrific level there are reports of migrants dying after having been hidden for smuggling in car boots or containers. There are also numerous reports of migrants being forced to become prostitutes and 'slaves' in destination countries in order to repay traffickers. The implication is that illegality can increase the vulnerability experienced by migrants.

Thus far the discussion has been fairly descriptive. The focus has been on defining what illegal migration is, who illegal migrants are and what illegality can mean to them, with the aim of developing a framework for the identification and interpretation of illegality in the context of migration. At a more conceptual level, another question that deserves attention is whether there are situations when illegal migration can be justified. There is a *prima facie* case for suggesting that one such situation arises in the case of refugees. For example, until recently it was in the political and strategic interest of Western European governments to accept refugees from the former Soviet bloc, even though these migrants had violated immigration laws both by leaving their countries and often by entering Western Europe clandestinely. There may be a case more generally for elevating humanitarianism in the form of the rights of refugees to exile above the national self-interests of receiving states as embodied in immigration control (Hathaway, 1991).

ASYLUM SEEKERS IN EUROPE: THE CHANGING POLICY CONTEXT

A brief analysis of the interaction between asylum policies and asylum migration in Europe is necessary to understand the obstacles in response to which asylum seekers are turning to illegality. Focusing specifically upon their implications for migration, recent policy initiatives can be categorized in a number of ways (see Table 10.1). First, a distinction can be drawn between policies which impact directly and those which impact indirectly upon the migration of asylum seekers. There are a range of policies aimed quite explicitly at preventing the arrival of asylum seekers in Western Europe in the first place. These include the growing list of countries from which visas are demanded; the promotion of so-called 'safe havens'; the requirement that asylum seekers submit their applications at a consulate or embassy in their country of origin ('in-country processing'); and carrier sanctions. Another such initiative is the definition of certain countries as 'safe' and from which applications for asylum can therefore be considered unfounded. At the same time, other policies have resulted in increasing restrictions upon asylum seekers once they have arrived in a European country, for example, concerning access to the refugee procedure or to refugee status, or access to state welfare. A supplementary aim of such measures is to make these receiving countries less than attractive destinations for asylum seekers, and so they can be considered to impact indirectly upon their migration.

Table 10.1   A schema of the impact of asylum policies on asylum migration

Impact	Policies
Nature of Interaction	
Direct	Visas, 'safe havens', 'in-country processing', carrier sanctions, etc.
Indirect	Exclusion from asylum procedure, exclusion from refuges status, exclusion from state welfare, etc.
Impact on Migration	
Scale	Visas and other direct measures, exclusion from asylum procedure and other indirect measures
Distribution	Closure of resettlement channels, Readmission Agreements, 'Safe third country', etc.

All of the above asylum policies are aimed to impact on the scale of asylum migration. A second distinction might be made between these and other policies aimed at changing the spatial distribution of asylum migration (Koser, 1996). For example, there have evolved a number of initiatives which shift the responsibility for dealing with asylum applications to other countries, usually outside Western Europe. One set of policies, which has impacted in particular upon countries in Southern Europe, involves the closure of traditional channels for resettlement in Western Europe so that 'transit' countries have become 'target' countries. Another example is the series of Readmission Agreements signed on a bilateral basis between countries in Western and Central or Eastern Europe which have facilitated the return of asylum seekers from the former to the latter (King, 1994). These latter measures are one example of the institutionalization of the notion of 'safe third country' (also known as 'country of first asylum' or 'host third country'). This notion denies access to national asylum procedures when an asylum seeker can be demonstrated to have travelled through other countries, deemed as safe.

THE CASE OF IRANIAN ASYLUM SEEKERS IN THE NETHERLANDS

Iran consistently has been one of the most important sources of 'spontaneous' asylum seekers in Europe since the 1980s (Hovy, 1993; IGC 1995*a*). There are many reports of the systematic abuse of human rights in Iran, targeted particularly on political opponents and religious minorities, but also on women and the disabled. Between 1992 and 1994 it is estimated that applications for asylum by Iranians in Europe numbered some 18,000 (IGC, 1995), and partial data for 1995 suggest that the relatively high rate of applications from this source continue. Some 30 per cent of applications from this source over the period have been lodged in the Netherlands, a proportion only exceeded in the case of Germany. More generally, by 1994 the Netherlands was numerically the second most important destination for asylum seekers in Europe behind Germany (IGC, 1994). In 1994 an estimated 6075 asylum applications from Iran were lodged in the Netherlands (IGC, 1995*a*).

The research upon which this paper draws was focused on two *Azielzoekerscentra* (AZCs) (Asylum Seeker Centres) in the Netherlands. Asylum seekers in AZCs have already passed through two earlier interview procedures, first in *Aanmeldcentra* (ACs) (Initial Reception Centres) and then in *Opvang en onderzoekscentra* (OCs) (Reception and Assessment Centres), and are at the stage where they are awaiting the outcome of a full assessment of their claims for asylum, or in some cases appeals against previous assessments. In-depth, semi-structured interviews were conducted with 32 heads of household, each lasting about 2 hours. Embarrassing or compromising questions including direct questions about reasons for flight were avoided and anonymity was guaranteed, these two methods being employed along with several other techniques to attempt to secure a degree of trust among the respondents. Given the sensitive nature of many of the issues discussed, a number of respondents at different stages of the discussion nevertheless declined to answer questions in detail.

Interview data were supplemented by information gathered during open-ended discussions with opinion formers and representatives from inside the asylum seeker populations. For approximately one quarter of the interviews the assistance of an interpreter was necessary. The interpreters employed were also from within the asylum seeker populations. Tables 10.2 and 10.3 respectively show the age and sex profiles of the 32 respondents interviewed. The predominance of young and female respondents reflects quite closely the demographic composition of the Iranian populations in the two AZCs visited, although it is a reversal of the gender profile of Iranian asylum seekers in Dutch AZCs as a whole at the end of 1995. All of the respondents left Iran between one and two years before the interviews.

Table 10.2 Age profile of the respondents

Age	n	%
0–17	0	0
18–29	13	41
30–39	9	28
40–49	6	19
50–59	4	12
60+	0	0
Total	32	100

Source: Field data (1995)

Table 10.3 Sex profile of the respondents

Sex	n	%
Male	11	34
Female	21	66
Total	32	100

Source: Field data (1995).

ILLEGALITY AND ASYLUM MIGRATION

Asylum seekers continue to arrive in Western Europe, albeit in numbers reduced since a peak in 1992, despite asylum policies aimed at excluding them. Empirical evidence presented below suggests that in the face of changing asylum policies, the migration of asylum seekers to Western Europe is becoming associated with illegal methods. Specifically, evidence is presented for an increasing dependence upon traffickers, and for the adoption by asylum seekers of a range of illegal migration strategies.

The Role of Traffickers

Europe-wide legislation on the trafficking of migrants has yet to be formulated. In the face of increasing evidence of individuals and syndicates being involved in such activities however, many governments in Western Europe, including the Netherlands, have passed legislation against human trafficking on a unilateral basis, with prosecutions now regularly reported (IOM, 1995; MNS, 1996). Of the 32 respondents in the survey, 29 reported that traffickers had been involved in their migration between Iran and the Netherlands. Apparently access to these traffickers in Iran is relatively easy. While some respondents reported having already known traffickers either personally or through other people, others said that they could be found in certain bazaars on certain days in most large cities in Iran, but especially in the capital Tehran. It was reported that they charged between US$4000 and US$6000 for their services. These payments had to be made in advance and in foreign currency.

Traffickers were reported to have been involved at each stage of the migration of asylum seekers between Iran and the Netherlands (Koser, 1997*a*). In the case of 19 respondents they had facilitated actually leaving Iran. These respondents reported having been under surveillance in Iran by the government's security service, such that the assistance of traffickers was required to leave Iran without interception.

Traffickers were also reported to have played a central role in the planning and facilitating of migration routes across Europe, including the arrangement of documentation and tickets where necessary. Only 18 of the 32 respondents were willing to answer detailed questions about their migration routes, of which all but one reported that traffickers had been involved in planning these routes. Only three of the 32 respondents reported having travelled directly to the Netherlands from Iran. The remainder had travelled via transit countries. Five arrived in the Netherlands via either Turkey or Pakistan, three arrived via either Romania or Hungary, while seven came through both sets of transit countries. A relatively restricted number of routes were therefore reported to have been used by the respondents. This may be an indication that a limited number of routes has become well established and maintained by traffickers. It was reported that a close international network of contacts operated along these routes. Most respondents were accompanied on each stage of their journey, and responsibility for them then handed on to another contact in the next destination.

A third function served by traffickers covered the choice of a final destination. In the case of only eight respondents were traffickers apparently not responsible in some way for the choice of the Netherlands as a final destination. Traffickers influenced the final destination for the remaining 24 respondents in two principal ways. The choice of the Netherlands for 13 respondents was reported to have been based on an impression formed before arrival there of general socio-economic conditions in the Netherlands, and particularly of a relatively lenient asylum policy. At the time of the respondents' arrival, these impressions can largely be described as justified. All of these respondents reported that traffickers had been primary sources of information about the Netherlands. It was repeatedly reported that traffickers had very up-to-date knowledge about changes in asylum policies throughout Europe. For the other 11 respondents, the choice of a final destination was effectively taken out of their hands, and determined by the routes across which traffickers were able to operate at the time. One woman was not even told when she left Iran to which country she would be taken, but simply assured that it would be in Western Europe.

In addition to advising on strategies designed to gain access to the Netherlands, most respondents reported that traffickers had also provided information concerning strategies for staying in the Netherlands, at least in the short term. Thus most had been advised as to how to respond appropriately during interviews with border police and immigration officials. For example, several knew with which countries the Netherlands had signed Readmission Agreements at the time of their arrival, so knew that they should avoid naming certain countries as transit countries.

Illegal Migration Strategies

The illegality surrounding human trafficking of the sort described above is often deepened by its association with syndicates involved in the illegal trafficking of arms and narcotics as well (Skeldon, 1994), or by evidence that trafficked migrants are recruited into illegal employment such as prostitution in their destination countries (IOM, 1995). The respondents were generally unwilling to respond to questions covering such issues; however it was clear that the strategies used by traffickers to facilitate the respondents' migration across Europe were illegal in their own right. The three principal illegal strategies reported were entry without passports; entry with false documentation, and clandestine entry.

These illegal strategies were adopted variously to gain entry into either transit countries or the Netherlands, and therefore depended largely upon the routes followed by individual asylum seekers. The three respondents who flew directly from Iran to the Netherlands did so with Iranian passports and short stay visas for the Netherlands. In two cases, respondents were visiting relatives in the Netherlands and in one case a respondent reported having bribed a contact in a Dutch embassy in Turkey to obtain her visa. They all then lodged a claim for asylum after their arrival.

Those respondents who initially went from Iran to neighbouring Turkey or Pakistan were obliged to do so illegally. Identification in Iran would in many cases have resulted in their detention, while several reported that other people apprehended in Turkey or Pakistan had been returned to Iran. As a result, most reported having been smuggled there overland, usually by night and always avoiding border posts. In contrast, eight of the ten respondents who came via Romania or Hungary, whether directly or indirectly from Iran, flew there. While four reported that they flew with Iranian passports, the remainder reported having been given Turkish passports by traffickers for this stage of the journey. It is not clear that a Turkish passport carried any advantage over an Iranian passport other than the hope that in the event of deportation, the respondents might not be returned immediately to Iran. Some respondents were adamant that their passports were forged, others that they were genuine passports obtained by traffickers from Turkish embassies.

All of those who flew from transit countries, either Turkey, Pakistan, Romania or Hungary, did so with false passports, as did approximately two-thirds of those who reported coming overland. The most commonly stated nationalities of passport used were Spanish, Portuguese and Polish. In contrast, about one third of those who came overland said they were smuggled across Europe and into the Netherlands without passports. They crossed borders secretly, normally hidden in cars or vans.

In practice the purpose served by passports was often to facilitate the journey to the Netherlands as opposed to actually facilitating entry into the Netherlands. Traffickers accompanied all but three of the respondents who paid them for assistance all the way to the Netherlands. Many reported that before passing through passport control there, they returned their passports to the trafficker. The implication is that these passports then re-entered the smuggling system. These respondents then lodged a claim for asylum without

passports. Other respondents who flew with false passports also succeeded in entering with them, and then claimed asylum after a short
time in the Netherlands, again normally having discarded their false
passports. There seem to be two advantages associated with lodging
an asylum claim without a passport. The immediate advantage of this
strategy is that the country of origin of the asylum seeker cannot be
identified straight away, so they are safe from immediate return there.
In addition, there is no evidence concerning countries of transit
through which asylum seekers have passed, so that they cannot be
returned to a 'safe third country' to seek asylum.

OUT OF THE FRYING PAN AND INTO THE FIRE

Perhaps unsurprisingly, every respondent in this survey reported that
their principal motive for leaving Iran was political vulnerability
there. They reported having either already experienced, or having
being under threat of, political persecution by the security forces or
police force in Iran. The reasons stated for this vulnerability varied
widely, but the two most often stated were affiliation with opposition
organizations and 'unIslamic' behaviour. Yet one of the central implications for the respondents of their illegalization during migration was
further vulnerability. It is suggested here that by leaving Iran and
trying to enter 'Fortress Europe', the respondents had effectively
'jumped out of the frying pan and into the fire'.

'Vulnerability' is a nebulous concept, which can been defined objectively by focusing on the character of a threat or crisis, or subjectively
by focusing on an individual's or group's capacity for coping with
stress. A useful analytical method is to think of vulnerability as
associated with the need for protection (Black, 1994). Relative to the
resources available to an individual, he or she might need protection
ranging from basic legal protection to social, economic or physical
protection. Based on this distinction between 'types' of vulnerability,
it is possible to distinguish various ways in which processes towards
illegalization during migration contributed towards the vulnerability
of certain respondents.

One of the main sources of political vulnerability for any asylum
seeker arises from the threat of deportation. Iran is one of a number
of countries where it is reported that repatriated asylum seekers often
face persecution from the government arising specifically from their
attempts to claim asylum in the first place (MNS, 1995). Nevertheless

a previous ruling having been recently overturned, deportations from the Netherlands to Iran are now reported to be occurring (MNS, 1996). In the case of asylum seekers who adopt illegal methods of entry, the possibility for repatriation is increased. A number of measures are currently being formulated in the Netherlands as well as elsewhere in Europe whereby asylum seekers can effectively be defined and treated as illegal immigrants instead. One such initiative is the refusal to consider claims not submitted immediately upon arrival (MNS, 1995). Illegal migrants are still dealt with on an *ad hoc* basis in most European countries, but usually face either detention, deportation, or both.

For many respondents, the political vulnerability associated with the rejection of a claim for asylum was heightened by the fact that they arrived in the Netherlands via one or more transit countries, these migration routes having been organized by traffickers. Regular deportations of Iranian asylum seekers have been reported from Turkey, and at the end of 1995, 150 Iranian asylum seekers were reported to have staged a sit-in at the headquarters of the United Socialist Party in Ankara demanding that deportation orders by the government be revoked. In addition, a Readmission Agreement is currently being negotiated by the Dutch government with Romania so that asylum seekers can be returned there under the concept of 'safe third country' (MNS, 1995). Romania, however, is one of several Central or Eastern European countries considered by many authorities to be ill-equipped properly to receive and protect asylum seekers (ECRE, 1995).

The role of traffickers in influencing the destinations of 24 of the respondents also gave rise in most cases to a source of what might be described as social vulnerability. Of these 24 respondents, 20 reported having friends or relatives in European countries before leaving Iran, and most said that their initial plans had been to join these people. In only three of their cases were these contacts located in the Netherlands, however. They were therefore effectively isolated from potential supportive social networks, in the short term at least, through the Netherlands being their final destination. Interviews with six other respondents who did have social networks *in situ* in the Netherlands confirmed that these had provided a variety of forms of assistance including emotional support, information, financial assistance and childcare. At a more qualitative level, there were quite clear indications that those without an immediate social network to which to turn for general support suffered to a far greater degree and far more frequently from depression and more regularly expressed concern about their future (Koser, 1997*b*).

Traffickers were reported to have charged between US$4000 and US$6000 for their services and meeting these costs also exposed many respondents to a form of economic vulnerability at various stages during their migration. First, even before leaving Iran, all but two respondents were obliged to turn to friends or relatives for financial assistance. Several reported that they had been forced to risk staying in Iran despite the very immediate threat of detention in order to raise money. It is quite clear that in the absence of financial support from social networks, most respondents would not have been able to migrate. Indeed many reported having known people in Iran with reasons equally as pressing as their own to leave, who simply had been unable to afford to do so.

Meeting the cost of traffickers also meant that some respondents left Iran with virtually no money, which exposed many to sources of economic vulnerability both in transit countries and in the Netherlands. Those respondents who came to the Netherlands via transit countries spent between one week and two months in the latter. About half of them reported that they had been obliged to work on the black market in transit countries, in order to derive sufficient income to live. This in turn exposed them to a source of legal vulnerability. In contrast other respondents had managed to borrow enough money before leaving Iran to cover the cost of living in transit countries.

Most respondents nevertheless arrived in the Netherlands without money. At the same time, most had no other source of income to supplement state allowances to meet basic expenditure, firstly because of isolation from social networks, and secondly because of restrictions upon entry into the labour market for asylum seekers in the Netherlands during their first two years there (Groenendijk and Hampsink, 1995). Although most respondents were unwilling to respond to questions about their income, several reported that they had worked illegally in the Netherlands. As payment to traffickers had apparently been made before leaving Iran in the cases of all the respondents in question, there did not arise the situation reported from other sources of asylum seekers being forced by traffickers to work illegally in order to pay them (IOM, 1995). Even in those few cases where respondents had found temporary employment after their first year in the Netherlands, in the majority of cases a substantial proportion of that income was regularly sent back to Iran to pay debts to friends or relatives from whom money had been borrowed initially.

CONCLUSION

This chapter has shown how changing asylum policies in Europe are forcing asylum seekers and refugees into illegality by denying them legal means of entry. A central implication of this illegality for the people concerned has been demonstrated to be increased vulnerability. These findings lend support to objections to the extension of restrictive immigration policies to cover asylum seekers, and give rise to worrying questions about the welfare and protection of refugees in the new Europe.

As their numbers have decreased, asylum seekers have nevertheless been replaced at the top of political agendas by illegal immigrants (IGC, 1995*b*). The findings in this chapter also stress the importance of taking a step back from knee-jerk policy responses towards illegal immigrants to understand who illegal immigrants are, what makes them illegal, and what illegality means to them. The processes which are forcing asylum seekers into illegality are directly comparable to those operating in the context of other migrants. There is no reason to think that the vulnerability found in this case to be associated with illegality is not applicable more generally. Policies towards asylum seekers have been found to be desperately inappropriate, and it remains to be seen whether any lessons will be learned when it comes to making policy for illegal immigrants.

REFERENCES

Black, R., 'Livelihoods under Stress: A Case Study of Refugee Vulnerability in Greece', *Journal of Refugee Studies*, 7(4) (1994), 360–77.

Collinson, S., *Europe and International Migration* (London: Pinter, 1993).

Cornelius, W.A., P.L. Martin and J.F. Hollifield (eds.), *Controlling Immigration: A Global Perspective* (Stanford: Stanford University Press, 1994).

Couper K., and U. Santamaria, 'An Elusive Concept: The Changing Definition of Illegal Immigrant in the Practice of Immigration Control in the UK', *International Migration Review*, 18(1) (1984), 437–52.

Dumon, W.A., 'Effects of Undocumented Migration for Individuals Concerned', *International Migration*, 21(2) (1983), 218–29.

European Council on Refugees and Exiles (ECRE), *Safe Third Countries: Myths and Realities* (London: ECRE, 1995).

Escalona, A. and R. Black, 'Refugees in Western Europe: Bibliographic Review and State of the Art', *Journal of Refugee Studies*, 8(4) (1995), 364–89.

198   *Khalid Koser*

Groenendijk K., and R. Hampsink, *Temporary Employment of Migrants in Europe* (Nijmegen: Faculteit der Rechtsgeleerdheid K.U., 1995).

Hathaway, J.C., 'Reconceiving Refugee Law as Human Rights Protection', *Journal of Refugee Studies*, 4(2) (1991), 113–31.

Hathaway, J.C., 'Three Critical Questions about the Study of Immigration Control', in W.A. Cornelius, P.L. Martin and J.F. Hollifield (eds.), *Controlling Immigration: A Global Perspective* (Stanford: Stanford University Press, 1994) 49–51.

Hovy, B., 'Asylum Migration in Europe: Patterns, Determinants and the Role of East–West movements', in R. King (ed.), *The New Geography of European Migrations* (London: Belhaven, 1993) 207–27.

Intergovernmental Consultations on Asylum, Refugee and Migration Policies in Europe, North America and Australia (IGC), *Overview of Asylum Applications as Reported by Participating States* (Geneva: IGC, 1995a).

Intergovernmental Consultations on Asylum, Refugee and Migration Policies in Europe, North America and Australia (IGC), *Illegal Aliens: A Preliminary Study* (Geneva: IGC, 1995b).

International Organization for Migration (IOM), *Trafficking and Prostitution: The Growing Exploitation of Migrant Women from Central and Eastern Europe* (Geneva: IOM, 1995).

King, M., 'Policing Refugees and Asylum-seekers in "Greater Europe": Towards a reconceptualisation of control', in M. Anderson and M. den Boer (eds.), *Policing across National Boundaries* (London: Pinter, 1994) 69–84.

Koser, K., 'Recent Asylum Migration in Europe: Patterns and Processes of Change', *New Community*, 22(1) (1996) 151–8.

Koser, K., 'Negotiating Entry into "Fortress Europe": The Migration Strategies of "Spontaneous" Asylum Seekers', in P.J. Muus (ed.), *Exclusion and Inclusion of Refugees in Contemporary Europe* (Utrecht: ERCOMER, 1997a).

Koser, K., 'Social Networks and the Asylum Cycle: The Case of Iranians in the Netherlands', *International Migration Review* (in press, 1997b).

Miller, M.J. (ed.), 'Strategies for Immigration Control: An International Comparison', *Annals of the American Academy of Political and Social Science*, 534 (1994).

Miller, M.J., 'Illegal Migration', in R. Cohen (ed.), *The Cambridge Survey of World Migration* (Cambridge: Cambridge University Press, 1995).

Migration News Sheet (MNS), various issues (1995).

Migration News Sheet (MNS), various issues (1996).

Skeldon, R., 'East Asian Migration and the Changing World Order', in W.T.S. Gould and A.M. Findlay (eds.), *Population Migration and the Changing World Order* (London: Belhaven, 1994) 173–93.

11 Illegality and Criminality: The Differential Opportunity Structure of Undocumented Immigrants
Godfried Engbersen and Joanne van der Leun

INTRODUCTION

Over the past ten years, politicians and the media in North America, Western Europe and Japan have become more concerned with the issue of undocumented immigration (Cornelius *et al.*, 1994; *Der Spiegel*, 1995; Espenshade, 1995; Groenendijk and Böcker, 1995; Meissner *et al.*, 1993; Morita and Sassen 1994). In most 'advanced' societies confronted with growing numbers of immigrants, both the public and politicians increasingly believe that the national absorption capacity is insufficient to accommodate all immigrants. People fear that a surplus of immigrants will disrupt the culture, economy and the level of public services of the welfare state. Most Western countries have therefore adopted more restrictive migration policies. Despite this, migration flows are still increasing. The new restrictions place special emphasis on the most feared immigrant, that is, the undocumented or 'illegal' immigrant.

Undocumented immigrants seem to make up a large part of the population of certain urban areas, although it is difficult to put exact figures on this category. For the United States, estimates vary from 3 to 15 million but the most reliable figure for 1990 is probably around 3 million (Passel, 1994). In 1991, the number of undocumented immigrants in Western Europe was assessed at 2.6 million (Castles and Miller, 1994). For Japan, estimates vary between 300,000 and 500,000 (Cornelius *et al.*, 1994; Sassen, 1995). In the Netherlands, the estimates range from 50,000 to 200,000. The

municipal immigration police of the three largest Dutch cities estimated the number of undocumented immigrants in Amsterdam to be
between 20,000 and 40,000, in Rotterdam 30,000 and in The Hague
20,000. This represents around 5 per cent of the total population of
each of these cities. It is likely that these figures are overestimates.
Based on our own research in Rotterdam, for instance, Jack Burgers
(1995) suggests that only around 10,000 undocumented immigrants
live more or less permanently in Rotterdam.

It seems that the attention currently given to undocumented immigrants also stems from a moral panic among politicians and parts of
the population (Goode and Ben-Yehuda, 1994). The 'illegal immigrant' has become a social symbol for immigrants who supposedly
abuse welfare state arrangements (social security, housing, education
and health care), commit crimes and jeopardize the employment of
established citizens (Gans, 1995). This moral panic leads to inflationary estimates of the number of undocumented immigrants. It also
casts a negative light on the legal immigrant and the recognized or
'tolerated' asylum seeker. The exaggerated estimates and assumptions
about the behaviour of undocumented immigrants are not supported
by empirical evidence (Espenshade, 1995; Groenendijk and Böcker,
1995; Passel, 1994; Zolberg, 1993).

This chapter focuses on the relationship between illegality and
criminality. The central question is whether (and how) illegality
might be associated with criminality. Are undocumented immigrants
more involved in crime than others or does their undocumented
status in fact cause them to refrain from criminality? The emphasis
of this chapter is on differences between different categories of immigrants and patterns of involvement in crime and how these patterns
can be explained. The chapter proceeds through five sections. In the
first section we discuss the conceptual framework and focus specifically on the differential opportunity structures of undocumented
immigrants. We present in the second section a brief outline of the
city of Rotterdam, the location of the case study. The third section
comprises our examination of the relationship between illegality
and criminality using our analysis of official statistics concerning
apprehensions by the police as well as expulsions of undocumented
immigrants. In the fourth section we attempt to explain the empirical
patterns of involvement in crime, while in the concluding section we
discuss some possible perverse effects of the current restrictive migration regime.

CONCEPTUAL FRAMEWORK

Undocumented immigrants are by definition the product of legislation. In short, undocumented immigrants violate laws or legislation designed to control migration. Legal definitions are not as clear as they may appear at first glance. Within the category of undocumented immigrants there are many differences. People may enter the country clandestinely, but more often they enter the country as a tourist and overstay their short-term visas. In addition, they sometimes work illegally, but this is not necessarily related to undocumented residence. The (il)legal status of a person can furthermore change over time and at some moments in time the (il)legal status of a person may be uncertain. For example, someone may be illegal simply because he or she has failed to undertake the procedures necessary to regularize his or her stay. Despite these difficulties, we have adopted a practical definition of illegality here. We define immigrants as 'illegal' or 'undocumented' where they did not have permission to enter or reside in the Netherlands at the time of the research.

When focusing on the relation between illegality and criminality, an important point to emphasize is that illegal residence in itself is not a penal offence. Criminality for the purposes of this research is defined as being apprehended for criminal offences. So far, there is little empirical evidence available about the extent to which undocumented immigrants in the Netherlands are involved in crime. Two contradictory assumptions can be made:

1. Undocumented immigrants refrain from committing crime for fear of being traced and expelled by the police. In other words, their illegal status encourages law-abiding behaviour.
2. Undocumented immigrants are more likely than others to commit crimes in order to survive, especially when they are excluded from public services and the formal labour market. In other words, the poverty and marginalization linked to their illegal status make them break the law.

Empirical findings thus far have been rather ambiguous. Evidence for both the above assumptions can be found. In the Netherlands, the first assumption finds some empirical support in the work of Aalberts and Dijkhoff (1993), who analysed the police records of 1285 apprehended immigrants (13 per cent appeared to be 'illegal' and 87 per cent to be legal). Aalberts and Dijkhoff argue that undocumented immigrants are less involved in criminal activities than legal immigrants. They conclude moreover that undocumented EU immigrants are more likely to commit crimes than undocumented non-EU immigrants.[1] The authors suggest that the crime rate among the latter is low because most are supported by their families or have jobs. The second assumption receives partial confirmation in the study *The Robbery of Passengers* by the Dutch criminologist, Willem de Haan. De Haan states that almost 25 per cent of the 960 cases of street robbery he studied were committed by undocumented immigrants. According to de Haan, 90 per cent of these undocumented immigrants committed crimes in order to survive in the Netherlands (de Haan, 1993).

Both Dutch studies have their limitations. De Haan studied a specific criminal offence, which does not occur very often, whereas Aalberts and Dijkhoff conducted a very broad study, which led to relevant but general conclusions. Little attention was paid to differences between the type and seriousness of the criminal offences committed or to intra-group differences.

In this chapter, we attempt to present a more detailed analysis of the possible linkages between illegality and criminality, combining the analysis of aggregate crime data with the preliminary results of the interviews and fieldwork conducted in the course of our 'Unknown City' project in the city of Rotterdam. This project shows that the 'typical' undocumented immigrant does not exist. The interviews demonstrate that undocumented immigrants occupy a wide variety of social positions ranging from those who are formally employed and in many respects integrated into Dutch society to those who are socially and economically marginalized. We also found that there are many ways of making a living. Undocumented immigrants who are unemployed – and many are – can often depend on their family or friends. Most are not involved in crime. Additionally, the interviews seemed to reveal systematic differences between undocumented immigrants from various countries in the degree to which they are integrated in Dutch society (Engbersen, 1996). The evidence was not strong enough, however, to draw any firm conclusions about the relationship between illegality and criminality, because of the 170 respondents we interviewed, only 13 claimed to be involved in criminality. Before turning to the quantitative data, we discuss the theoretical approach adopted.

Criminological Theories

The leading theories on marginal groups (for example the unemployed) and (legal) ethnic groups in Dutch criminological research are the 'social control theory' of Hirschi (1969) and the 'strain theories' based on the work of Merton (Jongman *et al.*, 1993; Junger, 1990). Additionally, some scholars make use of subcultural theories of migration and marginality (Buiks, 1983; Sansone, 1992; Werdmölder, 1990). Each of these theoretical traditions has its own specific shortcomings and has been subject to criticism. In our view it is difficult, for both theoretical and practical reasons, to apply these theories to the case of undocumented immigrants.

The social control theory – often focusing on juveniles – assumes that everyone has deviant tendencies. In short, the central question is not why some people commit crimes, but why everybody does not (Gottfredson and Hirschi, 1990; Hirschi, 1969). The answer lies in social bonds, the strength of which varies between people. The underlying assumption is that individuals with strong social bonds are unlikely to engage in delinquency. Hirschi specifies four elements of the social bond: attachment, commitment, involvement and belief. The most important element is said to be *attachment*, which refers to a person's sensitivity to the opinions of other people. *Commitment* refers to the rational element within social bonds. People invest time in their education or career and do not want to reduce their prospects. *Involvement* in conventional activities is supposed to prevent a person having time to participate in criminal activities, whereas *belief* refers to the extent to which a person believes s/he should obey the rules of society.

These four elements are typically studied in terms of an individual's relationships with family members, teachers and peers. Hirschi concentrated on minor delinquent acts committed by male high school students. With regard to undocumented immigrants who have left their home country and have often passed adolescence, these elements of the control theory are difficult to apply. Most undocumented immigrants have no social bonds with Dutch schools, whilst their ties with their parents are weakening. Furthermore, their 'illegal' status minimizes their chances of becoming fully integrated within an ethnic community or in wider society.

Subcultural theories assume that criminal behaviour is learned through interaction with others within relatively strong subcultures (Cohen, 1955; Miller, 1958). Within these subcultures people develop values that are 'deviant' from the point of view of society at large. These values condone or even actively encourage criminal behaviour. Cohen considers the delinquent subculture to be a lower-class boys' collective solution to the problem of status frustration: since they cannot acquire status by conforming to middle-class values, they reject those values. Little is known about the existence of specific subcultures of undocumented immigrants within the Netherlands. We assume that the uncertain status of undocumented immigrants obstructs an institutionalizing of subcultures. Moreover, although the level of integration varies, undocumented immigrants are not part of a separate subculture somehow severed from the rest of society (Engbersen, 1996).

Strain theories are based on the concept of 'relative deprivation'. Delinquency is thus seen as the result of incongruities between culturally embedded goals and the unavailability of legitimate means for immigrants to realize these goals. Crime, from this point of view, is an 'innovative' reaction to strain (Merton, 1957). School is considered to be the most important institution socializing people to cultural goals such as the pursuit of material success (Junger, 1990). To locate the undocumented immigrant within this framework of analysis is difficult. For instance, are the culturally embedded goals to which she or he refers those of the receiving society or those of his or her country of descent? In addition, the 'illegal status' of an immigrant often prevents him or her from making adequate use of legitimate and accepted means.

In sum, the commonly used criminological theories are either difficult to apply to the case of undocumented immigrants, or require methods of research other than those presently at our disposal. In general terms they present a possible motivation for crime among undocumented immigrants. After all, it is likely that undocumented immigrants do not have strong social bonds within the receiving country. In addition, it is difficult for them to achieve material success because they cannot make use of most legitimate means. From our interviews however we know that there is great variation among undocumented immigrants in terms of social position and level of integration.

The 'contexts of reception'[2] (Portes and Rumbaut, 1990) may be of relevance in explaining different patterns of involvement in crime. For these reasons it seems more promising to turn to the approach proposed by Cloward and Ohlin (1965) in *Delinquency and Opportunity*, in which they integrate the strain approach with the Chicago School tradition. In our view Cloward and Ohlin's concept of the 'differential opportunity structure' could help to explain patterns of criminal involvement or the absence of criminality in the case of undocumented immigrants. They point out that access to both the *legitimate* and the *illegitimate* opportunity structures of a society is characterized by inequality. Cloward and Ohlin used this concept to explain differences in crime patterns in specific urban neighbourhoods. We argue that it can also be adapted to explain differences in the social position and options of undocumented immigrants, provided it is used in an *institutional* way.

At first glance, it seems that the distinction which Cloward and Ohlin make between legitimate and illegitimate means does not really apply to (adult) undocumented immigrants, who are by definition excluded from many legitimate means such as formal labour, education and public housing. Our interviews with undocumented immigrants, however, show this assumption to be incorrect. The opportunity structure of undocumented immigrants may be divided along three institutional axes.

1. The first axis encompasses the degree of accessibility to the *formal institutions* of the welfare state: the labour market, education, housing and health care. For undocumented immigrants, the period of arrival in the Netherlands is important in this respect. In the 1980s and early 1990s, the Dutch migration regime was of a less restrictive nature (for example, undocumented immigrants were still able to obtain a social security number).
2. The second axis involves the degree of accessibility to *informal institutions*, three of which are particularly important. The first is the informal network of family, friends, acquaintances and relatives in the Netherlands as well as in the country of origin. This network is critical in finding accommodation, financial support, a possible partner and a first introduction to Dutch society. The second is the informal economy which represents possible employment opportunities for undocumented immigrants. The third is the extent to which undocumented immigrants are able to profit from the selective street-level administration of the law by the Immigration Police and other institutions such as those concerned with education and health care.
3. The third axis is access to *criminal circuits*, in which inequality also exists. Criminal circuits reflect the diverse settings in which various offences are committed: youth gangs, drug scenes, organized crime, and so on.

These formal, informal and illegal institutions play a role in the (semi-) integration of undocumented immigrants.[3] The informal sphere of the labour market and criminal circles offers undocumented immigrants an alternative to the formal labour market. In addition, street-level bureaucracies play a critical role in the passive and active toleration of undocumented immigrants. The discretion which institutions in the fields of immigrant surveillance, education, housing and health care allow themselves for reasons of capacity, control problems and humanitarian concerns opens up a social and economic sphere in which undocumented immigrants may become (semi-)integrated without being official members of Dutch society. The proposition we make in this chapter is that undocumented immigrants from different countries have access to different opportunity structures and that these opportunity structures may account for divergent patterns in involvement in crime. In the following section we present some information on the social composition of the population of apprehended undocumented immigrants in Rotterdam, before turning to the empirical patterns observed in our research.

THE CASE OF ROTTERDAM

With about 600,000 inhabitants, Rotterdam is one of the larger cities in the Netherlands. Extensive immigrant groups of non-Dutch origin have settled there, creating a population of some 240,000 immigrants. Our interviews with undocumented immigrants suggest that the population of undocumented immigrants in Rotterdam resembles to a certain extent that of established immigrants in the Netherlands in general (see Appendix 11.1). These immigrants are mainly Surinamese, Turkish and Moroccan and in Rotterdam also Cape Verdean. On the other hand, a comparison of *apprehended undocumented* immigrants and *registered legal* immigrants reveals a number of substantial differences (see Table 11.1). Among the apprehended undocumented immigrants, there are 40 per cent fewer Turks, almost three times as many Moroccans and almost 75 per cent fewer Surinamese compared with the legal immigrant group. The greatest difference is found among the Algerians: there are scarcely any Algerians among the legal immigrants, but a considerable number can be found in the undocumented population.

Table 11.1 Country/region of origin by sample

Country/region of origin	Legal immigrants		Apprehended undocumented immigrants	
	%	N	%	N
Turkey	15.1	89	9.0	29
Morocco	12.2	72	33.4	108
Algeria	0.2	1	7.4	24
Western Europe	19.9	117	17.6	57
Eastern Europe	7.7	45	8.7	28
Africa	17.5	103	11.2	36
Asia	11.9	70	6.8	22
Other	15.5	91	5.9	19
(Surinam)	(11.4)	(67)	(3.0)	(10)
Total	100.0	588	100.0	323

Source: Vreemdelingen Registratie Systeem (VRS) and Herkenningssysteem (HKS) (1994)

In many other respects, the undocumented immigrants in the sample (328 in total) form a relatively homogeneous group. This group consists mainly of men, the majority of whom are single. In most cases, they are semi-skilled or unskilled males between 20 and 30 years of age. Perhaps unsurprisingly, most of the undocumented immigrants live in neighbourhoods where large communities of immigrants exist.[4]

To recap, the social composition of the undocumented population partly confirms the well-known migration theories, in that a considerable percentage of immigrants comes from countries with which the Netherlands, or cities in the Netherlands (such as Rotterdam), maintained economic or political colonial relations (see Appendix 11.2). These immigrants come to the Netherlands with the help of their compatriots, who also take care of them once they have arrived. Some undocumented immigrants, however, come from African countries and do not belong to groups one might expect to see in the Netherlands (for instance, Algerians, Nigerians, Somalians, Indians). Some of them came to Rotterdam – after many detours – without the support of a migration network. We can conclude that the migration routes of *undocumented* immigrants are much more fragmented and unpredictable than some of the dominant migration theories presuppose (Portes and Rumbaut, 1990; Sassen, 1988).

THE RELATIONSHIP BETWEEN ILLEGALITY AND CRIMINALITY: APPREHENSIONS AND EXPULSIONS

In order to compare the apprehensions of undocumented immigrants with those of legal immigrants in the city of Rotterdam, we analysed three random samples drawn from the files of the Rotterdam police, including the files of the Immigration Police.[5] In the Netherlands, police officers in the Immigration Police, as well as police officers in other services, are charged with the supervision of immigrants and are authorized to stop them in order to verify their identity (Aalberts, 1990; Clermonts, 1994).

When using official crime data, certain reservations have to be expressed. Among criminologists there is an ongoing debate about the selectivity of these data. The central question is how well crime data measure crime rates. There is an unknown, but probably massive, amount of crime that never shows up in police files. This element is often termed the 'dark number' of crime. Methodologically, this dark number could perhaps be reduced by using self-report studies. But undocumented immigrants cannot easily be studied using self-report survey methods. Other criticisms of crime data cluster around the question of whether research on crime data actually measures crime, or whether it measures instead the bureaucratic activities of formal agencies such as the police. (Beirne and Messerschmidt, 1991). Our research indicates that to a certain extent the number of registered undocumented arrests is indeed the result of *selective* law enforcement (cf. Hagan and Peterson, 1995). Some undocumented immigrants run a higher risk of being apprehended and expelled than others. This practice has three major causes.

First, there is a discrepancy between legislation on the one hand and the enforcement of immigration policies on the other. Several studies point to such 'goal displacement' (Aalberts, 1990; Clermonts, 1994; Engbersen *et al.*, 1995; Merton, 1957). In practice, instead of targeting all undocumented immigrants, the immigration and local police target only those who cause inconvenience and display criminal behaviour. As a result of this selectivity, specific categories of undocumented immigrants rarely come into contact with the Immigration Police or local police departments. This is chiefly the case for those who work for businesses employing only a few undocumented immigrants and for those who live a shadowy existence and do not engage in crimes.

Second, the daily police routine of arresting immigrants also plays a role (Engbersen *et al.*, 1995). The police utilize informal rules and 'suspect typologies' to apprehend individuals and groups (Brown, 1988). These informal yet institutionalized rules lead inevitably to unequal probabilities of being apprehended by the police. It is less likely for undocumented Surinamese immigrants and immigrants from East and Middle Europe to be apprehended ('they will probably be legal') than for immigrants from Morocco, Algeria and other African countries. The use of these 'smart rules' – in contrast to 'proper rules' (Freilich, 1989) – can be seen as a form of statistical discrimination. These informal rules lead to disproportionately frequent arrests of immigrants from certain African countries.

Third, unidentifiable immigrants are constitutionally relatively invulnerable to expulsion.[6] This is the paradox of the current undocumented immigrant policy: those immigrants who are the primary target of apprehension and expulsion measures are the most successful in preventing their repatriation. Our research shows that certain groups of undocumented immigrants, especially those who are involved in drug-related crime and offences, are difficult to evict because they are able to hide their identity successfully by ridding themselves of their documents and pretending to come from countries unwilling to collaborate with the Dutch authorities. In the past the Dutch migration authorities had a poor working relationship with Morocco. Currently, the country they find most difficult to deal with is Algeria. In this case it is difficult to obtain a *'laissez passer'* for the undocumented immigrant in order to repatriate him/her.

Table 11.2 shows that undocumented immigrants who were apprehended for minor offences (for example, working illegally) or for living illegally in Rotterdam are expelled more frequently than undocumented immigrants who have committed more serious crimes. As a result, the deportation policy in the city of Rotterdam is quite the reverse of that which might be expected. The deportation rate of undocumented immigrants involved in misdemeanours is 53 per cent, while in the case of criminal offences it is only about 30 per cent.

The limits of the current expulsion policy become visible in the administrative category of immigrant termed here the 'revolving door illegal'. This is an undocumented immigrant who has been repeatedly arrested for criminal offences and who has been sent back on to the streets more than once, due to the shortcomings of the expulsion policy. In our research this was the case in 22 per cent of the dossiers.

Table 11.2   Classification of expulsions of apprehended undocumented
immigrants (N = 328)

Type of expulsion	Illegal residence %	Misdem- eanours %	Offences %	Drug-related offences %
Expelled to home country	43.3	52.8	32.5	27.4
Expelled in 'southern direction'	38.1	36.0	56.3	66.1
Various	18.6	11.2	11.3	6.5
Total number	N = 97	N = 89	N = 80	N = 60

Source: VRS (1994).

These three factors *partly* explain the over- and under-representation of specific groups of undocumented immigrants amongst those registered by the police. We argue however that the police data on apprehended undocumented immigrants give an important indication of the social mechanisms which underlie the interplay between illegality and criminality. At this point in time, these data form the best source of information available, especially when combined with the findings of the interviews we conducted during our empirical research.

The central question we considered was whether undocumented immigrants were more involved in crime than others, or whether – because of their vulnerability – they were more likely to refrain from crime. The collected data on illegality and crime make clear that the assumption that undocumented immigrants are only able to survive by committing crimes is incorrect. Nearly half of the *registered* undocumented immigrants in Rotterdam were apprehended for illegal residence (47 per cent) and an additional 13 per cent for misdemeanours such as illegal labour or fare-dodging. Another 26 per cent were apprehended for minor offences like shoplifting, theft from cars, 5 per cent for serious offences (robbery, murder, possession of firearms) and 9 per cent for offences against the Opium Act. It is important to compare these findings with data on the apprehension of legal suspects.

In our comparison of undocumented with legal immigrants, we limited ourselves to those arrested for criminal offences.[7] The conclusion we reached as a result of this comparison was that legal suspects are arrested more often for minor and serious offences, whereas undocumented suspects are apprehended more often for drug-related crime. Looking more closely (see Table 11.3), the three types of offence most frequently committed by undocumented immigrants are theft (47 per cent), drug-related offences (22 per cent) and the possession of false documents (14 per cent) (see Table 11.3). This seems to point to the fact that these groups of undocumented immigrants commit crimes in order to maintain themselves economically.

Table 11.3 Reasons for the most recent arrest for criminal offences of apprehended undocumented immigrants over the period 1989-94

Type of offence	Undocumented immigrants (%)
Traffic offences	0.8
False papers	13.8
Disorderly conduct	3.1
Non-aggravated theft	16.9
Aggravated theft	27.7
Robbery	2.3
Ill-treatment	1.5
Intimidation	3.8
Murder, manslaughter	1.5
Opium Act	22.3
Firearms Act	3.1
Other Acts/regulations	3.1
Total number	N = 130

Source: VRS (1994)

In a recent publication, Jankowski (1995: 83–4) outlined three general motives for the involvement of poor people in crime (cf. de Haan, 1993: 5–13). First, there are those who commit crimes in order to become socioeconomically mobile. Second, there are those who commit criminal acts to maintain themselves economically. Thirdly, there are those who engage in crime because they are addicted to drugs. In our opinion the first and third motives (socioeconomic mobility and addiction) seem to be less relevant with regard to undocumented immigrants.

Further questions arise as to whether (and how) different patterns of criminal involvement can be observed and whether there is any empirical evidence of differences between various categories of undocumented immigrants. The most important finding of our analysis was that the profile of arrests of undocumented immigrants differed significantly by country of origin. In the Rotterdam case, there is an over-representation of undocumented immigrants from specific countries when it comes to certain offences (such as drug-related offences by Moroccans and Algerians) and misdemeanours (for example, illegal labour in workshops by Turks). In the random survey of apprehended undocumented immigrants, the following differences may be noted (see also Table 11.4):

1. Turks and Eastern Europeans are mainly apprehended for *illegal residence and misdemeanours*;
2. Moroccans, Algerians and Eastern Europeans are arrested relatively frequently for *criminal offences* (theft, false documents);
3. Western Europeans (mainly French), Moroccans and Algerians are most frequently arrested for *drug-related crimes*.

Table 11.4   Classification of systematic sample of apprehended undocumented immigrants over the period 1989-94 by country of origin
(N = 323)

Reason for apprehension	Turkey (%)	Morocco (%)	Algeria (%)	Western Europe (%)	Eastern Europe (%)	Other countries (%)
Illegal residence	45	21	21	17	39	44
Misdemeanours	52	19	25	25	29	32
Criminal offences	0	34	29	19	32	17
Drug offences	3	26	25	29	0	6
Total	N = 29	N = 108	N = 24	N = 57	N = 28	N = 77

Source: VRS (1994)

We conclude that not every category of undocumented immigrants presents a criminal problem. Divergent patterns can indeed be found in the data on apprehended immigrants. In the case of Rotterdam, Turkish immigrants are rarely involved in (registered) criminality. Criminal problems seem to be caused mainly by undocumented Moroccans, Algerians and Western Europeans (especially by the French). If we compare these findings with the arrests of legal immigrants (see Table 11.5) we notice that both legal and illegal Moroccans have relatively high crime rates and are often arrested for drug-related crime. Legal Turks are often arrested for minor offences, undocumented Turks are never arrested for criminal offences. The latter are most frequently apprehended for misdemeanours such as illegal work. Both legal and undocumented Cape Verdeans have low crime rates, while legal Surinamese have relatively high crime rates in contrast with undocumented Surinamese. Undocumented immigrants from Algeria and Morocco are involved relatively frequently in the drug trade.

Table 11.5 Classification of arrested legal suspects (excluding traffic offenders) by country of origin (N=507)

Type of offence	Netherlands (%)	Turkey (%)	Morocco (%)	Surinam (%)	Other countries (%)
Minor offences	65	56	55	53	70
Criminal offences	33	40	35	46	29
Drug offences	2	4	10	1	1
Total	N = 271	N = 25	N = 49	N = 77	N = 97

Source: HKS (1994)

DIFFERENTIAL OPPORTUNITY STRUCTURES OF UNDOCUMENTED IMMIGRANTS

The central question raised at the beginning of this chapter was whether (and how) illegality might be associated with criminality. Are undocumented immigrants more involved in crime than others, or do they stay away from it because of their vulnerability? In addition, we were interested in different patterns of involvement, and how those patterns could be explained. After analysing samples from official records of apprehensions, we concluded that undocumented suspects were arrested less frequently for criminal offences than legal suspects. In drug-related crime, however, undocumented immigrants were more often involved. Moreover, divergent patterns of (non-)criminal activities amongst undocumented immigrants were found. We argue that the selective apprehension and expulsion policy described cannot account for the *systematic differences* between ethnic groups in the degree to which they are arrested for different offences. Our proposition is that undocumented immigrants from various countries have access to different opportunity structures which may account for divergent patterns in involvement in crime. In this section we present evidence to support this proposition by giving a general outline of the opportunity structures of Turkish, Moroccan, Algerian, Eastern European and Surinamese undocumented immigrants. This information was drawn from the 170 interviews of the 'Unknown City' project as well as from Dutch literature on (legal) ethnic groups (Gowricharn, 1993; Veenman, 1994; Vermeulen and Penninx, 1994).

Turkish undocumented immigrants, especially those who arrived before 1991 (and obtained a social security number), have relatively easy access to formal institutions, the labour market, council housing and education. Furthermore, Turkish undocumented immigrants often enjoy direct entry into the informal labour market. This is particularly true for those who work in ethnic enterprises within the catering business and the retail trade, for example coffee houses and butcher's shops (Vermeulen, 1984). Turkish undocumented immigrants can also rely on their own community, which is less divided than the Moroccan community (Bovenkerk, 1994). This community is also able to provide (legal) marriage partners (Böcker, 1994). As a consequence of their access to formal and informal institutions, Turkish immigrants do not have to engage in risky criminal activities in the Rotterdam drug economy. The other side of the coin is that undocumented immigrants are of low status within the Turkish community, which makes them vulnerable to exploitation (Staring, this volume).

Moroccan and Algerian undocumented immigrants, in contrast, have more limited access to formal institutions, especially to the wage labour market. This is not only because the unemployment rate among the settled Moroccan population is higher than among the Turkish, but also because informal employment generated by ethnic business seems to be far less available to Moroccans than to Turks (Blaschke *et al.*, 1990). Our research also confirms the findings of previous work showing that the embedding of Moroccans in their own community is problematic (Bovenkerk, 1994; Junger, 1990). The Moroccan community is a *divided* community in which discordant relations cause disruption and limit mutual solidarity and trust. Undocumented Moroccans appear to have a rather isolated social position within the community and run the risk of marginalization.

In the same way, there is no established Algerian community in Rotterdam on which Algerian immigrants can fall back in case of need and distress. Consequently, they are more prone to becoming involved in the drug economy. This drug economy – which is closely watched by the police – leads to crime and increases the likelihood that these undocumented North Africans will be arrested by the police. The undocumented status of immigrants makes them suitable for the most risky and lowest functions in the drug trade (van der Leun, 1995). Many of them have to take risks in order to survive in the Netherlands, often working as drug pushers or runners. Drug pushers do the 'dirty work' for the drug dealers; they carry the merchandise and deliver it to buyers. In the event of a police sweep it is they who get caught and not the dealer. Drug runners guide drug tourists to the retail buildings. They contact French, Belgian or German tourists on the highways and at the Central Train Station. Others walk along the main roads in the centre of the city. From our interviews with undocumented North Africans involved in the drug trade, we gathered that they often come from the larger Moroccan cities. Their migration process often contradicted the 'classic' one-stage movement. Several first went to Spain or France, and along the way became involved in the drug trade (van der Leun, 1995). Others were recruited by compatriots or attracted by the relatively liberal drug policy in the Netherlands.

Undocumented immigrants from Eastern Europe differ from the ethnic groups mentioned above. If they refrain from engaging in risky activities, they are arrested only infrequently. Some of these Eastern Europeans are rejected asylum seekers from former Yugoslavia. A number of Poles, Russians and Romanians were arrested because of illegal labour and certain offences (car theft). Most of them are in the Netherlands on a temporary basis and mainly operate from their own country. As a result of their recent arrival, they have little access to formal institutions, although some do work formally. They have limited access to the informal economy and they cannot fall back on an established community as their base is often elsewhere. On the basis of this research, little can be said about their access to criminal circles.

Surinamese undocumented immigrants scarcely appear in the records of the migration authorities. None the less, one may assume that there is also a substantial number of undocumented immigrants among the Surinamese. In research conducted by Vos *et al.* (1992) in The Hague, the Surinamese form a substantial category. The opportunity structure of the Surinamese group differs from that of the other ethnic groups. They have relatively easy access to formal and informal institutions, depending on the period in which they arrived in the Netherlands (van Niekerk, 1994). Thanks to the large Surinamese community in the Netherlands, young undocumented Surinamese often have the opportunity to obtain a legal status through marriage. For the older undocumented Surinamese, the chance of obtaining a

216   *Godfried Engbersen and Joanne van der Leun*

legal status, for example on medical grounds, is much smaller. Furthermore, they are able to profit from informal administrative practices which do not distinguish between legal and illegal immigrants from Surinam. The Rotterdam police records show that legal Surinamese are often arrested for criminal offences. This confirms recent studies which indicate that young Surinamese have higher crime rates than their Dutch counterparts with a similar socio-economic position (cf. Bovenkerk 1994).

To summarize, as a first explanation of the different criminal profiles of various immigrant groups, the differential opportunity structures perspective seems to be a promising approach. This is especially clear in the case of undocumented Turkish and Moroccan immigrants. Turkish undocumented immigrants have better access to both formal and informal institutions. They refrain from crime because they have other ways to survive. The greater involvement of Moroccans and Algerians in the drug trade seems to be linked to their limited opportunity structure. In the case of Western Europeans the relation between illegality and crime is the reverse: because of their criminal behaviour, they have acquired an illegal status. In sum, formal exclusion leads to marginalization and criminalization, especially for those groups which do not possess social capital (social networks) and do not benefit from the informal rules applied by street level bureaucrats.

THE CRIMINALIZATION OF MIGRATION

Although it is difficult to draw any firm conclusions about the effects of the current restrictionist migration policy from our research findings, it is likely that certain policy measures will influence the opportunity structure of undocumented immigrants and may generate some unintended and perverse consequences (Sciortino, 1991).[8] For example, it is likely that the implementation of the Compulsory Identification Act will lead to an increase in fraud. If identification documents are needed, then their falsification will become a lucrative business. Furthermore, the restrictive policy may lead to a marginalization of certain groups of undocumented immigrants. It is likely that many undocumented immigrants will switch from legal to illegal labour when they can no longer obtain a social security number. In other words, when undocumented immigrants are excluded from the formal labour market, they will go underground. They may look for work in the informal economy or seek refuge in criminal circles. Luciani (1993:

9) states: 'The criminalization of migration has the effect of increasing the incidence of criminals among immigrants.' This process of marginalization and criminalization of undocumented immigrants can be reinforced, as Staring (this volume) argues, by the exclusionary forces within established ethnic communities. In this chapter we have argued that it is also reinforced by the inability of the Dutch (migration) police to deal with criminal undocumented immigrants effectively.

In closing, we should like to return to the two contradictory assumptions on the relation between criminality and illegality which we presented at the beginning of this chapter. We can now argue that both of them have some relevance. The first assumption characterizes to a certain degree the period in which the legislation and the implementation of this legislation was of a symbolic nature. Undocumented immigrants were widely 'tolerated' and there was little interest in exposing the open secret of the existence of undocumented workers within the Dutch economy. The access to formal institutions was much easier for all undocumented immigrants. The second assumption might, in our view, increasingly characterize the current period in which migration policies are becoming more restrictive for undocumented immigrants.

Appendix 11.1 Apprehended undocumented immigrants by country/ region of origin, systematic sample over the period 1989–94

Country/region of origin	%	N
Turkey	8.8	29
Morocco	32.9	108
Algeria	7.3	24
Surinam	3.0	10
Cape Verde Islands	2.1	7
Spain	1.5	5
Portugal	0.3	1
Italy	0.9	3
(former) Yugoslavia	4.0	13
Greece	0.6	2
Poland	1.2	4
Great Britain	1.2	4
(West) Germany	2.4	8
India	1.5	5
Pakistan	0.6	2
Indonesia	0.3	1
France	9.1	30
China	0.9	3

Appendix 11.1   Contd.

Country/region of origin	%	N
The Gambia	0.3	1
Belgium	0.9	3
Ghana	2.1	7
(former) Czechoslovakia	0.9	3
Syria	0.3	1
Guyana	0.3	1
Ethiopia	0.3	1
Rumania	0.9	3
Russia	1.2	4
Colombia	0.6	2
Nigeria	2.1	7
Dominican Republic	0.3	1
Somalia	0.6	2
Singapore	0.3	1
Egypt	0.9	3
Togo	0.3	1
Zaire	0.6	2
Brazil	0.6	2
Tunisia	0.3	1
Finland	0.3	1
Israel	0.6	2
Liberia	0.6	2
Ecuador	0.3	1
Nicaragua	0.3	1
Lebanon	1.8	6
Cameroon	0.3	1
Burkina Faso	0.3	1
Bahamas	0.3	1
Iraq	0.3	1
Lithuania	0.3	1
unknown	1.5	5
Total	100.0	328

Source: VRS (1994)

Appendix 11.2   Ethnic groups in Rotterdam as a
percentage of the total 1995 population (N = 598, 275)

Ethnic group	% of Rotterdam's population
Dutch	60.0
Turkish	6.0
Moroccan	4.1
Cape Verdean	2.3

Appendix 11.2   Contd.

Ethnic group	% of Rotterdam's population
Surinamese	7.8
Antillean	2.0
Others	18.0

Source: Centrum voor Onderzoek and Stastiek, Rotterdam (COS) (1995) (new definitions)

NOTES

1. EU citizens have almost unlimited settlement rights in other EU states. Nevertheless, EU citizens can be 'illegal' within the EU territory if they do not fulfil certain conditions. If they commit crimes they can lose their legal residence permit and subsequently be evicted.
2. Portes and Rumbaut use this term to explain differences in the extent to which immigrants are incorporated within the receiving society. They specify three elements within this context: first the migration policy of the receiving country; second labour market factors; and third the characteristics of the ethnic communities.
3. According to Everett C. Hughes, criminal circuits and some of the above-mentioned informal institutions can be regarded as 'bastard institutions' (Hughes, 1994: 192–9). These bastard institutions form the illegal or shadow side of formal institutions (see also Peters, 1993: 175–6).
4. This finding may have significant consequences for the discussion of segregation processes and problems of domestic overcrowding in multi-cultural neighbourhoods (Burgers, 1995).
5. We took three samples from the files of the Immigration Police and the Rotterdam Municipal Police (1989–94). The first was a sample of 666 registered immigrants (76 undocumented and 590 legal immigrants), the second was a sample of 328 apprehended undocumented immigrants and the third was a sample of 639 suspects apprehended for indictable offences (16 undocumented immigrants were left out). Involvement in crime was measured in two ways. The type and seriousness of the offences were taken into account, as well as the development over time. The reasons for arrest were classified in to five categories. These were: (1) *illegal residence*, which according to the Dutch law is not a criminal offence, (2) *misdemeanours* such as fare dodging, prostitution or informal employment, which we did not classify as crime; (3) *minor offences*, for example shoplifting, theft from cars and houses and vandalism; (4) *serious offences* including violence and robbery; and finally (5) *drug-related crimes*, mostly trade in small quantities of hard drugs.

220   *Godfried Engbersen and Joanne van der Leun*

6. The apprehension of an undocumented immigrant is usually followed by
    expulsion. In practice, this is not always immediately possible. In order
    to expel someone it is necessary to prove their identity and, in some cases,
    to apply for certain documents. In general, three means of expulsion can
    be distinguished, depending on the circumstances: (a) an undocumented
    immigrant shows his or her passport (or a *'laissez passer'* document) so
    the person can be expelled 'effectively' to the home country by sea or air;
    (b) an undocumented immigrant has no relevant identification docu-
    ments. An investigation has to be started or an application has to be
    submitted for a *laissez passer*. In cases like this the return of individuals
    to their home country often entails lengthy procedures. This recurrent
    problem leads to an actual practice in which most of the unidentifiable
    immigrants are sent back to the streets through the backdoor of the
    Aliens Police Office. Police officers refer to this practice as 'sending
    away in a southerly direction'. Previously it was the custom to put
    them on a train to Belgium, but the Belgian authorities objected to this
    institutionalised practice; (c) in special circumstances expulsion is not
    possible because other measures have to be taken. The undocumented
    immigrant is sent, for example, to a detention centre or, in a minority of
    cases, to a (psychiatric) hospital.
7. In our sample of undocumented immigrants 130 people were arrested
    for criminal offences. The apprehensions of these people is comparable
    with the apprehensions of legal suspects.
8. The current policy concerning immigration in the Netherlands aims
    to exclude undocumented residents from public services, to
    prevent them from working and to intensify the national surveillance
    of immigrants. To support these objectives, a computerised registration
    system is being developed that will link all the relevant databases (of
    municipal records, social security, housing, and so on). Furthermore,
    the fines for employers who employ undocumented residents have
    become higher in recent years. Since November 1991, it has been
    impossible for an undocumented immigrant officially to obtain a social
    security number from the tax office if she or he does not have a valid
    residence permit.

REFERENCES

Aalberts, M.M.J., *Politie tussen discretie en discriminatie: operationeel vreem-
delingentoezicht in de praktijk* (Arnhem: Gouda Quint, 1990).
Aalberts, M.M.J. and N. Dijkhoff, 'Illegalen in de criminaliteit, criminelen in
de illegaliteit', *Rechtshulp*, 11 (1993) 24–8.
Beirne, P. and J. Messerschmidt, *Criminology* (Orlando: Harcourt Brace
Jovanovich, 1991).
Blaschke J., J. Boissevain, H. Grotenbreg, I. Joseph, M. Morokvasic and R.
Ward, 'European Trends in Ethnic Business', in R. Waldinger, H. Aldrich,
R. Ward *et al.* (eds), *Ethnic Entrepeneurs: Immigrant Business in Industrial
Societies* (Newbury Park: Sage, 1990).

Böcker, A., *Turkse migranten en sociale zekerheid: van onderlinge zorg naar overheidszorg* (Amsterdam: Amsterdam University Press, 1994).
Bovenkerk, F., 'Een misdadige tweede generatie immigranten?', *Jeugd en Samenlevi status of immig 487–504.*
Brown, M.K., *Working the Street: Police Discretion and the Dilemmas of Reform* (New York: Russel Sage Foundation), 1988.
Buiks, P., *Surinaamse jongeren op de Kruiskade* (Deventer: van Loghum Slaterus, 1983).
Burgers, J., *Niet thuis: De woonsituatie van illegale vreemdelingen in Rotterdam* (Utrecht: Onderzoeksschool AWSB/Research Paper 95/02, 1995).
Castles, S. and M. Miller, *The Age of Migration: International Population Movements in the Modern World* (Basingstoke: Macmillan, 1994).
Clermonts, L., *Inzicht in toezicht: De praktijk van het vreemdelingentoezicht in Amsterdam en Rotterdam* (Arnhem: Gouda Quint, 1994).
Cloward, R.A. and L.A. Ohlin, *Delinquency and Opportunity: A Theory of Delinquent Gangs* (New York: Free Press, 1965).
Cohen, A.K., *Delinquent Boys: The Culture of Gangs* (New York: Free Press, 1955).
Cornelius, W. A., P.L. Martin, and J.F. Hollifield (eds), *Controlling Immigration: A Global Perspective* (Stanford: Stanford University Press, 1994).
De Haan, W.J.M., *Beroving van voorbijgangers; Rapport van onderzoek naar straatroof in 1991 in Amsterdam en Utrecht* (Den Haag: Ministerie van Binnenlandse Zaken, 1993).
Der Spiegel, 'Leben im Untergrund Illegal in Deutschland', 49/1995 (1995).
Engbersen, G., 'The Unknown City', *Berkeley Journal of Sociology*, 40 (1996) 87–111.
Engbersen, G., J. Van der Leun and P. Willems, *Over de verwevenheid van criminaliteit en illegaliteit* (Utrecht: Onderzoekschool AWSB/Research Paper 95/03, 1995).
Espenshade, T.J., 'Unauthorized Immigration to the United States', *Annual Review of Sociology*, 21 (1995) 195–216.
Freilich M., (ed.), *The Relevance of Culture* (New York: Bergin and Garvey, 1989).
Gans, H.J., *The War against the Poor: The Underclass and Antipoverty Policy* (New York: Basic Books, 1995).
Goode, E. and N. Ben-Yehuda, *Moral Panic: The Social Construction of Deviance* (Oxford: Blackwell, 1994).
Gottfredson M.R., and T. Hirschi, *A General Theory of Crime* (Stanford: Stanford University Press, 1990).
Gowricharn R., (ed.), *Binnen de grenzen: immigratie, etniciteit en integratie in Nederland* (Utrecht: De Tijdstroom, 1993).
Groenendijk K., and A. Böcker, 'Het schatten van de onschatbaren: aantallen illegalen: beeld van een categorie of van de schatter?', *Migrantenstudies*, 11(2) (1995) 117–28.
Hagan, J. and R.D. Peterson, 'Criminal Inequality in America: Patterns and Consequences', in J. Hagan and R.D. Peterson (eds), *Crime and Inequality* (Stanford: Stanford University Press, 1995) 14–36.
Hirschi, T., *Causes of Delinquency* (Berkeley: University of California Press, 1969).

Hughes, E.C., *On Work, Race, and the Sociological Imagination*, edited and with an Introduction by Lewis Coser (Chicago: The University of Chicago Press, 1994).

Jankowski, M.S., 'Ethnography, Inequality, and Crime in the Low-income Community', in J. Hagan and R.D. Peterson (eds), *Crime and Inequality* (Stanford: Stanford University Press, 1995) 80–9.

Jongman, R.W. (ed.), *De armen van Vrouwe Justitia: Sociale Positie, criminaliteit en justitiele* (Nijmegen: Ars Aequi Libri, 1993).

Junger, M., *Delinquency and Ethnicity: An Investigation of Social Factors Relating to Delinquency among Moroccan, Turkish, Surinamese and Dutch Boys* (Deventer/Boston: Kluwer Law and Taxation Publishers, 1990).

Luciani, G., 'Migration: A Global Phenomenon Calling for Common Solutions', in G. Luciani (ed.), *Migration Policies in Europe and the United States* (Dordrecht: Kluwer Academic Publishers, 1993).

Meissner, D.M. *et al.* (eds), *International Migration Challenges in a New Era: Policy Perspectives for Europe, Japan and North America* (New York: Trilateral Commission. Triangle Paper, 44, 1993).

Merton, R.K., *Social Theory and Social Structure* (New York: The Free Press, 1957).

Miller, W.B., 'Lower Class Culture as a Generating Milieu of Gang Delinquency', *Journal of Social Issues*, 14(3) (1958) 5–19.

Morita, K. and S. Sassen, 'The New Illegal Immigration in Japan 1980–1992', *International Migration Review*, 28 (1994) 153–63.

Passel, J.S., 'Illegal Migration to the United States: The Demographic Context,' in W.A. Cornelius, P.L. Martin and J.F. Hollifield (eds), *Controlling Immigration: A Global Perspective* (Stanford: Stanford University Press, 1994) 113–18.

Peters, B., *Die Integration Moderner Gesellschaften* (Frankfurt am Main: Suhrkamp, 1993).

Portes, A. and R.G. Rumbaut, *Immigrant America* (Berkeley: University of California Press, 1990).

Sansone, L., *Schitteren in de schaduw: Overlevingsstrategie n, subcultuur en etniciteit van Creoolse jongeren uit de lagere klasse in Amsterdam 1981–1990* (Amsterdam, Het Spinhuis, 1992).

Sassen, S., *The Mobility of Labour and Capital: A Study in International Investment and Labour* (New York: Cambridge University Press, 1988).

Sassen, S., 'Labour Mobility and Migration Policy: Lessons from Japan and the US', in B. Unger and F. van Waarden (eds), *Convergence or Diversity? Internalization and Economic Policy Response* (Aldershot: Avebury, 1995) 108–32.

Sciortino, G., 'Immigration into Europe and Public Policy: Do Stops Really Work?', *New Community*, 18(1) (1991) 89–99.

Staring, R., ' "Scenes from a Fake Marriage": Some Notes on the Flip-side of Embeddedness', chapter 12, this volume.

van der Leun, J.P., *Patronen van illegaliteit en criminaliteit* (Utrecht: Department of General Social Sciences, 1995).

van Niekerk, M., 'Zorg en hoop. Surinamers in Nederland nu', in H. Vermeulen H. and R. Penninx (eds), *Het democratisch ongeduld; De emancipa-*

tie van zes doelgroepen in het minderhedenbeleid (Amsterdam, Het Spinhuis 1994) 45–80.

Veenman, J., *Participatie in Perspectief. Ontwikkelingen in de Sociaal-Economische Positie van Zes Allochtone Groepen in Nederland* (Houten/Zaventem/ Lelystad: Bohn Stafleu Van Loghum/ Koninklijke Vermande, 1994).

Vermeulen, H., *Etnische groepen en grenzen; Surinamers, Chinezen en Turken* (Weesp Het Wereldvenster, 1984).

Vermeulen H., and R. Penninx (eds), *Het democratisch ongeduld, de emancipatie van zes doelgroepen in het minderhedenbeleid* (Amsterdam, Het Spinhuis, 1994).

Vos, J., J. den Heeten and S. Santokhi, *Eens komt de dag... Een onderzoek naar leven, wonen en werken van Haagse* (Den Haag: Gemeentelijke Sociale Dienst, 1992).

Werdmölder, H., *Een generatie op drift* (Arnhem: Gouda Quint, 1990).

Zolberg, A., 'Are the Industrial Countries under Siege?', in G. Luciani (ed.), *Migration Policies in Europe and the United States* (Dordrecht: Kluwer Academic Publishers, 1993).

12 'Scenes from a Fake Marriage': Notes on the Flip-side of Embeddedness

Richard Staring

For what are we
Without hope in our hearts
That someday we'll drink from God's blessed waters

And eat the fruit from the vine
I know love and fortune will be mine
Somewhere across the border
(Bruce Springsteen, *Across the Border*, 1996)

INTRODUCTION

Just before April Fool's Day 1994, a rumour circulated amongst the Turkish community in the city of Amsterdam that undocumented migrants[1] with a job could apply for a residence permit. Approximately 1000 undocumented Turkish immigrants presented themselves at the Aliens Police office in the belief that they could acquire legal status in the Netherlands for 1000 guilders (approximately $581 or £373). It transpired that a permit to stay could not in fact be bought (*de Volkskrant*, 1 April 1994).

Incidents such as this point, rather poignantly, to the presence of undocumented migrants living and working in the Dutch welfare state.[2] They also draw our attention to the desire of large numbers of these undocumented migrants to legalize their stay in the Netherlands. The issue of Turkish undocumented migrants and their efforts to legalize themselves are the subjects of this chapter.[3]

Some social scientists have labelled the twentieth century 'the age of migration'. Others predict that international migration will be among the most important issues that governments will have to deal with in the

224

short term. In this respect, certain categories of migrants, such as refugees, asylum seekers and undocumented migrants are centre-stage. Although it is difficult to determine the exact number of undocumented migrants living in different 'developed' countries,[4] it is argued that the presence of these migrants is becoming more prominent (Miller, 1995). In most Western European countries the arrival of new immigrants is increasingly perceived as a threat to the welfare state. In response, most of these receiving countries have adopted similar, restrictive migration regimes (Burgers and Engbersen, 1995; Cornelius *et al.*, 1994). Although it is difficult to measure the success of these policies, it is clear that they have neither halted 'illegal' entry nor eliminated the presence of undocumented migrants in the receiving countries. These restrictive policies have, however, had certain effects on the socio-economic position of undocumented migrants in the Netherlands.

In this chapter I explore some of the consequences of these restrictive policies for undocumented migrants in their often laborious efforts to legalize themselves. I formulate an answer to the question of how undocumented migrants try to legalize themselves and in particular how the strategies they adopt relate to or are influenced by members of their ethnic communities. I thus begin in the following section with a short elaboration of network approaches. Undocumented migrants who want to legalize their status in the Netherlands are faced with only two possible strategies. They can either apply for a residence permit on the basis of their employment history or become a Dutch citizen by marrying a Dutch national. Both options are discussed in the third section of this chapter, although the remainder focuses largely on the marriage strategy. To illustrate the use of this strategy, I present in the fourth section of the chapter a case study of Erol,[5] one of the undocumented migrants I encountered during my research,[6] who tried to change his undocumented status by marrying a Dutch woman. In the fifth section I discuss some further implications of Erol's case, the restrictive migration regime and the role of Turkish communities. The chapter finishes with a brief discussion of what I term here the 'flip-side of embeddedness'.

INTERNATIONAL MIGRATION AND PERSONAL NETWORKS

The relevance of personal networks in the field of international migration has become widely accepted. Boyd, for instance, emphasizes the importance of family and personal networks in shaping migration outcomes and as 'conduits of information and social assistance' (1989: 639). Portes and Rumbaut (1990) define personal networks as an important link between sending and receiving countries through which the migration stream can continue, even after restrictive measures have been taken. Within the context of undocumented migration, personal networks seem even more relevant. Yücel writes that for undocumented migrants there is almost 'no severance of social relations as all the stages of migration, from taking the decision to migrate to finding a job abroad, are performed within the actor's social network' (1987: 124). The importance of personal networks is also undeniable in the process of settlement in the host country. According to Boyd (1989) these networks provide food, shelter, job information and contacts, information on health care and social services, recreation and emotional support.

It is striking that most of the above-mentioned studies emphasize the positive aspects of these personal networks in facilitating migration and rendering assistance in a variety of ways. They convey the image that merely belonging to a migrant network is enough to overcome all the difficulties one could possibly face. But this perspective overlooks those undocumented migrants who are not so well embedded in their community and those who are part of less supportive networks. How do such migrants cope with their problems in a new and strange environment? Portes and Sensenbrenner (1993) have developed some interesting concepts that could shed some light on such questions. In their search for mechanisms through which social structures affect economic behaviour, these authors introduced the concepts of 'bounded solidarity' and 'enforceable trust'. Bounded solidarity originates from the 'situational reaction of a class of people faced with common adversities' which can lead to internal solidarity and mutual support. Enforceable trust, on the other hand, can be seen as a source of social capital whereby individuals behave in certain predictable ways by anticipating and expecting rewards and sanctions linked to their group membership (Portes and Sensenbrenner, 1993: 1327–44).

Although both forms of social capital are linked to membership of an (ethnic) group, neither is a constant and omnipresent element within those communities as is suggested by a network approach. Instead, both are situational and have to be activated. In the context of the Dutch government' increasingly restrictive approach to immigration, undocumented labour and residence, it might be expected that the solidarity within ethnic communities would be strengthened and that undocumented migrants could profit from this situation. This scenario, however, corresponds only partly with what I observed during my fieldwork among undocumented Turkish migrants in Rotterdam. In addition to the solidarity displayed and help offered to these migrants, many were also confronted with distrust, disloyalty and deceit by members of their own community. This is what I term 'the flip-side of embeddedness'. Before going on to describe this phenomenon, I shall first discuss the two main paths to legalization open to undocumented migrants.

UNDOCUMENTED MIGRANTS AND FORMAL OPPORTUNITIES FOR LEGALIZATION

As stated above, undocumented migrants who want to legalize their stay in the Netherlands have only two options. The first is by means of the migrant's employment history and the second is by marriage to a Dutch citizen. Both routes to a legalized stay in the Netherlands are discussed here.

Since 1991, it has been possible to apply for a residence permit by referring to one's employment history. Although this route to legalization was not regulated formally by law, undocumented migrants have been able to use it successfully. Recently, after questions asked by the Judiciary Authority on Government Affairs, the Dutch Ministry of Justice tried to implement this informal rule by putting into writing several objective, verifiable standards. According to these standards, undocumented migrants who have worked for at least six years in the Netherlands, paying all their social security contributions and income taxes, can legitimately claim a residence permit.

The following three criteria for legalization have thus been established: first, a verifiable, uninterrupted stay in the Netherlands of at least six years; second, income from a formal job or benefit for which contributions have been paid over a minimum period of six years; and third, no contraindications, for example the possession of false papers, deportation, the giving of false information, or criminal antecedents. In addition, the applicant's ties with Dutch society in comparison to those with their country of origin are taken into consideration.

In the debate that followed the setting of these standards, the potential number of undocumented migrants who could apply for legalization through this regulation played an important role.

Schmitz, the State Secretary of Justice, repeatedly emphasized the relatively small number of 'illegal aliens' who would be eligible to apply, whereas opponents pointed out the possible attraction to other migrants. Examining the standards as described by Schmitz, one can hardly imagine this law giving rise to a massive regularization of undocumented migrants.

Several other recently implemented restrictive laws support this interpretation. For instance, before November 1991 everyone – undocumented migrants included – could acquire the social security number necessary for obtaining a formal job simply by registering as a resident of a city. After that date the issuing of a social security number was made conditional on the possession of a residence permit. This made it almost impossible for undocumented migrants to apply for a legal job in the usual way. At the same time the Dutch government introduced more restrictions on illegal work. Employers, for instance, can now be penalized for hiring undocumented workers. In this context, the introduction of the Compulsory Identification Act in June 1994 can also be seen as an instrument to prevent illegal labour, by directly limiting the opportunities of undocumented workers to work in the formal sector (Burgers and Engbersen, 1995). Consequently, the number of undocumented migrants who can apply for a residence permit by way of their employment history will fall.

The second option for obtaining a residence permit, still available to undocumented migrants, is marriage to a Dutch citizen. As a result of the introduction of new laws, the current situation is in many ways different from the period in which this research was conducted. During 1994 a new law concerning marriages of convenience was implemented, with the primary goal of preventing such marriages. In brief, this law gives the registrar the authority to refuse to conduct a marriage in certain circumstances, such as a lack of verbal communication between the prospective spouses (cf. *Migrantenrecht*, 1994).[7]

In summary, the number of undocumented migrants who can make use of the employment history regulation is set to decrease. For those undocumented migrants who have settled in the Netherlands after November 1991, this chance is still more remote because of the impossibility of obtaining a social security number in a legal manner. As an important consequence of these restrictive measures, undocumented migrants are increasingly excluded from formal job opportunities outside their ethnic community. A similar story can be told about the chances of undocumented migrants on the marriage market. Some Dutch researchers have described marriage as 'the easiest way of getting hold of a residence permit' (Vos *et al.*, 1992: 8). In the next section I present a detailed picture of the attempt of one of my respondents to enter such a marriage.

EROL AND HIS 'CONTRACT MARRIAGE'

I became acquainted with Erol in the tea-room where he worked as a waiter. While interviewing Ali (another of my respondents) Erol brought us our tea. After he had left the room Ali whispered, 'He is also a tourist'.[8] At that time Erol had been living for approximately one year at his sister's house in the city of Rotterdam. His sister, Ünzüle, had been widowed after a holiday in Turkey in which her husband and one of their two children were killed in a car crash. After spending several weeks with her family in Turkey, Ünzüle returned to the Netherlands where she suffered from acute mental problems. She visited the RIAGG[9] and a psychologist advised her to invite a family member from Turkey to support her during this difficult period.

As a result, Erol came to Rotterdam. Every three months he was issued with a temporary residence permit by the Aliens Police who retained his passport. Erol was a bookkeeper by profession and graduated from high school in Turkey. He is the eldest child in his family and is legally divorced from his wife, who now also lives in Rotterdam. After a year the Aliens Police discontinued his residence permit and told Erol to return to Turkey. According to the psychologist at the RIAGG Ünzüle would overcome her problems and would probably be able to remarry soon. At his sister's request Erol decided to stay on illegally in Rotterdam, although he knew that the Dutch government officially prohibits this.

In the meantime the Aliens Police, who still held Erol's passport, did not take any further action. Erol was anxious to stay in the Netherlands and wanted to take care of his sister. In addition to this, he is eager to learn the Dutch language so that he could apply for a job in the Netherlands. To achieve all this, Erol wanted to legalize his stay. According to Erol, the only way to fulfil this goal was to marry a Dutch citizen. Erol foresaw many difficulties in marrying a Turkish woman. First of all, he has a daughter from his previous marriage, who is being cared for by his parents in Turkey. His status as a divorced man and his age made him an unattractive partner within the Turkish community. Secondly, Erol was keenly aware of the distrust that exists among legal Turkish migrants which makes them reluctant to allow their daughters to marry undocumented compatriots. These parents fear – not always unjustly – that the suitor is motivated only by the prospect of a residence permit. Erol and Ünzüle were furthermore unacquainted with marriageable women from their home town, Samsun. In spite of several efforts, they had not succeeded in finding a suitable Turkish bride for Erol.

At this stage, Erol decided to try to find a woman willing to enter into a marriage of convenience, or in his terms a 'contract marriage'. He asked me whether I knew any suitable women, but I had to disappoint him. Erol's neighbours then introduced him to Selahattin, who promised him assistance in finding a willing parter outside the Turkish community. Erol and Selahattin did not arrange a fixed price in advance, but Erol thought 1000 guilders (approximately $581 or £373) at most would be paid for Selahattin's services.

A couple of weeks later, when I arrived at Erol's workplace, he seemed to be very excited and wanted to talk to me outside, where he told me the good news: Selahattin had introduced him to a relative of one of his colleagues who was willing to marry Erol for money. He did not want to tell me this inside because of the rumours which could flow from the news that he had found a woman for a 'contract marriage'. Erol did not know the woman's name at this point, and even later, after they had met several times, he kept forgetting it. He had, however, written down her telephone number in his address book.

Erol portrayed the woman as being of Surinamese origin and around 26 years of age. She was willing to marry Erol for the sum of 10,000 guilders (around $5810 or £3730). Erol had acquired scant fluency in Dutch and so it was difficult to imagine any verbal communication between them. They communicated through Selahattin, the marriage broker; Erol's sister also acted as an intermediary. Ünzüle could get by in Dutch, but did not speak the language fluently and furthermore thought that the Surinamese 'speak Dutch strangely and inaudibly'.

Erol knew scarcely anything about his future spouse, found it hard to think of her as trustworthy and at the same time did not understand her motives. Initially she demanded the money in advance, but Erol refused. After conferring with Selahattin he proposed paying the first instalment after the wedding ceremony and the rest at a later date. They contacted each other several times by telephone in an attempt to make an appointment, but most of these appointments were cancelled.

By this time, I had become acquainted with Erol's future spouse. Her name was Cindy and she was not from Surinam but from Aruba, in the Antilles. Erol still found it difficult to remember her first name. He made another appointment with her at the Legal Advice Centre and asked me to be there too. The meeting with Cindy was to take place at the nearby subway station at 10 o'clock in the morning after which an appointment had been made with a staff member at the Advice Centre. Erol, Ünzüle and I arrive at about the same time, but there was no sign of Cindy. At 10.30 Ünzüle decided to telephone Cindy at home but nobody answered. We decided to wait a little longer, but the subway station was crowded with inspectors whom Ünzüle mistook for police officers. After waiting for an hour and a half, by which time there was still no sign of Cindy, we decided to leave.

A couple of days later I received another 'phone call from a troubled Erol. Cindy had hinted that she wanted to call off the marriage. Erol asked me to go with him and Selahattin to Cindy's home in a nearby village to sort out the problems. Selahattin, who works as a driver for the sanitation department, has lived in the Netherlands for ten years and possesses both Dutch and Turkish nationality. But despite his lengthy stay in the Netherlands his Dutch is still poor. During the drive to Cindy's home however, Selahattin blamed Erol for not speaking Dutch. Since I speak Turkish as well as Dutch, Selahattin urged me to put pressure on Cindy's sister and brother-in-law to help – in exchange for money – bring about the marriage. He also wanted me to point out to Cindy that she, in order to make the marriage more genuine to the Aliens Police, should adopt a more positive attitude.

The meeting with Cindy was supposed to take place at the home of Cindy's elder sister. When we arrived, Cindy's sister, her two young children and a colleague of Selahattin were present, but not Cindy. Cindy's sister offered to look for her and Selahattin told Erol to give her some money, which he did, taking a 25 guilder (about $14.50 or £9.33) note from his wallet. Selahattin's associate told me that Erol should learn some Dutch to satisfy the Aliens Police. In his opinion, they would never agree to the marriage if Erol and Cindy could not communicate with one another. While I talked with him, Erol sat nervously on the sofa, unable to understand anything of the conversation. He had begun to think that Cindy has changed her mind about the marriage, saying in Turkish, 'I don't have a chance, I don't have a shadow of a chance, she refuses doesn't she?' Eventually Cindy was found, but she had no time for the meeting and yet another appointment was made.

Over the following two weeks, several appointments were made and broken, each producing the same sense of disappointment for Erol. After not hearing anything from Erol for a couple of days, I received a call from Erol in Istanbul. He told me the story of his dramatic arrest by the Aliens Police at his sister's home, after which the police had deported him. Erol suspected that his former parents-in-law had seen his presence in Rotterdam as a threat to his ex-wife, and had reported him. According to Erol they had known of his 'contract marriage' and had informed the Aliens Police. At the time of writing Erol is living in Turkey with his daughter.

EMBEDDEDNESS: SOLIDARITY, DEPENDENCY AND DISTRUST

Erol's case-history illuminates some general problems which undocumented migrants have to cope with in their legalization efforts. First, it illustrates the complexity of organizing a marriage of convenience. Even disregarding the formal rules as outlined above, such an attempt can be described as a real *tour de force* for the people involved. In his efforts to find a bride within his own community, Erol received only limited support from his legal compatriots. In his search outside the community, he was totally dependent on the help of a member of that same Turkish community.

Second, Erol's experience is a good example of the dependent position in which most 'tourists' find themselves. This dependence, particularly on legal compatriots, is not unique to Erol but characteristic of most undocumented migrants, who are often invited to Europe by family or friends or have persuaded these relatives to help them. Many undocumented migrants, like Erol, enter Holland on a tourist visa, thus becoming 'illegal' residents only after some months. Migrants' relatives or friends usually look after their guests for an initial period. Unemployed 'tourists' are also financially dependent on their legal compatriots. Ill or uninsured 'tourists' have to rely on sympathetic GPs or the loyalty of their family or friends who put up their 'medical insurance card'. This dependency on legal members of the Turkish communities is sustained and reinforced by the lack of fluency in the Dutch language, which characterizes most 'tourists'.

Third, this dependency also expresses itself in the domain of labour. As we have seen, 'tourists' are increasingly thrown back on the assistance of their legal compatriots in their search for paid work. As a result of more restrictive policies regarding illegal labour, formal jobs are becoming scarcer. Informal employment opportunities available within the ethnic group are therefore becoming more important for these undocumented migrants. As many ethnic entrepreneurs prefer employees from within their own ethnic group (cf. Waldinger 1986), the rising ethnic entrepreneurial activity among Turkish migrants is important for 'tourists'. As vacant places are scarce, however not everyone manages – as Erol did – to find a job within the community.

> When we came, we thought that we would work here for a couple of years and then return. It's been two years now and I haven't found work. We get depressed. The problems increase, and you think of committing suicide. In the Netherlands there are human rights, according to the media, the television, everybody. But it is all fake.
>
> (Salim, a married 'tourist')

Eventually, six months after our conversation, Salim returned, disenchanted, to his home village in Turkey. About half of the respondents in my research are married and have children. The households, of 'tourists', which almost always remain in Turkey, are often dependent on the remittances made by the 'tourists'. Unemployment, therefore, not only threatens the position of the undocumented migrants in the Netherlands, but can also have far-reaching consequences for the families left behind (cf. Böcker, 1994: 80–1).

Erol's case is also a good example of the flip-side of embeddedness since he ultimately seems to have been betrayed by his former parents-in-law (cf. Clermonts, 1994). A similar example is presented by Riza, an older married 'tourist' who has spent more than ten years in various European countries. Riza managed to get a formal job in a small factory owned by a Dutchman. Owing to his intervention three other Turkish migrants also obtained jobs there. During our conversations Lütfi was on sickness benefit, because his employer had dismissed him. The tragedy of this example lies in the fact that one of the 'işçi' whom Riza had helped in this way caused his dismissal by telling his employer of Riza's undocumented status, thus creating a vacant position for his brother-in-law. Owing to their vulnerable legal position, and the restricted availability of opportunities outside their ethnic group, 'tourists' increasingly have no choice but to comply with rules set by their legal compatriots. This means that they often have to accept badly paid and dirty jobs and that they have to tolerate discrimination from compatriots. In doing so, however, they still run the risk of being caught or betrayed by members of their own community.

For Erol life would have been more bearable if he had succeeded in finding a marriageable Turkish woman. Intra-ethnic marriages however confront 'tourists' with their own specific set of problems. One of the main obstacles 'tourists' have to surmount is the distrust they face when marrying a woman from their own ethnic community (cf. Böcker, 1994; Everaert and Lamur, 1993; Rişvanoğlu-Bilgin, 1987; Yerden, 1995). 'Tourists' can, however, conquer this distrust in at least three different ways.

The first option is to disseminate information, as this kind of distrust is largely the result of the 'tourist' being a stranger. If there is some degree of acquaintance with the 'tourist' this distrust can be overcome. If the daughter's parents do not know the 'tourist' involved, relatives of the 'tourist' can supply them with information. For Erol this was a true disadvantage, since only his younger sister lived nearby and all his other relatives who could have supported him were far away in Turkey.

Yet success is not always guaranteed even when a 'tourist' has relatives within immediate reach. Kadir, who had lived 'illegally' for nearly two years in Rotterdam at the home of his elder, married brother, wanted to marry a Turkish girl. When I met him, things had evidently gone wrong.

Richard: Where have you been?
Kadir: We went asking for this girl, to make an offer of marriage...
Richard: Yes, and your family went with you?
Kadir: No, my family didn't come, my brother's father-in-law went. They [the girl's parents] had to find out certain things about me, they had to ask my family questions. He [his brother's father-in-law] said 'he is of no use'. He spoke negatively about me. That's why they didn't give the girl [he curses].

During our conversation Kadir showed me his arms which he had mutilated with a knife out of sheer frustration. His dream of a stable future in the Netherlands had been shattered by a non-cooperative relative. Two months after this I received a photograph showing Kadir in combat-gear, fighting in the war against the Kurds in eastern

Turkey. Personal dramas such as this in which disloyal compatriots play a leading role are for 'tourists' like Kadir an important reason for returning to Turkey.

A second possible way for 'tourists' to deal with distrust can be characterized as an informal insurance policy. Some 'tourists' mention the fact that Turkish parents ask an unusually high bride price in the case of marriage to an undocumented migrant.

They [legal Turks] feel themselves superior to us. They don't trust us, they think that we will abandon the girl. You know that in Islam virginity is very important. If you marry a girl, she has to stay with you. If you marry for a second time, you will be disparaged within the community. To maintain the marriage, they want money. To keep everything under control.... Just for safety.

According to this 'tourist', the extra costs that accompany a marriage for undocumented migrants can be as much as 10,000 guilders (the equivalent of some \$5810 or £3730). 'Tourists' who are able to pay this extra amount of money can overcome the distrust of legal Turkish migrants. For most undocumented migrants however this is not a viable option.

A third, culturally acceptable way of circumventing the distrust of 'işçi' is by abducting a woman. Traditionally this is an opportunity for a man to force a marriage by running off with a woman either with or without her consent. By carrying off a woman, the abductor threatens the honour of her family and the only way to 'repair' this honour is for them to grant permission for the marriage (Gailly, 1983: 147). Some Turkish parents thus fear the abduction of their daughters by 'tourists' hoping to force a marriage (cf. Böcker, 1992: 75; Yerden, 1995: 9). Only one 'tourist' I spoke with had eloped with a Turkish girl. This abduction finally resulted in a religious marriage. A marriage by abduction implies a certain degree of consensus in cultural norms. A number of social scientists however have observed a slow and gradual change of these traditional values in favour of more Western ideas among established Turkish migrants (cf. Yerden, 1995). One wonders how much longer a marriage by abduction will be tolerated by Turkish migrants in the future.

Several different strategies among undocumented migrants in coping with this persistent dependency on their legal compatriots can be identified. Clearly, the most successful way for undocumented migrants to reduce their dependence on other, legal migrants is to exchange their illegal status for a legal one, as Erol tried to do, thereby depriving their compatriots of their main source of power over them. Financial freedom generated through jobs, preferably from outside their community, also adds to a feeling of independence.

Among other strategies of coping with this dependent and subordinate position is the adoption by 'tourists' of a superior attitude towards their legal compatriots. Employed 'tourists' are especially likely to adopt this strategy.

> ... only *'tourists'* work here. Those who possess a valid residence permit, they just lie down. The coffee shops are packed. Only we *'tourists'* really work for the Dutch economy.

> The 'işçi' play the fool with us because of our illegal status. But if you are in possession of a residence permit, you've got to work. That is better than doing nothing. I see a lot of 'işçi' the whole day long they sit here or in another coffee shop. They play games and throw away their time.

Undocumented migrants with a (steady) job, develop a desire to stay legally in the Netherlands and feel they have earned their residence permit (cf. Chávez, 1994). By blaming and stereotyping the Turkish 'işçi' who supposedly are not willing to do their often dirty and badly paid work, 'tourists' try to cope with their inferior position. Refusing to mix with established Turkish migrants, for instance in attending special social occasions such as weddings or circumcisions, is another way of dealing with dependency. Participating in these gatherings without meeting the (financial) expectations of the hosts increases a sense of dependency and some 'tourists' therefore withdraw from these social gatherings.

Finally, another tactic used can be captured by the term secrecy. Some 'tourists' try to conceal their undocumented status by lying about it to their compatriots whenever necessary. A good example here is Erdal with whom I made an appointment for an interview, but who at the agreed time did not show up. When I met him a couple of days later, he explained that he otherwise would have disclosed his undocumented status in front of a large Turkish audience:

> *Erdal*: The worst here, is to be 'illegal', it's the worst.
> *Richard*: Why?
> *Erdal*: Because they [legal Turkish migrants] don't speak with you, they treat you as a totally different person. Nobody says anything to you. In my case, for example, nobody knows that I'm a 'tourist'.... Because you are a 'tourist', they don't treat you with any respect.... Here, even dogs are worth more than 'tourists'.

The negative implications of this largely one-sided dependency do not have the same impact on all undocumented migrants. The impacts vary, for instance, with the migrant's perspective on the future. Those 'tourists' who see themselves as short-term migrants often develop a kind of indifference or immunity against their inferior treatment. The temporary nature of their stay thus makes it possible for them to endure the sometimes difficult circumstances.

DISCUSSION

I began this chapter with the question of how undocumented migrants try to legalize themselves, and ended it by pointing to the ambiguous position in which 'tourists' find themselves. Within the Turkish community these 'tourists' are not only hard-working and motivated employees but often they are brothers, family members, friends, neighbours, and always compatriots. Sometimes the distinction between legal and undocumented is blurred as some 'tourists' have lived for more than a decade in the Netherlands. By focusing on the legalization options of undocumented migrants, the constructed nature of the concept of 'illegal migrant' becomes evident. Migrants, as the case of Erol illustrated, can travel from a legal to an 'illegal' status, and vice versa. Seen in this way, undocumented migrants truly are products of restrictive migration policies (cf. Cohen, 1995: 5).

Most of the undocumented migrants I encountered are well embedded in their ethnic communities and 'enjoy' some of the advantages that go with this group membership. Within this community and with the support of relatives and friends, these migrants experience (emotional) support and can find a place to live and work. It is striking that, whereas undocumented migrants from other countries make use of charities or agencies such as the Salvation Army, Turkish 'tourists' largely do not. This observation illustrates the basic solidarity displayed within the Turkish community. This solidarity has little to do with the 'bounded solidarity' I described earlier in this chapter, but comes closer to what has been described by Portes and Sensenbrenner as 'value introjection'. According to the definition used by these authors, individuals are expected to behave in certain predictable ways, directed by internalized, consensually established beliefs (Portes and Sensenbrenner, 1993: 1323–6).

These norms, however, are not fixed, and many migrants do not subscribe to them in the same way that they did in their home country.

During their stay in the Netherlands, Turkish migrants change their attitudes (cf. Böcker, 1994) and although 'tourists' expect a kind of 'old-fashioned' solidarity from Turkish migrants this expectation is not always met. In this chapter I have described the flip-side of embeddedness. As the social lives of 'tourists' revolve around their compatriots, they are confronted with a community in which they occupy an inferior position and which 'keeps them in their place'. A new package of restrictive measures introduced by the Dutch government has served to increase the dependent position of 'tourists'. As a result of the new legislation, 'tourists' increasingly have to focus on opportunities that are offered within their communities, which in turn heightens their dependent and subordinate positions within the community. As Böcker (1994) observes, Turkish migrants often feel overstretched by their relatives and friends in Turkey, and the same observation could be made about their relationship with 'tourists'. Just as Turkish migrants manage to deal with those left behind in Turkey, they also adopt strategies in dealing with 'tourists'. As I have shown, this can result in solidarity and assistance, but also in deceit, disloyalty and betrayal. This leads to the conclusion that ethnic communities not only support and encourage migration but are also capable of deterring or preventing migration. Although I have identified several strategies through which undocumented migrants cope with their dependent position, many such migrants return home due to the lack of opportunities available to them and a disloyal community.

John Steinbeck once wrote, 'Okie use'ta mean you was from Oklahoma. Now it means you're a dirty son-of-a-bitch. Okie means you're scum. Don't mean nothing itself, it's the way they say it' (Steinbeck, 1939: 239). Like 'Okies', the term 'tourist' has a specific connotation within the Turkish community. As one of my respondents told me, he often feels like a 'third-class citizen without any rights'. Many 'tourists' seem to be trapped within their ethnic group in an unfamiliar country, unable to find the fortunes they had imagined across the border.

NOTES

1.   Several different terms are used to denote those migrants who reside in a country without a valid residence permit. In this chapter I use the

term undocumented migrant, and the emic term 'tourist' interchangeably. I also use on occasion the term 'illegal migrant'.

2. Most 'developed' countries, as well as 'developing' countries in Africa, Asia and South America are confronted with the presence of undocumented migrants (Lohrmann, 1987).

3. I should like to thank N. Van Bemmel, L. Brunt, K. Groenendijk, D. Kalb, J. Kehla, S. Kingma, R. Kloosterman, G. Kroese, T. Müller and D. Van der Ree for their comments on earlier versions of this chapter.

4. For a critical discussion of the various estimations of undocumented migrants, see the recent contributions of Böcker and Groenendijk (1996), Burgers (1996) and Groenendijk and Böcker (1995).

5. In order to protect the anonymity of my informants, I use pseudonyms throughout this chapter.

6. Trained as an anthropologist, I conducted fieldwork among Turkish migrants in several different neighbourhoods in Rotterdam between winter 1993 and summer 1995. During this period I interviewed and subsequently maintained contact with 43 Turkish undocumented migrants, most of them male adolescents. My research is part of a larger research project, 'The Unknown City'. The contribution of Engbersen and van der Leun (this volume) also draws on work which forms part of this project.

7. Another obstacle for undocumented migrants was the introduction of the requirement of 'Authorization of Temporary Residence' . This law was implemented in April 1994 and retracted nearly a year later (*Migrantenrecht*, 1995). During this period every foreigner who wanted to marry a citizen of the Netherlands first had to return to his/her country of origin and apply there for an 'Authorization of Temporary Residence'.

8. Within the Turkish community the word 'tourist' is the common term used for undocumented migrants, whereas 'işçi', literally meaning 'worker', refers to Turkish migrants who reside legally in the Netherlands. (cf. Böcker, 1992; IOT, 1993).

9. The regional institute of mental welfare.

REFERENCES

Ahmad, A., 'Enkele aspecten van het MVV-beleid nader belicht', *Migrantenrecht*, 8 (1994) 151–3.

Böcker, A., 'Gevestigde migranten als bruggehoofden en grenswachters: kettingmigratie over juridisch gesloten grenzen', *Migrantenstudies*, 8 (1992) 61–78.

Böcker, A., *Turkse migranten en sociale zekerheid: van onderlinge zorg naar overheidszorg?* (Amsterdam: Amsterdam University Press, 1994).

Böcker. A, and K. Groenendijk, 'Vuile handen en verbrande vingers?', *Migrantenstudies*, 12 (1996) 27–32.

Boyd, M., 'Family and Personal Networks in International Migration: Recent Developments and New Agendas', *International Migration Review*, 23 (1989) 638–71.

Burgers, J., *Niet thuis. De woonsituatie van illegale vreemdelingen in Rotterdam* (Utrecht: Onderzoekschool AWSB, 1995).

Burgers, J., 'Natte vingers en vuile handen. Over het schatten van het aantal illegale vreemdelingen. Een reactie op Böcker en Groenendijk', *Migranten-studies*, 12 (1996) 14–26.

Burgers J., and G. Engbersen, 'Mondialisering, migratie en illegale vreemdelingen', *Amsterdams Sociologisch Tijdschrift* (Groningen: Wolters Noordhoff, 1995), 225–50.

Chávez, L., 'The Power of the Imagined Community: The Settlement of Undocumented Mexicans and Central Americans in the United States', *American Anthropologist*, 96 (1994) 52–73.

Clermonts, L., *Inzicht in toezicht. De praktijk van het vreemdelingentoezicht in Amsterdam en Rotterdam* (Antwerpen: Kluwer rechtswetenschappen, 1994).

Cohen, R., 'Prologue', in R. Cohen (ed.), *The Cambridge Survey of World Migration* (Cambridge: Cambridge University Press, 1995) 1–9.

Cornelius, W., P. Martin and J. Hollifield (eds), *Controlling Immigration: A Global Perspective* (Stanford: Stanford University Press, 1994).

Everaert, H. and H. Lamur, *Alles wat geheim is, is lekker: seksuele relaties en beschermingsgedrag van Turkse mannen* (Amsterdam: Het Spinhuis, 1993).

Gailly, A., *Een dorp in Turkije* (Brussels: Cultuur en Migratie, 1983).

Gölpinar, O., 'Duizendtal Turken wacht uren tevergeefs op verblijfsvergunning', *de Volkskrant*, (1 April 1994).

Groenendijk K., and A. Böcker, 'Het schatten van de onschatbaren. Aantal illegalen, beeld van een categorie of van de schatter?', *Migrantenstudies*, 11 (1995) 117–28.

Inspraakorgaan Turken in Nederland (IOT), *Illegalen in het overheidsbeleid. Een ongevraagd advies aan de Nederlandse regering* ('s Gravenhage: IOT, 1993).

Lohrmann, R., 'Irregular Migration: A Rising Issue in Developing Countries', *International Migration*, 25 (1987) 253–65.

Migrantenrecht, various issues, 1994.

Migrantenrecht, various issues, 1995.

Miller, M., 'Illegal Migration', in R. Cohen (ed.), *The Cambridge Survey of World Migration* (Cambridge: Cambridge University Press, 1995), 537–40.

Portes, A. and R. Rumbaut, *Immigrant America: A Portrait* (Berkeley: University of California Press, 1990).

Portes, A. and J. Sensenbrenner, 'Embeddedness and Immigration: Notes on the Social Determinants of Economic Action', *American Journal of Sociology*, 98 (1993) 1320–51.

Rişvanoğlu-Bilgin, S., L. Brouwer and M. Priester, *Verschillend als de vingers van een hand. Een onderzoek naar het integratieproces van Turkse gezinnen in Nederland* (Leiden: COMT, 1986).

Steinbeck, J. *Grapes of Wrath* (London: Mandarin Books, 1939).

Vos, J., J. den Heeten and S. Santokhi, *'Eens komt de dag . . .' Een onderzoek naar het leven, wonen en werken van Haagse illegalen* (Den Haag: Gemeentelijke Sociale Dienst, 1992).

Waldinger, R., *Through the Eye of the Needle: Immigrants and Enterprise in New York's Garment Trades* (New York: New York University Press, 1986).

Yerden, I., *Trouwen op z'n Turks. Huwelijksprocedures bij Turkse jongeren in Nederland en hun strijd om meer inspraak* (Utrecht: Jan van Arkel, 1995).

Yücel, A., 'Turkish Migrant Workers in the Federal Republic of Germany: A Case Study', *Migrants in Europe: The Role of Family, Labour and Politics* (New York: Greenwood Press, 1987) 117–48.

13 Controlling and Disciplining the Foreign Body: A Case Study of TB Treatment among Asylum Seekers in the Netherlands

Mirjam van Ewijk and Paul Grifhorst

INTRODUCTION

In this chapter we explore some of the ways in which Dutch institutions produce knowledge and power about and over refugees' bodies. These include the construction of images of 'otherness'. Our focus is on the role of medicine in this process, particularly the provision of care for asylum seekers during their application for asylum, their mandatory screening for contagious tuberculosis (TB) and the treatment of asylum seekers suspected of being multiple drug-resistant tuberculosis (MDR TB) carriers.[1]

In the first section, we develop a theoretical concept of medicalization, drawing on Foucault's notions of how modern medicine's disciplinary mechanism works. Although Foucault located the 'discipline societies' in the eighteenth, nineteenth and early twentieth centuries (Deleuze, 1992: 59), his considerations of 'disciplinary' power, which involve acts of confinement, surveillance and detailed organization of human action, are still relevant in understanding the reactions of modern democracies towards asylum seekers and refugees in the 1980s and 1990s. In the second part of the chapter, we discuss how Dutch authorities 'read' the 'foreign' bodies of asylum seekers who try to apply for refugee status and construct them as the contagious and diseased 'other' who is a threat to public health. We go on to evaluate some of the effects of the application by health providers of concepts such as 'compliance' and 'culture' in addressing their clients' problems with medication.

Finally, drawing on the literature of critical medical anthropology, we suggest a different reading of the 'foreign' body and sickness.

THE CONCEPT OF MEDICALIZATION

A growing body of literature has evolved on the health consequences of migration and resettlement. Mental health issues are perhaps the most studied of migration-related health issues (Morrisey, 1983). In the last two decades Post-Traumatic Stress Disorder (PTSD) has become the health model on which the problems of asylum seekers and refugees are based (van Dijk, 1995; Ong, 1995). The causes of dislocation, the hardships of the forced journey, and the conditions of reception and life at the place of resettlement all pose dangers for personal and social well-being (Desjarlais *et al.*, 1995; van Willigen and Hondius, 1992). Experts assume that a substantial part of the refugee population suffers trauma-related somatic and mental health problems in one way or another (Desjarlais *et al.*, 1995).

PTSD is a diagnostic tool used by Western medical workers 'as the lens through which refugees... are viewed, represented and treated' (Ong, 1995: 1246). PTSD symptomology includes: recurrent nightmares, feelings of sadness, social withdrawal, restricted affect, hyperalertness and startle reflex, sleep disorders, loss of memory, guilt and avoidance of activities that prompt recall of stressful events. This universal diagnostic model has come under scrutiny only recently by academics and professionals working in the field of refugee mental health (van Dijk, 1995: 3).

Several authors have criticized the cross-cultural pretension inherent in the PTSD approach, largely because it neglects cultural differences in people's expression of post-traumatic stress through its emphasis on universality in people's reaction to traumatic events. For example, Eisenbruch states 'health and ill-health are defined by the culture and a psychiatric taxonomy should allow for variations in cultural background and the circumstances surrounding the trauma' (van Dijk, 1995: 129–30). A more general critique, for example that expressed by Kleinman and Kleinman (1991: 291), is that 'the very idea of post-traumatic stress as a disorder invalidates the moral and political meaning of suffering'. Similarly:

the ways in which psycho-social needs are addressed do little to empower survivors of flight, violence, and destruction and, instead ... when people become cases, when expressions of hurt become symptoms, and when processes of healing become treatment, I worry that it is professional definers who are empowered rather more than the people we work with.

(Stubbs, 1995: 64)

This process of 'medicalization' is also increasingly recognized by Dutch professionals and helpers: 'The trauma concept represents the colonization of [refugees'] life world ... by a rigid Western conceptual framework ...', and also, 'a "traumatized refugee" seems to have become a pleonasm' (van Dijk, 1995).

'Medicalization' has been defined as 'the way in which the jurisdiction of modern medicine has expanded in recent years and now encompasses many problems that formerly were not defined as medical entities' (Gabe and Calnan, in Helman, 1987: 137). Medical sociologists, including Freidson (1970) and Zola (1972), have discussed in different ways how medicine, 'as an institution of social control', is involved in the management of modern society. These authors are concerned with the controlling effects which medicalization had as a result of its repression of deviant behaviour. They argue that, far from being a neutral scientific concept, the concept of sickness is ultimately a 'moral' one, establishing an evaluation of normality or desirability (Freidson, 1970: 208). Helman also notes that 'the notion of an "unhealthy lifestyle" has replaced the earlier religious concepts of "sinful behaviour" leading to divine retribution' (1987: 138).

Medicalization can also be viewed from the broader perspective of normalization. Foucault, for instance, studied the capacity of modern societies to control and discipline populations. In these disciplinary societies, he suggests, the operations of modern power, in the domestication of the individual body, are productive rather than repressive. As Desjarlais summarizes:

Although the Panopticon was never built in its ideal, original form, Foucault contends that the 'model' or 'diagram' of power inherent in this system of visibility 'spread' throughout the industrial age to pattern the technologies of prisons, medical practices, and educational reforms, all of which were – and, to some extent, still are – predicated on the production of tangible knowledge and 'docile' bodies suited for capitalist production. To wit, the disciplinary mechanism created 'individuals' whose histories, pains, and anatomies were classified in the service of technologies of production and reformation.

(Desjarlais, 1995: 143)

Medicine has thus played a pivotal role in shaping people's life-worlds. Modern industrial societies have allowed medicine and psychiatry to assume a hegemonic role in responding to human distress. Doctors and psychiatrists can shape and transform negative and hostile feelings into symptoms of new diseases such as PTSD (Young, 1995) and pre-menstrual syndrome (Martin, 1987). Through a proliferation of disease categories and labels in medicine and psychiatry, resulting in ever more restricted definitions of the normal, social life and imagination have become infused by health ideologies and practices (Lindenbaum and Lock, 1993; Lock, 1993). This includes the modern ideology of prevention in which:

> it is no longer necessary to manifest symptoms of dangerousness or abnormality, it is enough to display whatever characteristics the specialists responsible for the definition of preventive policy have constituted as risk factors.
>
> (Castel, 1991: 288)

Medical interventions in the reception of asylum seekers in the Netherlands have become substantial. This is in the context of a period of 'crisis' of the welfare state and a shift from a 'welfare' to a 'boarder' state in which criteria for citizenship have become increasingly important (Detrez and Blommaert, 1995). As a result of exclusionary asylum policies (see Koser's chapter, this volume) refugees may spend months, or even years, waiting in Dutch camps, denied access to legal work, study and decent housing, all of which leaves them particularly vulnerable to medicalization. Their apparent readiness to submit themselves to medicalization should be understood within this context. Evidence from the clinical practice of asylum seeker medicine however suggests that medicalization may better be perceived as a creative force, rather than merely a controlling force. In other words, as we shall see, medicalization creates different patterns of experiences.

SCREENING AND DISCIPLINING BODIES

Legal Screening

People wishing to apply for asylum in the Netherlands are sent by the Aliens Police to one of three Registration Centres (ACs). Here requests for asylum are submitted and evaluated to determine eligibility for a detailed review. Once eligibility is established, the asylum seeker is transferred to a screening centre (OC). All this has to be accomplished within 24 hours of the asylum seeker's arrival. The screening centre is the first place of residence for many asylum seekers in the Netherlands. Detailed information about the legal process and general regulations is provided during the first few days. As is made clear in the government information sheet, *Basic but Humane* (1995), however, 'No programmes are offered to help asylum seekers adjust to their surroundings during this period, as this practice might inspire false hope that they will be allowed to remain in the Netherlands.' After several weeks, Ministry of Justice officials make a first decision on asylum requests. These decisions are based officially on extended in-depth interviews conducted by Immigration and Naturalization Service (IND) officers, although in practice all applicants are suspected of not revealing their real identity or motives. The IND's main task is to expose the 'truth' to legal sanction. In other words, they aim to select the few 'real' refugees among the many, assumed economic migrants who are excluded from refugee status.[2]

Those asylum seekers who are not expelled immediately, or who receive provisional leave to remain in the Netherlands, are transferred to an Asylum Seekers' Centre (AZC), or, if no beds are available in an AZC, to temporary accommodation. None of these displacements is voluntary. In the event that people reject their displacement, they are deprived of their right to accommodation and financial support from the Dutch authorities. When they are transferred, asylum seekers can do nothing but await the final decision on their application, which for many can take months or even years. This system, according to many, including a director of one of the centres, can hardly be described as humane. 'This is no luxury . . . little chance that they will be pampered. The facilities are basic . . . nothing more nothing less . . . only that they have to be obedient . . . and wait' (field notes, 1995).

Mortland has referred to the anthropological idea of 'liminality' to summarize the situation in which Southeast Asian refugees find themselves while staying in US refugee camps:

> the refugee . . . exist[s] in a state of 'inbetweenness,' in which any previous status or position he [*sic*] possessed no longer obtains... This liminality . . . is reinforced by . . . the total social context of a . . . centre [and] encourages the powerlessness and dependency of refugees both in the camp and in the country of resettlement.
>
> (Mortland, 1987: 379–80)

We should stress, however, that this kind of liminality carries few of the qualities of transcendence and sacred power that often comes with liminality in religious and initiation rites. For many asylum seekers in Dutch camps, moreover, it seems more a state of 'limbo' – a place or condition in which people are neglected and forgotten – which explains why waiting is so integral to their situation. For most, their waiting is rarely rewarded with permission to resettle. Among many others, Mohamud, a Somali refugee, exclaimed desperately: 'Why did they let us in first... let us wait in hope and fear... and then... send us back again?' (field notes, 1995).

Medical Screening

The construction of asylum seekers as the contagious and diseased 'other' is part of the social debasement they experience. Asylum seekers are considered to be a high-risk group for communicable diseases and, therefore, a danger to Dutch public health until medical screening proves otherwise. This construction, however, appears to be based only partly on epidemiological evidence. For example, in the Netherlands, asylum seekers and refugees from the age of 12 were until recently screened routinely for syphilis (*Staatstoezicht op de Volksgezondheid*, September 1992).[3] The health authorities discontinued this screening programme only after a large serological research project conducted in 1992 (among 1300 asylum seekers), found no evidence whatsoever for this disease amongst refugees. Despite this, the framing of refugees and asylum seekers as disease carriers has continued in other areas.

During their stay in the screening centre, all asylum seekers are requested to fill in a health questionnaire to provide the centre's medical staff with intimate knowledge with which to assess their current state of health. In addition, they are offered a medical examination, unrelated, as is stressed in a covering letter, to their asylum procedure.[4] The consonance of this well-meant information with the actual experiences of refugees who find themselves fully dependent on the centre's staff may however be questioned. For instance, the government brochure, *Medical Reception of Asylum Seekers* (1992), states that, 'Special attention is paid to diseases and abnormalities that might cause serious harm for the individual and the community in the short run.' This includes tropical and transmissible diseases and mental disorders, which are often claimed to be associated with migrants (for example, Kraut, 1994). In acute cases, treatment begins immediately. Finally, the vaccination status of all underage refugees is checked. In the event of a (suspected) gap in vaccinations, an age-specific 'catch-up' programme is initiated. Every newborn infant is signed automatically into the Dutch immunization programme. Additionally, a hepatitis B vaccination and a BCG are given.

AZC staff also focus on the problematized body of refugees. Health education is thus an important task of the centre's health staff. Workshops are organized around general topics such as hygiene, tuberculosis, sexually-transmitted diseases (especially AIDS) and psychosomatic complaints, or are focused on group-specific topics such as substance abuse (for example Qat and alcohol). In addition, informative materials are handed out on topics such as dental care, head lice, and also on issues such as 'correct' perinatal care and the prohibition of female circumcision in the Netherlands. The organizers generally complain about the poor attendance of centre residents at health meetings. The assumed low priority of this information among the refugee population ('AIDS is the last [thing] they have on their mind') and the 'cultural inappropriateness of the materials offered' are two of the most frequently heard explanations of this.

A variety of incentives are used to motivate people to participate. Some health staff prefer the alternative of a more individual approach, particularly when sensitive issues such as female circumcision are involved. Overall, the health education in the AZCs promotes Dutch ways of healthy living, which includes teaching asylum seekers medical concepts to understand their bodily and emotional experiences, and, by the same token, behaviour appropriate to Dutch standards of hygiene. In other words, visits to the centre's medical unit often imply lessons in (Dutch) culture (Ong, 1995).

TB Screening

The World Health Organization (WHO) claims that nearly half the world's refugees may be infected with TB (WHO, 1996). Screening for TB among refugees and asylum seekers is therefore highly prioritized in many receiving countries. Consequently, in the first weeks of their stay in a Dutch screening centre, asylum seekers are X-rayed to screen for infectious tuberculosis (TB). This is the start of a series of four X-rays of the lungs, taken periodically over the two years (with an interval of six months) following the refugee's arrival in the Netherlands. Since 1993 the first screening has been mandatory. If a suspicious shadow is detected on their thorax-photo, asylum seekers are placed directly under medical surveillance. If the diagnosis is confirmed, the legal procedure of asylum seeking coincides with a long (6–9 months or more) and intrusive treatment with TB chemotherapy. These people, moreover, are directly classified and treated as potentially contaminated with TB strains resistant to multiple drugs (MDR TB). In brief:

> MDR TB occurs when naturally occurring mutant strains become favoured during the course of erratic or poorly conceived therapy. In contrast to the normal drug susceptible strains, the drug-resistant strains are 'notoriously difficult to treat'
>
> (Farmer, 1995: 4)

A case study of TB serves to illustrate some of the mechanisms involved in the larger process wherein asylum seekers are transformed into individual clinical as well as juridical cases. TB is an airborne communicable disease caused by... the tubercle bacillus. It is spread primarily by tiny airborne particles (droplet nuclei) expelled by a person who has infectious TB. If another person inhales air containing these droplet nuclei, transmission may occur.

> (CDC 1994: 5)

The WHO suggests that nearly three million people died from TB in 1995, exceeding the worst years of the epidemic in the early years of the twentieth century, when an estimated 2.1 million people died annually, and warns that if no immediate action is taken, as many as half a billion people could become infected with TB in the next 50 years (WHO, 1996). Despite the fact that effective drug treatment has now been available for 30 years, tuberculosis remains the leading infectious cause of preventable deaths of youth and adults in the 'developing' world (Farmer, 1995). Brandt argues that in this respect the discussions on conquering infectious disease have always disguised a deep ethnocentrism. Clearly, to be successful drugs must first of all be delivered effectively to those who need them. However,

> the persistence of TB... represents more... TB flourishes in conditions of poverty and degradation, in environments in which humans become increasingly vulnerable to the microbes that cause disease.
>
> (Brandt, 1993: 6)

Improved standards of living, better nutrition and improved housing explain the decline of TB in the 'developed' world long before the organism was identified and effective drugs became available. In poor countries TB has persisted in epidemic proportion. For decades the annual decrease of the incidence of tuberculosis in the Netherlands was 6 per cent. Similar trends have obtained in other wealthy countries. In general, since the mid-1980s this decline has halted. Entering the 1990s, the total number of tuberculosis cases diagnosed increased by as much as 30–50 per cent in some 'developed' countries of Europe and North America. Consequently, tuberculosis has returned as a major issue on Western health agendas.

Significant outbreaks of MDR TB in homeless shelters, prisons and medical facilities in 'developed' countries such as the USA have encouraged the world's public health authorities to take radical precautions. Although large numbers of health and social workers and prison personnel have been among those infected with MDR TB, the contours of the 'new' risk groups were instantly set by the US public health community along old lines: 'being born outside the United States, being homeless, a substance abuser, being incarcerated, or being a migrant worker is a risk factor for (MDR-) tuberculosis infection' (OTA, 1993: 5).

These risk-group categories have been adopted quickly by the remainder of the Western countries and special treatment protocols have been developed. Public health authorities continue to debate which groups constitute real risks, yet from the start, people from the southern hemisphere have been included amongst the various groups considered as high risk factors. The mandatory screening for TB shortly after refugees' arrival in the Netherlands is an effective method of identifying TB cases. The default rate of 13 per cent for TB treatment is, however, in the light of the risk of developing an MDR TB, considered unacceptably high. Unlike AIDS, the spread of the tubercle bacillus is not attributed to risk behaviour, although this is not the case for MDR TB. Patients' non-compliance with TB treatment, for example, has been directly linked with the emergence of drug-resistant tuberculosis. Although public health officials admit that structural factors, such as the Dutch asylum policy, are to blame for the high rate of defaulters among asylum seekers (in fact, placing them at extra risk of developing an incurable tuberculosis); in health workers' narratives, as we shall see, the problem of 'asylum seekers' poor compliance' is mainly constructed as a 'behavioural problem', articulated in terms of patients' unwillingness, irresponsibility or foreign culture.

NON-COMPLIANCE WITH TB TREATMENT: COLLISIONS BETWEEN REALITIES?

Abdi, a 2-year-old boy from Somalia diagnosed with lung TB, was temporarily transferred from an asylum seekers' centre to the residence of resettled family members. After a month the nurse locally responsible for TB cases found out about the existence of the child in her district and visited the family. As the family were having difficulties organizing the child's therapy, the TB nurse, together with a volunteer who had already known the family for several months, and a local primary health nurse, established a therapy management group.

(field notes, 1995)

Salient details in this case include the fact that Abdi was transferred by the centre's authorities without the necessary measures, such as informing the responsible local TB services in time, being taken. Even his medicines were overlooked on his temporary displacement from the centre. Abdi's case is no exception. Factors causing the interruption of therapy – such as the frequent movement of asylum seekers from centre to centre, from centres to other housing facilities (ROA), and vice versa – are among the main complaints of all the providers involved with TB services we have interviewed. All kinds of problems, partly resulting from an ambiguous Dutch asylum policy, and exacerbated by communication difficulties, complex regulations and procedures, unclear responsibilities, and conflicting interests, often require a great deal of effort and creativity on the part of public health nurses, volunteers, family members and patients in order to pursue successful therapy management.

Most of the health providers interviewed during our research project were themselves acutely aware of the health-threatening effects of these structural factors, of which Abdi's case is emblematic. Their approach to non-compliance as an individual 'behavioural' problem should partly be understood therefore as stemming from pragmatic reasons. Their focus on patient agency also has a precedent, however, in medicine's celebrated focus on individual patients, which is inevitably desocializing (Farmer, 1995). Consequently, a (potentially stigmatizing) set of disciplinary techniques has been promoted in the health field and sociomedical literature on non-compliance. Recently, Direct Observed Therapy (DOT)[5] and forced compliance, even to the extent of forced hospitalization, have become key terms in the conceptual framing of the treatment of 'uncooperative' TB patients. Below, a nurse discusses her responsibility:

> It's the public health nurse's task to pursue collective prevention ... which includes: promoting healthy living, tracking and eliminating health-threatening factors ... The elimination of seats of infection and the prevention of multiresistance are of general interest. Thereby patient's co-operation is extremely important. The public health argument, in my opinion, legitimatized forced treatment in dealing with uncooperative patients.
>
> (field notes, 1995)

The general meaning of the word 'uncooperative' is well illustrated by the following instance we discussed during an informal talk with several members of an AZC's staff:

> Ousmani is a 16-year-old boy from Somalia. Diagnosed with lung TB in the centre. According to the centre's nurse the boy lacks every motivation to take his pills. He doesn't feel sick. Despite many attempts of the nurse, the physician, the public health nurse and the group leader to educate O. about the consequences of poor compliance with TB therapy, the boy persists in not taking his drugs regularly. It is said he even uses his pills to blackmail the staff; by threatening not to take his tablets he tries to get things done.
>
> (field notes, 1995)

This preoccupation with individual agency (conceptualized in terms such as non-compliance, negligence and irresponsible behaviour) and with individualistic solutions, including patient education, behaviour change and alteration of provider–patient relations, seems to be a very powerful force underlying the production of images of the sick and needy. Nurses, however, who see their major task as one of caring, in the light of potentially conflicting physicians' mandates and patient expressed need, have been considerably more open (than physicians) to the inclusion of psycho-social concepts and perspectives borrowed from psychology and other social sciences (Singer, 1995: 85–6). Their willingness to include cultural issues in their educational curricula, directed at patients from different countries who are assumed to possess different cultures, is one strategy. Terms such as 'culture' and 'cultural difference' thus have rapidly found their way into health workers' vocabulary in reflecting on deviant illness behaviours among their refugee-patients.

Mahanni, a 17-year-old girl from Zaire seems to be very reluctant to take her TB medicine. One of the health care providers of the centre told us that the girl completely lacks insight into the seriousness of her condition. Another member of the staff is convinced that M. knows the consequences, but it seems that she doesn't care at all: 'When I warn her that she will probably die if she should persist this way... M. replies solely that she doesn't mind dying.' The nurse hurried to express her thought, that warnings like this do not always appeal to unwilling patients, 'especially when they come from cultures where people are more at ease with death and dying'.
(field notes, 1995)

Whether conceived of as a set of customs, traditions, ideas or beliefs, the cultural idiom has become an important element in providers' assessment of the possible motives of foreign patients in noncompliance. By the end of the 1980s, one Dutch anthropologist felt compelled to warn health workers (and social scientists) about the use of cultural information to explain away the problems in the provision of health care to migrants. Knowledge of the traditional culture thus misleads health workers into blaming cultural factors for a failing health care system, at the same time disregarding structural deficiencies (van Dijk 1989: 131).

Van Dijk's plea for a more dynamic concept of culture in analysing the interactions between migrants and health care workers has since been echoed many times; but has not resulted in any significant new local research programmes on 'migration and health' in the Netherlands, either in nursing, medical anthropology or sociology. Health workers who are interested in cultural issues still have to depend on so-called 'recipe book' approaches, or, social-medical and medical anthropological studies conducted in the countries from which their clients originate. The question of whether such studies offer an antidote vigorous enough to counterbalance medicine's somewhat reductionist and rigid view of human distress remains. Social scientists have a clear responsibility here in (re)producing images of 'otherness' which is inevitably inherent in their contribution to the production of knowledge and power over bodies.

In much of the social science literature on 'compliance' on which health care providers can rely, however, there is a persistent inclination to focus merely on the characteristics of the individual patient (see for example, Sumartojo, 1993). Medical anthropologists too, in explanatory models, health beliefs or cognitive scripts of patients, their families and their providers, have often echoed the concern of many physicians and other providers with the individual agency, which is assumed to exhibit (irrational) behaviours and (illicit) thoughts (Good, 1994; Farmer and Good, 1991). In a review of sociomedical studies on non-compliance (performed in 'developing' countries), Farmer concludes that 'it is social science that has under-lined the importance of contextualization, and so our failure to com-plement clinicians' view with more robustly contextualized ones is all the more significant' (Farmer, 1995: 27–8).

In Singer's view the failure of studies like the ones discussed by Farmer, lies in their lack of 'appreciation of the social structure as a configuration of power alignments embodied in all personal relation-ships and social institutions, including the various sectors of the health system' (Singer, 1995: 86). Besides, as Trostle argues, 'the basic problem with research on medical compliance is that it is domin-ated by a series of ideological conceptions of the proper roles of patients and physicians' (Trostle, 1988: 1305). These assumptions about patient–doctor relationships can be summarized as follows: the physician is the proper ultimate authority over the actions of his or her patients; in exchange for a physician's services a patient owes fees, co-operation, and compliance; non-compliance is usually the patient's fault; and physicians offer therapeutic partnerships to patients, not vice versa (Trostle, 1988: 1305).

In fact, thinking about patient behaviour in term of 'compliance' obscures the variability and denies the legitimacy of behaviours that differ from medical prescription (Trostle, 1988). Trostle urges researchers to take 'an omniscient position outside the physician–patient relationship' in order to understand that non-compliance is often 'an unavoidable by-product' of collisions between the clinical reality and the competing social realities of patients, for example financial constraints, or an inability to function adequately under a medication's side-effects:

> Joa is a 15-year-old asylum seeker from Angola. At first he felt miserable: weakened, tight in his chest, and suffering from a persist-ent cough. After five months of medication he is quite satisfied that these complaints have disappeared. Another four months of pills seem to him a necessary evil. Jao finds it difficult to keep up with his new peer group. His medication does not allow him to drink beer and the side-effects are causing him drowsiness. Sometimes he deliberately forgets to take his medication because he is angry at

himself, the whole situation, or, just because he wants to be able to drink and smoke among friends.

(field notes, 1995)

Within critical anthropology, there is an abundant literature that has studied sickness as a performance, as just one of numerous everyday forms of resistance of subordinate classes or peoples throughout history, who have rarely been afforded the luxury of open, organized political activity (Lock and Scheper-Hughes, 1990; Martin, 1987; Richters, 1991; Scott, 1985). This argument can, of course, readily be extended to the situation of the majority of refugees and asylum seekers living in a prolonged situation of enforced liminality. This is not to suggest that people suffer from TB in order to 'articulate resistance', but that 'non-compliance' with TB treatment can indeed acquire this quality; especially for people living in a situation of extreme powerlessness. This can apply even when people themselves are fully aware of the possibly devastating health consequences of not taking TB medicines properly. The numerous newspaper reports on hunger strikes, (attempted) suicides and self-mutilations among asylum seekers suggest that the same body that is subject to a systematic colonization by bio-medicine and the state often seems to be one of the very few tools left through which protest, resistance and despair can be articulated. During a seminar addressing the problem of compliance among asylum seekers, one nurse recalled how one of her patients refused to take his medication at all as long as his legal procedure was postponed: 'It doesn't make any sense, telling him that he is allowed to stay in the Netherlands during the time of his treatment to motivate him to co-operate! Does it?' (field notes, 1995).

Adopting a performative stance allows a very different representation of the 'non-compliant' asylum-seeker to emerge. For example, stories such as Ousmani's can be read as acts of resistance rather than acts of ignorance, deviant behaviour or non-compliance. Cases in which health providers and asylum seekers are seen to be involved in struggles for control over the patient's body, can also be interpreted differently when we understand what is at stake for those involved:

According to the centre's physician, Fharid is a very stubborn and irresponsible person. 'Don't know what he really wants.' Always finding ways to upset the staff. Now, admitted to the hospital because of serious complications resulting from his TB medication, Fharid assured us that he would rather flee again than go back to the camp where, as he sees it, he contracted his TB. After weeks of isolation and treatment, Fharid refuses to leave the clinic. Earlier on, he expressed his worries to us: 'In here, I'm in the Netherlands... in a centre, life is so degrading... how can they send sick people back to a camp?'

(field notes, 1995)

FINAL REMARKS

Although serving as a good example of a more contextualized approach to sickness, the concept of resistance remains a problematic one. There is a real danger of dichotomizing complex human behaviour into simple resistance/non-resistance categories. This is also at odds with the variety of experiences we have recorded. During our conversations with health workers a recurrent theme was that asylum seekers tend to manipulate medical resources for non-medical reasons such as obtaining housing permits, or prolonging their stay in the Netherlands. By decontextualizing and individualizing these practices, however, refugees are being blamed for what is actually the outcome of the interplay of their individual agency and the operation of the 'system'.[6] Illustrative of this is the fact that the medical argument – proving that one's present state of physical and mental health is largely due to persecution – has become increasingly important in appeal cases (Galensloot, 1994).

Medicalization works in different and complex ways. In many ways, it seems, it is linked with a refugee's (liminal) position in society. It could be argued that people are pushed into a medicalized path when they try to escape persecution or forced repatriation, because (they feel that) there are no other options left, or, at least to win back some of their lost social status and dignity. It is better therefore to conclude that, besides being a controlling force, medicalization is also both adhered to and contested by its subjects, in pursuing what is at stake for them in their particular circumstances. In other words, medicalization when adhered to may be a 'strategy' or 'tactic' for asylum seekers to overcome their liminal situation, to survive at the margins of the 'boarder' state; or, when contested, perhaps one of the few options open to them (the powerless) to articulate protest and resistance.

NOTES

1. This chapter is based on open interviews conducted during 1995 with refugees living and employees working in Dutch asylum seekers' centres. By using pseudonyms to avoid identifying specific individuals, we have woven fragments of their stories into this account to support our argument. We would like to thank all the people who were willing to share their experiences with us. Thanks especially to Bob Desjarlais, Paul Farmer, Annemiek Richters, Jamie Saris and Joke van der Zwaard for their constructive critique. We are also grateful to Sjaak van der Geest, Khalid Koser, Helma Lutz and Ann Phoenix for their editorial (and otherwise inspirational) comments.

2. The IND also looks for doubt about facts such as age and nationality. If a minor single asylum seeker is suspected of lying about their age, for instance, their dossier is marked 'ZAMA' (alleged minor single asylum seeker) and the applicant is subjected to bone and teeth X-rays to determine their real age (see for example, *De Volkskrant*, 8 December 1995). It is assumed by the IND that some asylum seekers are aware that minor single asylum seekers receive 'better' treatment in the Netherlands than adults. If an applicant's country of origin is doubted by the IND, they are dubbed a 'Ligerian' by IND officers (Lassen and Kloosterboer, 1995; *Vrij Nederland*, 20 January 1996).

3. In this context, it is unsurprising that migrant labourers, as well as homosexuals and teenagers, have since the 1960s been stereotyped in the Netherlands as carriers of venereal disease, based on dubious epidemiology (Mooij, 1993:170–6).

4. This letter states that: 'Your information will be handled in confidence at all times. The medical examination is completely unrelated to your asylum procedure. For this reason, the doctors and nurses under no circumstances provide information to the judicial authorities.'

5. 'Direct observed treatment (DOT), short-term is the key to curing the patient and controlling the TB epidemic' (WHO, 1995).

6. Or, often more accurately, several 'systems' both in the Netherlands and abroad.

REFERENCES

Brandt, A.M., 'TB, again', unpublished paper (1993).
Castel, R., 'From Dangerous to Risk', in G. Burchell, P. Gordon and C. Miller (eds), *The Foucault Effect* (Chicago: The University of Chicago Press, 1991) .
Deleuze, G., 'Postscript on the Societies of Control', *October* 59 (1992) 3–7.
van Dijk, R., 'Cultuur als excuus voor een falende hulpverlening', *Medische Antropologie* 1 (2) (1989) 131–43.
van Dijk, R., 'Cultuur en trauma: culturele variaties in de omgang met schokkende Gebeurtenissen', *Medische Antropologie* 7 (1) (1995) 128–42.

van Dijk, R., 'Trauma als redding', *PHAXX.* Kwartaalblad Gezondheidszorg en Vluchtelingen 4 (1995).

Desjarlais, R., A. Kleinman, L. Eisenberg and B. Good, *World Mental Health. Priorities and Responses in Low-income Countries* (Oxford: Oxford University Press, 1995).

Desjarlais, R., 'Struggling Along: The Politics of Life and Language in a Shelter for the "homeless mentally ill"', unpublished manuscript (Boston, MA, 1995).

Detrez, R. and Blommaert, J. (eds), *Nationalisme. Kritische Opstellen* (Berchem: EPO, 1995).

Farmer, P., 'Social Scientists and the New Tuberculosis', unpublished manuscript (Cambridge, MA, 1995).

Farmer, P. and B. J. Good, 'Illness Representations in Medical Anthropology: A Critical Review and a Case Study of the Representation of AIDS in Haiti', J.A. Skelton and R.T. Croyle (eds), *Mental Representation in Health and Illness* (New York: Springer-Verlag, 1991) 132–62.

Foucault, M., *Geschiedenis van de seksualiteit. De wil tot weten 1* (Nijmegen: SUN, 1985).

Freidson, E., *Profession of Medicine* (New York: Dodd-Mead, 1970).

Galesloot, B., *Bevindingen van de medische onderzoeksgroep van Amnesty International* (Amsterdam: Amnesty International, 1994).

Good, B. J., *Medicine, Rationality and Experience. An Anthropological Perspective* (New York: Cambridge University Press, 1994).

Helman, C. G., *Culture, Health and Illness* (Oxford: Butterworth Heinemann, 1987).

Kleinman, A. and J. Kleinman, 'Suffering and its Professional Transformation: Towards an Ethnography of Interpersonal Experience', *Culture, Medicine and Psychiatry* 15 (3) (1991) 275–301.

Kraut, A. M., *Silent Travelers. Germs, Genes and the 'Immigrant Menace'* (New York: HarperCollins, 1994).

Lassen, B. and Kloosterboer, K., *Het leven in Nederland is niet zacht als zijde. De sociale en juridische positie van alleenstaande minderjarige asielzoekers* (Amsterdam: Defence for Children, 1995).

Lindenbaum, S. and Lock, M. (eds). *Knowledge, Power and Practice* (Berkeley: University of California Press, 1993).

Lock, M. 'Cultivating the Body: Anthropology and Epistemologies of Bodily Practice and Knowledge', *Annual Review of Anthropology* 22 (1993) 133–55.

Martin, E., *The Woman in the Body: A Cultural Analysis of Reproduction* (Boston: Beacon Press, 1987).

Mooij, A., *Geslachtsziekten en besmettingsangst. Een historisch-sociologische studie 1850–1990* (Amsterdam: Boom, 1993).

Morrissey, J. A., 'Migration, Resettlement and Refugeeism: Issues in Medical Anthropology', *Medical Anthropological Quarterly* 14 (1983) 10–14.

Mortland, C. A., 'Transforming Refugees in Refugee Camps', *Urban Anthropology,* 16 (3–4) (1987) 375–404.

Ong, A., 'Making the Biopolitical Subject: Cambodian Immigrants, Refugee Medicine and Cultural Citizenship in California', *Social Science and Medicine,* 40 (9) (1995) 1243–57.

Richters, J. M., *De medisch antropoloog als verteller en vertaler* (Delft: EBURON, 1991).

Scheper-Hughes, N. and M.M. Lock, 'The Mindful Body: A Prolegomenon to Future Work in Medical Anthropology', *Medical Anthropological Quarterly*, 1 (1) (1987) 6–41.

Scott, J., *Weapons of the Weak: Everyday Forms of Peasant Resistance* (New Haven: Yale University Press, 1985).

Singer, M., 'Beyond the Ivory Tower: Critical Praxis in Medical Anthropology', *Medical Anthropological Quarterly*, 9 (1) (1995) 80–106.

Stubbs, P., 'Working with Refugee and Displaced Children', in ESSOP, *From 'Trauma' to 'Safety'. Child Health Care for Migrants and Refugees* (Programme and Abstracts) (ESSOP: Rotterdam, 1995).

Sumartojo, E., 'When Tuberculosis Treatment Fails: A Social Behavioral Account of Patient Adherence', *American Review of Respiratory Diseases* 147 (1993) 1311–20.

Trostle, J. A., 'Medical Compliance as an Ideology', *Social Science and Medicine* 27 (12) (1988) 1299–308.

World Health Organisation (WHO), *TB, Groups at Risk. WHO Report on the Tuberculosis Epidemic* (Geneva: WHO, 1996).

van Willigen L.H.M., and A.J.K. Hondius, *Vluchtelingen en gezondheid. Theoretische beschouwingen. Deel 1* (Amsterdam: Swets and Zeitlinger, 1992).

Young, A., *The Harmony of Illusions: Inventing Post-traumatic Stress Disorder* (Princeton: Princeton University Press, 1995).

Zola, I. J., 'Medicine as Institution of Social Control', *Sociological Review* 20 (4) (1972) 487–504.

Index